Juice Jargon
How to talk about wine

by
Stephen Reiss, Ph.D, C.W.E.

B&C Publishing
a division of

Enterprises

Where Bacchus Computes

B&C Publishing
Box 10206
Aspen, CO 81612
www.BandC.com

First Edition Published by AuthorHouse 2004,
Second Edition Published by B&C Publishing 2005

ISBN: 0-9761237-0-3

Library of Congress Number: 2004095138

Printed and Bound in the
United States of America

Acknowledgments

*To all of the women who helped
to make this possible, and to
everyone that helped to make the
first edition a success.*

*With an extra thank you to
Sue and April, for their sharp
eyes.*

Introduction

I never thought I was going to become a wine professional. I was a cook. Even that was an accident. I moved to Aspen, Colorado, the ski town, and fell in love. I knew that I would do whatever it might take to live in this resort community, and I knew that my previous education was not going to help. So, I cooked. At first I cooked breakfast (and 25 years later people still come up to me and tell me they miss my hash browns!) I moved up the culinary ladder and eventually became the apprentice to a French trained chef.

It was in this classic culinary environment that my epiphany occurred. The waiters liked to play "guess this wine" with any wine that might be left over. Since this was a very exclusive restaurant (it only sat 20 people, twice a night, and the menu changed daily) the wine tended to be of the highest quality. I was young, and my wine experience was essentially non existent. I never had any way of knowing what we were tasting, until one night. On this fateful night the head waiter poured me a glass, and with a smirk, told me to try to guess what it was. I looked at it, smelled it, and tasted it. I pronounced rather sheepishly "It is a 64 Margaux." The waiter looked at me with shock, and asked how I could possibly know. "We tasted it last month" I replied innocently. I expected that to settle the matter, but it just led to greater disbelief. "You remember something you tasted a month ago?" he asked. To which I replied "Of course, don't you?" His unprintable reply was my first indication that I have a gift, a gift of palate memory, and it turns out to be rare.

Armed with this new knowledge that I had a gift, I began to read everything I could about wine. Knowing that reading is never enough, I arranged to spend the summer in France with my wife. I was cocky and young (at least I am not as young now) and I was full of book knowledge. I had never been to a winery, or tasted wine in any sort of professional environment. I would like to think it was my poor understanding of the French language that led to my first memorable faux pas, but it was mostly lack of experience.

One of the first wineries we visited had a rain barrel full of water and wine for the proprietor to spit his wine out into. Previously I had dutifully spit on the floor like the others in the winery, and I was unclear on the purpose of the barrel. The gentleman gestured at the barrel with his wine glass, and said something in French. To this day I am not sure what he said, but I took it to mean that I should rinse my glass in the rather nasty rain barrel. He laughed at me, and kindly fetched me a clean glass, and through pantomime I realized I was to spit in the barrel and not stick my glass in it. After 20 years I still feel the shame of what was a silly, but minor faux pas.

I wanted to share this with you to demonstrate a basic fact that is easy to forget. No one is born knowing about wine. Most of us do not even encounter wine until we are well into our 20s, and the first time we look at a wine list we are completely overwhelmed.

Eventually, if we persevere, we learn a few favorite styles and producers, and for some, this is only a beginning. Soon we are stopping at every out of the way liquor store to see if a forgotten bargain is hiding inside. Then we move on to wine tastings, and "serious" wine appreciation. A few of us are so struck with the wine bug, it becomes our vocation.

Somewhere in there we decide we want to learn to refine our wine vocabulary. For me, that meant reading the college texts that are available on the subject. Not only did this cover quite a bit more than I was planning to learn, but they tended to contradict one another. I quickly realized that the language of wine was not well defined, and that it ultimately was more a matter of opinion than convention.

After teaching and writing about wine for two decades, I decided it was time to share what I had learned. The language of wine has not become any more defined, and I am not pretending to have written the definitive book on the subject; rather, I have attempted to blaze a new trail. To teach people that talking about wine does not have to be any more complicated, or detailed than you wish it to be.

We all have to start somewhere, and no matter where you are on your wine journey, this book can help. It may not stop you from embarrassing yourself, but at least you will smile and know you are in good company.

How to use this book

The first chapter covers the basics. The minimum you need to know to be able to tell someone why you like or dislike a wine. This is a great section for the beginner, and you may want to read it several times, with a glass of wine in hand. For those more familiar with wine, or even the wine professional, the first chapter acts as a review, and will introduce you to a way of speaking about wine that may be more disciplined, but easier, than the vocabulary you are using now.

The second chapter is an alphabetical list of words used when talking about wines. For those that want to say more than the basic about how a wine tastes, this is a must read. For others, it is a reference. A place to look up a word they encountered, or to find a word that helps convey their meaning more efficiently.

In the chapter entitled "Where it comes from," the book details the most common grape varieties, and wine regions of the world. Learn what grapes are found where, and what to expect before you taste the wine. This section is a great reference, and is designed to help you determine what the wine label says about the wine.

There is even a chapter for those that love the technical side of things. It not only covers the words used in wine making and grape growing, but gives a glimpse of the process as well.

Finally, the glossary is an alphabetic listing of the words and terms used throughout the book. This is where you go to look up a specific word or abbreviation.

Whether you read the book from cover to cover or use it as a reference, I hope you enjoy it and refer back to it for years to come.

WineEducation.com

Since 1996 I have been rambling on about wine on the World Wide Web, in fact I have been teaching and learning about wine on-line since 1984. Wineeducation.com has been the test bed for much of what has been written here, although this book contains original material that has never appeared on the web site. The site will continue to be updated, and will evolve to act as a companion to this and my future wine books. If you have never visited, come on by. Sign the guest book and say hi. Those of you that have signed the guest book, and are a fan already, thank you for your continued support. Stop by to see what is new.

Aspen Wine Program

Twice a year, in the beautiful mountain town of Aspen, Colorado, I teach a wine school. The classes are limited to 10 people at a time (private courses are available) and last for one week of basic instruction, and optionally a second week of professional training. We taste over 100 wines in the two weeks, 9 a day. We go out to dinner, and sometimes even tour wineries. It is fun, it is work, it is an unparalleled way to learn about wine.

To learn more, please visit AspenWineProgram.com

To Order this Book

Visit www.JuiceJargon.com to purchase additional copies today. We are more than happy to ship to multiple addresses, so you can get all of your gift shopping done in one stop.

Juice Jargon
How to talk about wine

Contents

How to talk about
Wine the easy way

Talking about wine

For some people talking about a wine brings them pleasure, for others tasting wine is its own reward. Most of us either know someone that seems to be able to talk forever about a wine, or at least have seen such a character in the movies or on television. Many of these people seem to know what they are talking about, too many more do not. It is easy to be intimidated by the blend of poetry and technical mumbo jumbo that seems to surround the language of wine. It need not be.

We talk about wine because we want to communicate our experience to someone. We use special words, because every day speech seems ill equipped to convey the nuance of something as personal as what you taste in a wine, and how you feel about it. Some wines can inspire us to speak volumes, and others can be summed up in a few words.

A little confidence can go a long way. Start out easily. Read through this first chapter a few times until you are comfortable with the basic terms I use, and then if you are up to it, you can begin to expand your descriptions. Only a few words are really needed to give someone a good idea of what you thought of a wine. The thousands of other words used by wine lovers are mostly there to fill in the details.

It is important to know that there are no real rules to what words to use and which to avoid. Personally, I try to avoid words that assign action to something inanimate (i.e. anthropomorphic words). Wine doesn't do anything, or act any way, it just sits there. If you feel a word conveys meaning and understanding, use it, don't let my, or anyone else's rules get in the way.

To get the most out of this book, open a bottle of wine and enjoy, as we learn how to talk about what you are tasting.

Balance

Wine is all about balance. It is primarily a balance between the three main components of wine: fruit, tannin and acidity. It can also be a balancing act with food, or special circumstances. If someone shares a special bottle of wine with you, the circumstances and the situation may make the wine more memorable.

Acidity

Acidity and acid are words you will come across throughout this book, and everywhere wine is discussed. Some people cringe when acid is mentioned. Perhaps they conjure up images of battery acid. The acid in wine is like lemon juice, it tastes sour. Lemon has to be balanced by sugar when you make lemonade. Too much lemon, or too much sugar, and the lemonade will be out of balance.

As the grape ripens, the amount of sugar in it increases, and the amount of acidity decreases. This is true for all fruits. The wine maker wants the grapes to be picked when they are at their perfect balance between sugar and acidity.

The sugar will be turned into alcohol by the yeast during fermentation. Too much sugar and the wine may be alcoholic, or have problems during production (stuck fermentation). If there is too much acid and not enough sugar, you will get a wine that is sour and unpleasant.

This same balancing act is what we are paying attention to when we taste wine. We want to determine if the wine has a pleasing balance between sweet and sour, and something not quite bitter - tannin.

Tannin

When you taste a red wine that you would call heavy or hard or rough, it is the tannins you are tasting. These come from the grapes themselves, and you have tasted them if you have ever peeled a grape and eaten the skin. It is bitter, but not really, it is almost more something you feel than taste.

Tannins soften with time. A young wine that is intended to be aged will often have tannins out of balance with the rest of the wine. That is because tannins soften with time, and the wine is not ready to drink yet. This is what that whole aging wine thing is primarily about. A well aged wine has very soft tannins, and one that is too old has lost all of its tannins. Most wines are not made to age, or at least not for very long. These wines usually have less tannin, and they either have more fruit, or the impression of fruit is more noticeable.

Fruit

Fruit is the third part of the wine balancing act. One could characterize fruit as everything that is pleasant in wine. It is what balances the sour acids and bitter tannins. Fruit is a catch-all phrase for the smells and flavors that you find in wine, even if they smell more like wood, or anything other than fruit.

Different kinds of grapes have different characteristics. Some are tart and firm, some sweet and juicy. The flavors the wine ends up with are due in part to the grapes that are used, where the grapes were grown, how the wine is made, and even who the person is that made it. These all contribute to the style of the wine. The acidity and the tannins are part of that style, but it is the fruit you notice.

The list of things people have smelled or tasted in wine is endless. The important thing to remember is that these smells and tastes are fleeting and subtle. Few wines strongly resemble any single type of fruit. It is usually a mix of things you smell and it is often difficult to put a finger on exactly what it reminds you of. Whatever it is, in wine, we call it fruit.

The 5 senses

The term "tasting" is applied to the act of experiencing wine, although in truth all five senses are used when you "taste" wine.

Taste

This is the first sense that comes to mind, but it turns out your tongue can actually only taste four things:

Sweet - It is alcohol and the perceived sweetness of the fruit flavors in wine that act to balance the other tastes. In sweet wines, there is sugar that also needs to be balanced.

Sour - The taste of acidity. Acidity not only keeps wine fresh, it offers a balance to the sweetness of the alcohol, as well as to any sugar that may be in the wine. Acidity is required to help wine age, so the greatest wines, those few that will last for decades, always have a good deal of acidity in their youth.

Bitter - A result of tannins in wine. White wines tend to have few tannins. Tannins come from the skins and seeds of the grape. Tannins can also come from aging the wine in oak barrels. Grape tannins along with oak tannins are common in red wines, with oak tannins being primarily responsible for whatever amount of tannin a white wine has.

Salty - With very few exceptions salty is not a flavor you find in wine. Salty foods are rarely complimentary with dry wines, although a wine that contains a small amount of sugar will balance salty foods nicely.

Smell

The world is full of smells. Most of the time we hardly notice them, and in many cases, this is a good thing. Wine too is a complex mix of smells. To make matters slightly confusing, when we talk about flavor we are also talking about smells. Since there are only four tastes, where do all the other flavors come from? It turns out that we actually smell what is in our mouths. There is a connection between our nose and mouth (retronasal passage). As we eat, we draw small amounts of air across the food or drink, into our nose, where receptors identify the aromas. Since the food is in our mouths, our minds consider these smells to be flavors. A common example of this is when you eat something while you are suffering from a cold. You can't taste it because your nose is stuffed up, and you can't smell it either.

Smell is the great memory trigger. Nothing can make your mind wander like a smell. It is for this reason that so many smells are associated with wine. The subtle, fleeting aromas of wine trigger a memory and the taster is treated to an image of what they smelled. This may or may not be related to what others smell in the same wine. Almost any aroma or flavor you can imagine, good or bad, can or has been applied to wine by someone.

Sight

The most obvious aspect of sight in wine is color. There are a few other aspects that the casual observer would tend to overlook.

Opacity - This is a measure of how much light passes through the wine. A good way to judge this is to tilt the glass over a well lit page, and see if you can make out the words through the wine. All but the darkest of wines let some light through, while few white wines stop more than a small amount of light. Opacity is a clue to how intense the flavors will be, and in many cases, which grapes are used and how the wine was made.

Clarity - There was a time when wines were often cloudy, they were full of particles that floated around. While an old wine can throw sediment, and a shaken bottle with sediment will look cloudy, young wines rarely suffer from clarity issues any more. The wine making techniques used now should eradicate all potential for a wine to become cloudy. Even wines marked "unfiltered" should be clear. Any wine that is not clear (unless it is an old red wine) should be considered faulty.

Brilliance - Another visual aspect of wine that should rarely be an issue, due to modern wine making. Few wines are dull, but even today, some are shinier, and more brilliant than others.

Color - Wines in youth are a different color than they will be once they have aged. A young red wine will often have hints of blue, but will turn brown with age. White wines start life nearly colorless, but they too, yellow, or even brown, with age. Oxygen is the culprit that turns wine brown and the mechanism is one we are all familiar with. Bite into an apple, and put it down for a time, and it too will brown from oxidation. Had you squeezed some lemon juice on that apple, the browning would have slowed due to the citrus acid in the lemon. Acid in wine works the same way, as an antioxidant to help preserve the color and freshness of the wine.

Touch

As aroma is to smell, haptic is to touch. It is the word we use to describe all sensations relating to touch. In wine, haptic sensations range from the temperature of the wine, the tickle of the bubbles in sparkling wines, or the burning sensation in your nose from high alcohol content. There is even a mouth feel to wine, especially older wines. Some of these sensations are easier for someone to understand if they have tasted a lot of wines. Others will be obvious at once.

Sound

On the surface, this would seem to be the least of the senses used in wine tasting. In fact, this is the sense that this book is most concerned with. The sound of wine is that of discussion. Lively discourse on how the wine tastes, what it is, where it came from, and for some, how it was made. It is telling that the word "Symposium" which has come to mean a gathering where topics are discussed, originally meant a wine tasting party.

There is another aspect of sound as it relates to wine. This is found in the joyous clink of wine glasses raised to punctuate a heartfelt toast.

Tip: To ensure you get the ringing clink, and not a dull clank, always hold your glass by the stem when you toast.

The tasting ritual

Wine is a food. We enjoy it with meals, or with company. It does not have to be expensive to be enjoyable or even to want to talk about it. The tasting ritual exists because wine is complicated, and it helps to take it one step at a time. Wine appeals to everyone, and there is no reason it should be for a privileged few. In most of the rest of the world, it is just another food item on the table.

The Steps

Figure 1.1 illustrates the order that wine is tasted and talked about. This hand-out is from my school, the Aspen Wine Program, and is given to each student as a reminder to explore each aspect of the wine. At the end of this chapter, you will find something similar to keep in your wallet.

Step 1 - Look at the wine, judge its appearance. What color is it? How opaque is it?

Step 2 - Swirl the wine and then smell it. Do it twice, the first time inhale from just outside the glass, slowly and long. The second time inhale sharply from inside the glass. This will help you to smell both the aromas that escape the glass and those that stay inside. Don't worry yet about what you smell, just how strong the smell is. This is the degree of fruit. If the wine burns your nose hairs it is "hot" and this means it has a lot of alcohol. This is usually a sign of quality in wine, if it is not too overwhelming. You also want to notice and comment on any strange or bad smells the wine may have.

ASPEN WINE PROGRAM
Wine Speak Check List

Appearance	Color	
	Opacity	
Odor/Aroma	Degree and type of fruit	
	Hot or not	
	Off odors	
Taste	Flavor	Balance of components
		Amount and type of fruit
Finish	Aftertaste	Good or bad
		Look for bitter
	Linger	Long or short
Overall	Like or dislike	
Impression	Typicity	
	Value	

Figure 1.1 - A handy reminder card

Tip: Swirling a wine glass takes practice. As you are learning, the best way to do it is to leave the wine glass on the table, place two fingers on either side of the stem, and make small circles with the base. Start slowly, and as you gain confidence swirl more vigorously. Learning to keep the wine in the glass and off your clothes is the goal. Practice with water, to minimize stains.

Step 3 - You finally get to taste the wine. Place a small amount of wine in your mouth, and perform the famous wine tasting slurp. This will increase the amount of aromas that reach your nose, through your mouth, increasing the intensity of the flavors. The flavor of the wine is defined by the balance of the 3 tastes: fruit, acid and tannin. It is further defined by the specific type of fruit you experienced, usually this is first noticeable in the smell, and often, but not always, carries through to the flavor.

> **Tip**: The slurping technique is another one that takes practice but is very important. Place a small amount of water or wine in your mouth. Do not swallow. Place your lower lip between your teeth, and raise your upper lip. You can now draw air in through your teeth and over the wine. Practice until you can do it easily, and without so much force that you choke. Beware of dribbling.

Step 4 - Look for any tastes that follow swallowing (or spitting) the wine. Are the flavors pleasant? Is there any bitterness? We are looking for actual bitterness here as opposed to the rough flavors of the tannin, and it is somewhat rare. Drinking coffee and other bitter drinks tends to dull one's palate for bitterness, so not everyone can catch it when it is there. If you do notice it, make a comment about it, because it is a sign that the wine may not age well. After the flavor and even the aftertaste have faded, can you still taste a sense of the wine? If so, this is the linger, and how long it lasts is one of the most important indications of quality in a wine.

Step 5 - Pronounce your judgment upon the wine. Did you like it or not? If you are up to it, say why. If you have tasted enough wines to compare this one to others of its class, do so, how typical is it? Finally, consider everything you have said and experienced about the wine, and if you know how much it cost, decide if the wine is a value or not. A wine that cost many hundreds of dollars should surprise no one with its quality, but a memorable wine that is affordable is a find, and you want to make sure to remember it.

A few good words

Now that you have learned the concepts, it is time to learn the words you will use.

The language of wine can be rich and varied. While this adds poetry and excitement to discussions of wine, it does not always lend itself to the complex task of conveying something as subjective as how a wine tastes. The trick to communicating is to use a few choice words rather than to use as many as you can conjure up.

For each of the aspects of wine you will be given just a few words to remember. Aroma and taste have many words associated with them, and so, many words will be listed in the next chapter. Most are so familiar you will not have to worry about remembering them.

The words will be broken down into the various aspects of wine we discussed above.

<u>Appearance</u>

Color - From youngest to oldest, although some young wines may start anywhere on the scale.

Red wine:
Purple ➤ Violet red ➤ Garnet ➤ True red ➤ Bright red ➤ Brick red ➤ Orange red ➤ Tawny

White wine:
Clear ➤ Pale green ➤ Straw ➤ Yellow ➤ Pale gold ➤ Golden ➤Amber ➤ Maderized

Opacity - From letting a lot of light through, to letting no light through.
Transparent ➤ Light ➤ Translucent ➤Dark ➤ Opaque

Brilliance - From not at all, to very.
Dull ➤ Bright ➤ Brilliant

Odor (Aroma / Bouquet)

Degree of Fruit - From not at all, to very.
Closed ➤ Tight ➤ Fruity ➤Perfumey

Hot or not - does it burn your nose hairs? If so it is high in alcohol.

Aromas - In the next chapter is a list of smells / flavors commonly found in wines. Some are pleasant, some not so. You may not find any of these in wine, or you may find something completely different. This is the most subjective part of wine.

Off Odors - Sometimes when you smell a wine, it seems somehow wrong. It may be subtle, or it may be overwhelming. The moldy smell of a corked wine is one of the most common. There are many other smells and flavors that are considered "off" and are mostly due to spoilage or some sort of mistake in the wine making.

Taste

Flavor - Here are a few words to use to describe each of the three components in a wine, fruit, acidity and tannin. The first word relates to wine that has too little of the taste in the balance, and the final word is for too much of that taste.

For fruit:
Dry wines: Sour ➤ Tart ➤ Balanced ➤ Fruity ➤Jammy
Sweet wines (for sugar): Sour ➤ Tart ➤Balanced ➤ Sweet ➤ Cloying

For Acidity: Flat ➤ Thin ➤ Balanced ➤ Tart ➤ Sour
For Tannin: Thin ➤ Light ➤ Balanced ➤Hard ➤ Rough

Notice that there is overlap with the words that relate to acidity. Acidity is the most readily recognized aspect of taste, and one of the most important in wine. You will almost always have something to say about the acidity of a wine.

> **A note about balance:** When a wine is in perfect balance it is very hard to talk about, since no one aspect of it stands out from the others. Should you find the rare wine that seems perfectly in balance, simply say so and move on. When it comes time for you to give your overall impression of the wine, look back at more than the balance. If it was complex (had many different aromas and flavors) as well as balanced, it is a great wine. If it is balanced and has nothing else going for it, it may simply be boring. I have a special term for boring wines: No Vice - No Virtue.

Finish

Aftertaste - The most important aspect of a wine's aftertaste is simply to ask yourself "Is it pleasant?" Some chemical flavors or other less pleasant flavors tend to show up in the aftertaste, so a wine that has been good up to this point may not finish as well as you would like. Bitter is one of those tastes that tends to show up at the end. Bitterness should be rare in wine, and since many people have grown used to the bitter taste of coffee and tea, they may miss it. That true bitter flavor (as opposed to the roughness of tannin) is a sign that something went wrong in the wine making process (usually the maceration period was too long) and the wine may suffer for it over time.

Linger - The best wines have an incredibly long, lingering taste. It remains after you have swallowed or spit. The flavor is almost always pleasant, and is more a shadow of all that has come before, rather than a new taste. When you taste a wine that has a long linger, you feel compelled to enjoy the taste until it fades, and then you want to try the wine again, just for the sensation of that long linger. Most wines do not linger so long as to be memorable, so make a point of mentioning it when you do find a wine that lingers forever. Low quality wines almost always have a short linger, or even no linger at all. Sweet dessert wines linger longer than dry wines, so expect more from them.

Overall impression

Like or dislike - When someone asks you what you think of a wine, they expect you to jump right to this point. Fortunately, it is usually pretty easy to tell if you do or don't like a wine, just from a sip or two. If you are not speaking with someone that expects a detailed reply, just answer this question with a simple yes or no. If you are speaking to the wine maker, or you are at a wine tasting, expect to have to add why you like or dislike the wine. When you justify your preference, it will help to be able to mention each aspect of the wine, as a way to bolster your opinion. The more you taste wine, and the more comfortable you are talking about it, the more detailed your "why" will become.

> **When good wines turn bad:** As you taste more wines, and become quite familiar with one or more types of wine, you are certain to run into a favorite wine that is not "showing well." Usually it is a shock to find a familiar wine that tastes completely different than you remember. Before you blame your palate, keep in mind that some wine is subjected to environments that may alter, or even ruin, the wine.
>
> The most common culprit are the twin plagues of shipping and storage. Not all wine is treated as well as it should be before you get it. If you are a serious wine lover you will eventually create a wine cellar of some sort. You will coddle your wines, and do everything you can to protect them. Unfortunately, you do not always have control over what has happened to the wine before it came into your possession. Chances are, the wine was not so lovingly cared for before you got it.

Rather ironically, wine tastings are a place where a wine may not show well. It may have been shipped to the tasting that day, and it may even have come to the tasting in the trunk of a car. If you taste a wine that you know, and it tastes odd, especially if it tastes as if the acid, tannin, and alcohol have all been separated, it is likely to be suffering from "bottle shock" due to the move. The good news is that wine is incredibly resilient, and given time, usually a month or two, it will be back to its own self.

Finally, a word about a "corked wine." If you taste a wine and it has a suspicious moldy smell, open another bottle and compare. If the smell is not in the second bottle, the first was corked, and was just subjected to bad luck, you do not have to write off the wine entirely. If the second bottle smells the same as the first, the barrels used to age the wine were old and moldy, and you should avoid that wine from now on. In a restaurant or a wine tasting, there should never be an issue with opening a new bottle when it is suspected the first was corked. If they do give you a hard time, do not give them your business in the future.

Typicity - Typicity is a measure of how typical a wine (or other subject of scrutiny) is for its class.

As you taste more wines, and become familiar with regions, grape varieties, or even wine makers, you can determine how typical this wine is compared to others. The important part of this is to make the decision of how typical the wine is, without judging its overall quality, or how much you like it.
In Europe many wines must be tasted by a panel of experts, to decide if the wine is typical of wines that would bear similar labels. In Italy, where new wine making trends and techniques have created many wines that are not typical of the region, the Italians have instituted a new designation for those wines which are not typical, but are still of high quality.

If you have tasted enough wines to determine if this wine is typical for wines of its class, say so. Sometimes being atypical is a bonus, often times it is not, since the consumer may be getting something other than what they expect.

Value - The ultimate pronouncement for any critic. Sure the wine was good, but was it worth it? This is in many ways the most subjective part of talking about wine. If you earn millions a year, and the greatest bottle of wine you ever tasted cost you an hour's salary, you may consider it a bargain. If you earn a more modest wage, and that same bottle of wine cost you a week's, or even a month's salary, you are not likely to consider it a bargain, no matter how good it was.

As with typicity, determining the value of a wine is made easier if you have tasted a great number of wines. You can then tell by tasting it approximately how much a similar wine would cost. Compare the wine you are tasting, against the ideal price, and see how it fares.

For those just learning about wine, keep this step simple. When it comes to value, just decide if you would pay the same amount for the wine again. If so it is a decent value.

Sample wine tasting notes

The goal in talking about wine is to share your impressions with other people. What is important is communication. The trend among wine writers has been to shorten their prose, but they still do not always communicate their experience of the wine.

Here is an actual tasting note for a Pinot Noir from a leading publication:

Earthy, decadent flavors weave through the dark cherry and orange peel notes. $18.

The wine earned 80 points. While that sounds high, it was actually one of the lowest scores of any wine they have ever listed.

This would be my tasting note for the same wine:

Light true red, and very translucent. Not much on the nose, low alcohol. Slightly dirty aroma may be a form of spoilage. Dark fruit in the mouth. Tart acid balance, no tannins, and slight fruit. Not much in the aftertaste, with perhaps a hint of citrus notes. Short linger. Overall I was not impressed with this wine. It is light compared to other Pinots from the region, and at $18 it was no bargain.

Their tasting note was much shorter than mine, but they left me with the impression they liked the wine, even though it received a low score.

Ultimately, how you talk about wine is a matter of style and personal choice. Just try not to lose sight of your objective, which is to communicate an experience.

Keep it simple

The above tasting notes are an example of what I would write or say about wine. I am a wine professional with many years practice at describing wine. It is unlikely you would describe a wine with the detail I did, nor is there any real reason to do so.

Using the terms I have outlined in this book, this same wine could easily be described as:

Tight, with a tart balance. Light tannins, short linger.

This is a perfectly reasonable thing to say about this wine, and it communicates your experience with the wine as well, or better than I did.

Written notes vs. talking about wine in person

When you write about a wine you have time to reflect on what you tasted. When you are prompted for an answer to "what do you think of it?" you will be put on the spot and you will have to talk about each aspect of the wine as you taste it.

Written tasting note for a fictional Chardonnay:

Light golden color. A ton of fruit on the nose. Hints of bright tropical fruits, as well as woody notes from oak aging. My first impression of the wine was that it smelled better than it tasted, but it soon developed a near explosion of fruit in my mouth. Well balanced, with just a hint of oak tannins leading me to think that this wine could use some more aging. Pineapple and cloves notes are predominant, with hints of ripe melon and other bright fruits. The aftertaste is rich and pleasant, with a long linger that seems to go on forever. The fruit in this wine is typical of a well made Chardonnay. At this stage in its aging the oak gets in the way. A very good wine that will be excellent in another year or two. At $50 it is not a bargain, but it is what I would expect to pay for this quality.

The same wine, described in person:

I love the golden color, since the wine isn't that old I would guess it has seen a lot of oak. *(after smelling the wine)* Wow, that is a huge nose. *(after tasting the wine)* Hmm, not much to it at first... wait here it comes. Everything that was in the nose is in the mouth now, and the balance is great. I am tasting a little more oak than I like, but that will probably go away if the wine ages a bit more. Nothing is standing out in the finish, but it sure keeps going. Nice wine, if a tad pricey.

Finally

There are many ways to talk about wine, and many words you can use. The words we have just covered will be all most people ever need to know. For those who love technical things, or wish to advance their knowledge of wine, the rest of the book will cover many more aspects of talking about wine. For those who just wanted the confidence of having something to say when tasting wine, continue to review the past section whenever you feel the need.

If you have now learned everything you wanted to know in regards to talking about wine, or even if you plan to keep reading and become an expert, there is something that you should consider doing from now on. Take notes whenever you can. Even if you never look back at the notes, it will force you to pay attention to what you are tasting, and will be good practice to help you taste every aspect of a wine.

Tape

Wine Tasting Card
Make note of each of these in order

Appearance	Color		
	Opacity		
Odor/Aroma	Degree and type of fruit		
	Hot or not		
	Off odors		
Taste	Flavor	Balance of components	
		Amount and type of fruit	
Finish	Aftertaste	Good or bad	
		Look for bitter	
	Linger	Long or short	
Overall Impression	Like or dislike		
	Typicity		
	Value		

Fold (left margin)   *Fold* (right margin)

	Too Little	A Little	Balanced	A Lot	Too Much
Aroma	Closed	Tight	Balanced	Fruity	Perfumey
Fruit:					
Dry	Sour	Tart	Balanced	Fruity	Jammy
Sweet	Sour	Tart	Balanced	Sweet	Cloying
Acidity	Flat	Thin	Balanced	Tart	Sour
Tannin	Thin	Light	Balanced	Hard	Rough

Tape

Figure 1.2 A wine tasting card to copy and keep

How to talk about
What you are tasting

The Details

In the previous chapter we covered the basics that are required to talk about wine. While that brief vocabulary is sufficient to allow you to convey the general essence of the wine, it fails to fill in the gaps and provide the tools necessary to really describe a wine. For this, you need all the words you can get.

The most obvious missing words are those that describe the flavors or smells you are experiencing. We will start with an aroma chart that will not only list the most commonly used words, but will show the general groups the aromas belong to. Following the aroma charts is an alphabetical listing of those wine tasting words you are most likely to need or encounter.

Pick those words that you find suit you, and do not feel the need to use words that feel clumsy, or awkward for you. In time your vocabulary will grow, and your confidence as you talk about wine will grow with it.

Aroma Chart

The following charts contain many of the words that people commonly use when they describe wine. You may find flavors or smells in the wine that remind you of something that is not here. Or it may just be hard to determine exactly what you smell or taste.

This is common, in fact it may be more common to not know what to call a smell or flavor than it is to be definite about the name. Since there are no actual strawberries in wine (as a random example), it would be unusual to smell or taste a wine and get an overwhelming impression of strawberries. Rather, there tends to be very subtle flavors and aromas that in some way suggest, or remind you of one or several of the words on the following charts.

Pleasant Aromas, by Group

Fruity

Grapefruit	Citrus
Lemon	Citrus
Orange	Citrus
Melon	Bright fruit
Pineapple	Bright fruit
Apple	Light fruit
Apricot	Light fruit
Banana	Light fruit
Fig	Light fruit
Green apple	Light fruit
Peach	Light fruit
Pear	Light fruit
Currants	Red fruit
Raspberry	Red fruit
Red cherry	Red fruit
Strawberry	Red fruit
Dark cherry	Dark fruit
Plum	Dark fruit
Prune	Dried fruit
Raisin	Dried fruit
Blackberry	Bramble fruit
Wild berries	Bramble fruit

Floral

Lemon blossom	Bright floral
Linden	Bright floral
Orange blossom	Bright floral

Pleasant Aromas, by Group *cont.*

Floral

Honey	Sweet floral
Honeysuckle	Sweet floral
Rose	Rich floral
Violet	Rich floral

Vegetal

Green bell pepper	Green
Olive, Green	Green
Freshly cut grass	Grassy
Dried grass	Hay

Herbal

Anise	Anise
Basil	Anise
Fennel	Anise
Licorice	Anise
Black pepper	
Mint	
Tea leaves	

Earthy

Black truffle	Mushroom
Mushroom	Mushroom
White truffle	Mushroom
Soil *(if light)*	Forest floor
Wet leaves *(if light)*	Forest floor
Flint	
Olive, black	

Pleasant Aromas, by Group *cont.*

Animal

Butter	
Leather	
Musk	

Nutty

Hazel Nut	Nutty

Woody

Cedar	Woody
Oak *(if light)*	Woody
Cinnamon	Wood spices
Clove	Wood spices
Vanilla (Vanillin)	Wood spices

Burnt

Cigar box *(somewhat woody as well)*	
Chocolate	Dark aromas
Coffee	Dark aromas
Tar *(if light)*	Dark aromas
Tobacco	Dark aromas
Smoke *(if light)*	Smokey

Less Pleasant Aromas, by Group
(*some smells are not so bad if they are not too strong*)

Fruity

| Grapes | Foxy |

Vegetal

Cabbage, cooked	Sulfur
Asparagus, canned	Green
Green leaves	Green

Earthy

| Dirt | Forest floor |
| Wet leaves | Forest floor |

Animal

Dog, wet	Spoiled
Horse, or horse blanket	Barnyard
Sour milk	

Nutty

| Hazel nut *(if strong or old wine)* | Oxidized |

Woody

| Oak *(if strong)* | Over oaked |

Burnt

Caramel	Oxidized
Charcoal	
Smoke *(if strong)*	Smokey

Less Pleasant Aromas, by Group *cont.*
(some smells are not so bad if they are not too strong)

Chemical

Alcohol	Hot
Chemicals generally	
Pine cleaner	Pitch
Pricked	Sour
(tickles your nose like vinegar)	
Rotten eggs	Sulfur
Shower cap	Rubbery
Soap	
Sulfur	Sulfur
Tar *(if strong)*	Tar

Moldy

Mold	
Wet cardboard	Corked
Wet dirt with mold	Brett

Yeasty

Beer
Bread, freshly baked
Yeast

Example usage: If you smell or taste something that reminds you of "Cherries," you may instead want to say "Red Fruit." In this way the person you are talking to will have a better chance of understanding than if you say "Cherries," and they taste "Strawberries."

Bouquet vs. Aroma: Odor encompasses all smells, and even flavors. In wine the two words aroma and bouquet are often used, but rarely defined. Aroma are those smells that come from the grapes, and are most noticeable in youth.

Bouquet are those smells that develop from wine making, and aging. If in doubt, avoid the word bouquet.

Tasting glossary

What follows are a collection of words that are used by wine tasters. Some of them are words that probably should not be used, even if they commonly are. Some words are foreign, especially French, since the vocabulary of wine is richest where they have a long tradition of making and enjoying wine. Almost all of the words are appropriate for more advanced wine tasters.

Acidity The tart taste in wines. When there is too much acidity the wine can taste sour.

Aroma The smell of a young wine. Different from bouquet, in that Aroma is the smell that comes from the grapes, and bouquet, which takes time to develop, is the smell that comes from the finished wine. Technically there are 3 forms of aroma. Primary aroma, which originates in the grape itself. Secondary aroma, those which are aerobic (happens in air) and are due to the wine making process (this includes barrel aging). Finally, tertiary aromas are those which develop in a reductive environment (without air) in the sealed bottle, over time, these are what is usually called "bouquet."

Aftertaste The taste that stays in your mouth after swallowing the wine. It should be pleasant and in fine wines it should last a long time after the wine is gone.

Astringent That mouth puckering feeling that some wines give you. Related to, and usually caused by tannins. The sensation is accentuated by the acid in wine.

Balance A much used, but rarely defined term in wine tasting. A wine is said to be balanced when no single component is overwhelming the wine, and the overall impression is pleasing.

Bitter Wine tasting term for the sensation in the finish of a wine. This is different than astringency (q.v.) which is a dry feeling in the mouth. Bitterness is very hard to spot, it is rare and undesireable in wine. As well, the taster gets used to the bitterness quickly, so the impression goes away after a few sips.

Body The overall mouth feel or weight of a wine. Some tasters incorrectly attribute it to glycerin or glycol in wine (there is not enough in wine to make wine thick). The term may be related to the amount of dry extract in a wine (what is left when you remove the water).

Bouquet Used generically to indicate how a wine smells, or more specifically to indicate aromas associated with bottle aging. A more technical term for this later definition is "tertiary aromas."

Clean In wine tasting this term refers to wines that do not have any noticeable unpleasant or out of the ordinary odors or flavors. Modern wine making has ensured that most wines today are clean. Some may complain that New World wines can be clean to a fault. The lack of faults as a fault in itself is an interesting argument, and one that implies that a few faults in wine give it "character."

Cloudy A wine with particles floating in it from the wine making process. Modern wine making has made this very rare; however, some wine makers skip the filtering process and their wines may exhibit this fault. Wine that has "thrown sediment" with age is not said to be cloudy.

Cloying Overly sweet, to the point of being faulty. Wine should be balanced. The sweet flavors should be balanced with the sour flavors of the acids (much as lemonade is).

Color The color of wine tells us much about its origin and wine making. Deeper colors usually relate to longer wine making practices and higher quality wines. Red wines range from blue-red, through red and as they age towards orange red (or brick red). White wines range in color from clear to deep golden, with hints of greens common in lighter wines. As whites age they tend to turn towards brown.

Corked / Corky The most common fault in wine and the reason for the tasting ritual at a restaurant. The characteristic smell is a moldy, wet cardboard aroma. The cause is bacteria from the cork that has reacted with the bleaching process. Synthetic corks are free of this defect and this is a leading reason for their increasing adoption.

Coulant *(coo-lahn)* A rather poetic French wine tasting term that literally means flowing. It is used for wines that are easy to drink. In the US we may say "quaffable."

Crackling The English language term for a wine that is slightly sparkling, or bubbly, due to dissolved carbon dioxide. The French use the term "pétillant" and the Italians use the term I prefer "frizzante." The slight sparkle in crackling wines is intended to add freshness, and these types of wine are not uncommon in Italy. Some wines that exhibit this slight sparkling character do so less from intent than by accident. Dissolved carbon dioxide that may be unnoticeable at sea level is quite distinct at the high altitude of our offices (almost 9000 feet or 3000 meters). Wine makers are often surprised to find this in their wines when they visit.

Crisp A wine tasting term used to imply that a white wine has a refreshing acid balance. It is used much the same way one may say the taste (not texture) of a fresh green apple is "crisp."

Dry The opposite of sweet in wine parlance. This term is used to denote a wine that has no residual sugar. Often this word is misused to refer to a wine with a minimal amount of "fruit." Most wines are dry with sweeter varieties being primarily white.

Dulce *(dool'th-eh)* Literally sweet in Spanish, the term usually refers to the sweetening agent added to some Sherry.

Dumb A wine tasting term to mean a wine that is not showing up to its potential. Dumb, in this context, refers not to intelligence but to the inability to speak. While trying to avoid words that are anthropomorphic, this one seems particularly well suited.

Earthy A wine tasting term. It means just what it sounds like, a slight taste or aroma of soil. The French use a term "goût de terroir" that is often used to mean the same thing; although it can also mean that the wine has typical tastes for the region.

Elegant A dubious wine tasting term. It refers to a well balanced wine that has subtle complexity. I say it is a dubious term because it is anthropomorphic (giving human traits to inanimate objects) and should be avoided. That said, I am guilty of using the word myself.

Faded A wine tasting term for a wine that has lost all or much of its flavor and aromas over time.

Fat In the US this term often infers that the wine is lacking in acidity. In other parts of the world the term fat is used to indicate a full, well balanced wine, and is a compliment.

Fatigue When a wine is subjected to shaking and jostling, either through the winemaking process, or shipping, it becomes fatigued. The further the wine has travelled, or the more severe the trip, the longer it will take to recover. Also called Bottle Shock or Bottle Fatigue. Usually a temporary condition which a month or more of rest will cure.

Finesse One of the wine tasting terms I most recommend avoiding because it is vague and anthropomorphic. When not applied to wine the term suggests "subtlety in performance, skill" (Random House Dictionary). Wine is inanimate, it has no skills, and does not perform. Subtlety is further defined as "elusively thin or tenuous" (Random House Dictionary) and these terms are not a compliment for wine. I suspect the term is most used to express admiration for the balance of a very fine wine, one where the balance between the fruit, acidity and tannins are harmonious enough to keep any one from standing out.

Finish The final flavors you taste in the wine. Often confused with "aftertaste." I distinguish the finish as being the taste you notice just as you swallow or spit a wine, as opposed to the aftertaste which are those flavors you notice after you swallow the wine, and which linger in your mouth for some time. Tannin is one of the common components that are noticeable in the finish of a wine.

Foxy A wine making term for the smell of native American grape varieties. The best example is the Concord grape that most Welch's grape juice is made from. The term originated with the early settlers who called the native grapes Fox grapes.

Fresh Most wine is intended to be enjoyed young. When this young wine has ample acidity in the balance, it is often referred to as fresh.

Frizzante *(free-zahn'-teh)* The Italian term for a wine that is slightly sparkling. Some wines may exhibit this spritz or sparkle by accident, but more often it is intentional. The French use the term "pétillant" although I prefer this Italian term.

Fruit Wine basically has three components. Fruit, acidity and tannin. All three must be in balance to make a decent wine. The fruit encompasses all the tastes and smells that that are not sour (acid) or bitter (tannin). Every grape variety and style of wine exhibits different fruit. In some wines such as Zinfandel the fruit can be very noticeable (Zin has so much fruit it is often described as jammy). Other wines such as Cabernet Sauvignon have less obvious fruit.

Fruity Some young wines have an aroma that can only be described as fruity. Beaujolais is one of the best known examples.

Goût de Terrior *(goo-de-tare-wah)* A much used, little defined French term. Literally it means "taste of the soil." Often used to describe the earthy flavors found in some wines. Just as often used to credit the conditions of soil and climate, for the particular taste of a wine or region.

Green A wine tasting term for wines made from under ripe grapes. The wine will have the smell of vegetation and be highly acidic.

Hard In wine tasting terms this relates to a wine that is tannic, particularly one that is so tannic that it is out of balance. This is a function of youth for some wines, and these wines will "soften" with age.

Harsh A hard wine with excessive acidity will be "harsh." The acid accentuates the tannins and increases the drying sensation known as astringency.

Heavy Used in wine tasting to imply that the wine is out of balance towards the tannins. This type of wine is more than just "hard" it is tannic to a fault, and may not soften enough with age to be enjoyable.

Herbaceous A green, vegetable smell in wine. For example, Sauvignon Blanc is grassy when subtle, herbaceous when overpowering. It is considered a negative attribute when it is more than slightly noticable.

Hot The burning sensation of excessive or out of balance alcohol in wine. Usually found in the nose, rather than the taste.

Legs A much over used and meaningless wine tasting term. It refers to the streams that are seen on the side of the glass after swirling (also called tears). While too many so called experts explain this as being related to the body, or the amount of glycerin in the wine, it is actually a function of the alcohol, and has no relation to the quality of the wine at all.

Light The opposite of heavy. A wine without much tannin in the balance. The wine may still be complex, and full of flavor. Such wines are often enjoyable young, but rarely age. Uncharacteristically, there is a legal meaning for Light Wines in the US. They must be less than 14% alcohol. This is the same alcohol limit for all table wines in the US, making the legal definition of Light Wine somewhat redundant.

Limpid Literally this word means transparent, as in pure water. Used in wine tasting to imply a wine that is clear and bright. Occasionally misused by those who associate the homonym "limp" with the word, and assume it must mean something negative. It may be best to avoid this term, using "clear" instead.

Maderized A wine tasting term for a wine that has been affected by oxidation. In extreme examples the wine (usually white wine) has begun to turn brown. This process is identical to the browning that occurs in an apple that has had a bite taken out of it. The term comes from the wines of Madeira, which are very brown, due to a great deal of oxidation, and being baked.

Moelleux *(m'wah-luh)* A French term for a wine that is ever so slightly sweet. There is no real English equivalent. The term "threshold" is applied in the US to wines that have measurable residual sugar, but do not taste sweet to most people.

Moldy Just what it sounds like. Wines (usually red) that were affected by mold and used to make wine anyway will have this off taste and odor.

Mou *(mooh)* A French term for a wine that is soft or thin to a fault. Not well known in the US, but a good term to know as there is not really an English equivalent.

Mousse *(moose)* The French term for the foam found on sparkling wines or beer. Often called "head" in English.

Mousy A wine tasting term for the smell and taste of a particular bacterial spoilage in some faulty wines.

Musty The off smell of a wine that has been in contact with old or poorly cleaned wooden casks. It is similar to a moldy smell, or even the "corked" smell of an off wine. If you experience this smell, and think it may be a corked bottle, try opening another bottle of the same wine, if it still exists, it is likely musty, and not corked.

Nutty A wine tasting term for a wine that exhibits flavors reminiscent of nuts, especially hazelnut. In some cases this can be a sign that the wine is oxidized. Sherry and Tawny Ports are both very nutty, and very oxidized (hence the brown color).

Oeil de Perdrix *(uh'y duh pair-dree)* Literally eye of the partridge in French. The term is used to connote a color of wine. It is a browning pink color. The term is old, and rarely used much anymore, but seems to have referred to rosé wines that were slightly oxidized. You may run across the term in reading old notes, or from overly poetic wine writers.

Off A very general word for any wine that is not quite as it should be. Usually used by a taster familiar with the wine, who is pronouncing that this bottle or sample is somehow damaged. Especially used to describe an odor that may be due to a problem with the wine.

Oxidized A wine tasting term for a wine that has absorbed oxygen. In extreme examples the wine (usually white wine) has begun to turn brown. This process is identical to the browning that occurs in an apple that has had a bite taken out of it. Also known as "maderized."

Perfume Used by some wine tasters to describe the abundant floral quality of some white wines. It should be used exclusively for those aromas that derive from the grape itself (primary aromas).

Perlant *(pehr-lahn)* A French term for a wine that has some, but very little sparkle. It is for wines that are less sparkling than what the French call "pétillant," and the Italians call "frizzante."

Pétillant *(peh-tee-yahn)* The French term for a wine that is slightly sparkling. Equivalent to the Italian term "frizzante."

Piqué *(pee-kay)* A French term, it means a wine that has begun to sour.

Plonk A common slang term for bulk or jug wines.

Rancio In an odd twist of wine jargon, this term, which literally means "rancid" in Spanish is used to describe the browning effect, and nutty taste that wines take on when purposefully exposed to air during aging. It is not considered a negative trait in these wines. Madeira is one such wine, and it has lent its name to the term "maderized' which has a similar meaning, but is used with a negative connotation for wines that were not meant to be oxidized. Common sense would dictate that these two terms are reversed, and yet, this is how they are used. Tawny Port, Marsala and Banyuls are all wines that could be described as rancio.

Robe *(roab)* A French wine tasting term. Usually translated to mean color, it seems to also refer to the overall appearance of a wine.

Robust A commonly used wine tasting term which belongs to the group of terms I would suggest you avoid. Anthropomorphic and vague, it seems to be used for a wine that is not showing any signs of fault, and is high in dry extract (rich and mouth filling). It is not clear if this term applies to or alludes to the amount of tannins in the wine. It is also not clear if it indicates quality or just the "weight" of the body of the wine.

Rotten Egg The odor of hydrogen sulfide (the additive to household gas that allows you to smell it escaping). Rare in wine, and most unfortunate when it occurs. Almost always attributed to poor handling of grapes and the wine during production.

Rough A wine tasting term for a wine that is astringent, and tannic out of balance. Mostly a term for young wines. Rough wines rarely soften enough with age to be really enjoyable. By the time the roughness has gone, so has all of the fruit.

Round A wine tasting term applied to a wine that is well balanced. Often used as in "a well rounded wine."

Sediment In a young wine still being made, the sediment is the remnants of the wine making process itself. These tiny particles drop to the bottom of the barrel or tank, and the wine is then racked - moved to a fresh tank or barrel - and the sediment left behind. If the wine is not perfectly clear when bottled, rare in modern winemaking, the particles are called haze or clouds rather than sediment. In a wine that has been bottled, sediment is the collective solids that form at the bottom of the bottle over time. This is made up of the tannins and coloring agents (phenolic compounds) that have precipitated out of solution. This is why a wine becomes lighter in color, and less tannic as it ages. Wine is decanted when it has sediment so that the clear wine can be enjoyed, and the sediment thrown away. Sparkling wine made in the champagne method has its own form of sediment. This forms after the yeast have created the bubbles in the wine during a secondary fermentation. The process of riddling and degorging is used to remove the sediment. On the bottom of a cork or in white wines there can be another form of sediment. This comes from the harmless crystals of potassium bitartrate (cream of tartar in the spice section of the grocery store) which precipitate out of the wine when the temperature is dropped. Because these crystals are sometimes mistaken for sugar, or even glass, most white wines are cold stabilized to allow this crystal to be removed before bottling. A commonly used expression is to say that a wine has "thrown sediment", meaning that sediment has accumulated.

Sharp A wine tasting term used when the acid in a wine is out of balance or strong. It would fall between "tart" and "sour" on a scale of perceived acidity.

Short One of the most important measures of quality in fine wine is how long the flavors stay in your mouth after swallowing or spitting. A short wine is one of poor quality, that does not linger.

Sick An old fashioned wine tasting term for a wine that is very faulty, such as being cloudy with an odd smell. This term is anthropomorphic, and implies that the wine can somehow become well again. It is best avoided.

Silky A wine tasting term for a specific mouth feel that is evident in the very finest of red wines. It is related to balance and is usually used when the wine is old enough for the tannins to have softened.

Simple A wine tasting term for a wine that has very little complexity. That is, it doesn't have a lot of different flavors. Most wines are simple to some degree, with only the greatest wines being complex.

Smooth A wine tasting term that refers to a tactile sensation in the mouth (mouth feel) associated with the acids, rather than the tannins in the wine (see soft). Technically a wine is smooth due to the presence of lactic acid, which in turn is present in the wine due to malo-lactic fermentation. This secondary fermentation turns the tart, "sharp" malic acid, found in green apples, into the "smooth" lactic acid found in milk. The opposite of smooth is sharp.

Soapy An off odor in some faulty wines. Technically, it may be due to fatty acids produced by the yeast that end up as salts in the wine, notably caprylic acid salts. The term "soapy" is also used for a wine that has very little acid in the balance. There is some debate on the use of the term, as flat seems to cover the meaning.

Soft A wine tasting term that refers to the lack of apparent tannins in a wine. If the wine is well aged, or in a style that is enjoyed young, soft is a plus. If the wine is meant to age, and is soft in its youth, it is a minus, as one would expect to find tannins to help the wine age.

Solid A rather vague, but commonly used wine tasting term. Usually used when the wine is showing no obvious flaws and is in balance. It is not clear if this is to be considered a compliment, or just a way of saying there is nothing wrong with the wine.

Sophisticated A wine term that should almost certainly be avoided. Originally it was a euphemism that meant that the wine had not been tampered with to make it seem better. This meaning is largely forgotten, and was never well known outside of professional circles. It is more likely to be used now to mean a wine that is complex. When used in this way the term is anthropomorphic and vague. When used in the original context it is more specific, although few people will understand that it means unadulterated.

Sound A wine tasting term that means the wine is free of defects. It is the minimum expected of a wine, and therefore can not be construed as a compliment.

Sour A wine tasting term for a wine that has too much acidity in the balance. This is beyond tart, and usually means the wine has a serious defect, such as it is turning into vinegar (technically it has too much volatile acidity). This should be considered rare, and marks a wine that is not drinkable.

Spice / Spicy A wine tasting term. Use carefully. Gewürztraminer (which means spicy traminer) is the only grape that you should use the unqualified term spice for (in reference to its aroma). For every other type of wine, it is important to specify what kind of spice you mean (after all there are many spices). Black Pepper spice is common in red wines, and woody spices (such as clove and cinnamon (from aging in oak barrels) are found in some white wines.

Spritz The English language term for slightly sparkling. The French call it "pétillant," the Germans "spritzig" and the Italians use my favorite term "frizzante." Some wines, such as Moscato d'Asti are made to have very light carbonation. Other wines may have a small amount of dissolved carbon dioxide by accident. This term applies to both conditions.

Steely A wine tasting term used primarily for very crisp, dry, white wines. The high acid balance of these wines can leave a metallic impression on the palate. Chablis, the great Chardonnay of the Burgundy region of France, is often said to be "steely." Flinty is another term that seems to have the same or similar meaning.

Stemmy A wine tasting term for the flavor of stems in some wines. The taste is bitter and full of chlorophyll and so is sometimes also called "green." This should be considered a fault in wine, as it rarely improves the flavors.

Sturdy A rather vague wine tasting term. It seems to be used for wines that are tannic, but not to a fault, and are otherwise well balanced.

Supple A very common wine tasting term. As with many wine tasting terms, it is rather vague. It literally means "compliant or yielding." When applied to a wine it seems to mean a wine that is easy to drink without being too simple. The lack of tannins in the balance seems to be one of the primary requirements for a wine to be supple.

Sweet There are four basic tastes: sweet, sour, bitter and salty (all other flavors are actually related to smell). Of these, only sweet is pleasant. In dry wine the alcohol adds a slight sweet taste to help balance the tannins and acids. Sweet being the opposite of dry in wine, sweet wines contain some amount of sugar. This can vary from a barely noticeable 1% up to an intense 10% or more. Since too sweet is the definition of "cloying" all decent sweet wines have a good deal of acidity (which is sour) to balance out the sugar. The best sweet wines are actually more "sweet-tart."

Tannin Those compounds responsible for the bitter and astringent tastes in wine. They are found primarily in the skin and seeds of the grape, as well as stems (which are not always included in the wine making process). Because white wines have little to no contact with these parts of the grape, white wines have little tannin. Aging in oak barrels can also add (oak) tannin to wines. Tannin is required for aging red wine. Not all tannic red wines will age well, but few red wines without strong tannins will age well either. Technically the tannins are known collectively as "phenolic compounds."

Tar / Tarry Some wines have a dark flavor that wine tasters call tar. It is not the overwhelming stench of a tarred road, rather it is a flavor so dark, that only tar seems to fit. Rhône wines can have this, as well as the Barolos of Italy. If it is too pronounced it is not a positive thing.

Tart A wine tasting term for a wine that is noticeably acidic. As long as the acid is not overwhelming, it is only tart. A stronger acid flavor would be harsh and a very strong acid flavor would be sour. Dessert wines are often sweet/tart as the acid and residual sugars balance each other.

Tears Another name for "legs." A much over used and meaningless wine tasting term. It refers to the streams that are seen on the side of the glass after swirling. While too many so called experts explain this as being related to the body, or the amount of glycerin in the wine, it is actually a function of the alcohol, and has no relation to the quality of the wine at all.

Terroir *(tair-wah'r)* While this literally means soil in French, it has many more implications. It may also be used to mean the surrounding weather patterns such as the English language term "microclimate." For some, the term may mean how typical the wine is of the region the "expression of terrior." Like many French wine tasting terms this one has been adopted by English speaking wine professionals, although it is no more easily defined when used in English. It is often used in conjunction with the French word for "taste" as in "goût de terroir."

Thin A wine tasting term for any wine that has little flavor. Technically it is used for a wine that has little dry extract (what is left after you remove all the liquid).

Usé *(oo-zay)* A wine tasting term from the French for "worn out." A more common English language term is "over the hill."

Vert *(vair)* French for green. A wine that is green will have the smell of vegetation and be highly acidic.

Vinous *(vin-us)* A wine tasting term used for wines that have no real flaws, but the best thing you can say about them is that they taste like wine.

Woody When a wine has had extensive aging in a barrel, it takes on the barrel taste, hence it is "woody." The taste of wood, usually oak, should not dominate the flavor of the wine. It is there to help the wine age, and will diminish over time. Some winemakers disguise the taste of their wines with wood, especially in regions where the grapes do not ripen completely. In the New World this taste has become synonymous with Chardonnay for many wine lovers, although one may debate that this is not a positive thing.

Yeasty A wine taster's term for a wine that has a pronounced flavor or aroma of yeast. Reminiscent of fresh bread, this flavor is common in sparkling wines and wines aged "sur lie." For all other types of wine, this flavor should be considered a fault. It should never be too pronounced, and in sparkling wines, it should be more toasty (like burnt bread) than a freshly baked loaf.

Young A designation for any wine that is not quite ready to drink. In the case of lighter wines, this may be directly on release; but for Cabernet Sauvignon based wines, and others designed for prolonged aging, the period of youth may last a decade or more.

How to talk about
Where it came from

What is that wine called?

For most wine drinkers in the US, it is the grape that gives the wine its identity. Clearly marked on the bottle, the name of the grape is usually the largest text on the label. This is true for most wines that are made in the New World. European wines by contrast, tend to emphasize the place name where the wine was made. Even the European wines tell you what the grapes are, or at least what the grapes are likely to be, if you know enough about the regions.

By reading through the list of grapes first, and then the sections on the regions of the world, you will have a better chance of determining what a wine will be like, just by looking at the label.

Grapes, and regions can give you a clue as to where it came from before you open it, but it is the producer and even vintage that will ultimately determine the quality of the wine. Producers and vintages change with alarming regularity, and this book would have to be republished every year in order to keep up. It is up to you then, to keep track of the trends in weather, and producers. This is one of the most important reasons to keep notes of the wines you have tried.

The grapes

Stone age man knew about grapes. Evidence for this has been found in ancient caves and dwellings. The grapes our early ancestors enjoyed were almost certainly closely related to the Muscat grape of today. The Muscat is one of the few wine grapes that is also good to eat, which is important since early man ate grapes long before he discovered wine. Almost every grape in the following list can trace its existence back to the original Muscat grape.

Wine was discovered, not invented. All other alcoholic beverages had to be invented, but grapes, left to their own devices, will ferment, and turn into a simple wine. It is likely that this is how wine was discovered. A clay pot with grapes was forgotten about, and when it was found, the grapes had transformed into wine. Not only did techniques to improve wine develop, so did different types of grape come into being as early civilization learned about domestication and cross breeding. Over the millennia the original Muscat grape, while still around today, has been bred into a profusion of varieties that boggles the mind.

Thousands upon thousands of grape varieties were produced, each with different characteristics, as well as benefits and weaknesses. Over time some grape varieties were found to perform better in a certain climate than others, and regional preferences started to take shape. By the time the 20th century began, most of the grapes we use today had been developed, and most had a home in some part of Europe. With the expansion into the New World, these grapes followed the immigrants to the far corners of the world. In some climates the old grapes thrived, and in others they did not. By process of elimination a handful of grape varieties were found to perform better than others, and these have become the grapes that you are most likely to encounter.

Key to grape charts:

Old world: Where in Europe the grape is found.

New world: Where in the rest of the world the grape is found.

Color: General color of wine made from this grape.

Aroma: Most commonly used words to describe the smell and flavors.

Body: How much tannin wine made from this grape usually has.

Blended with: What other grapes it is regularly blended with.

Other: Any other information about the grape.

Red wine grapes

Cabernet Sauvignon

Old world: Bordeaux, primary in Haut-Medoc.

New world: Pervasive.

Color: Dark red with blue hints when young.

Aroma: Cassis and bramble fruit.

Body: Heavy.

Blended with: Merlot, Cabernet Franc, Malbec, Petit Verdot, Syrah (Australia).

Other: Increasingly being planted in Italy where it only recently has gained an official status. Often heavily oaked, but incorporates well into the wine.

Merlot

Old world: Bordeaux, primary in St.-Emilion and Pomerol.

New world: California, Washington State and South America.

Color: Tends towards medium dark and very blue.

Aroma: Green bell pepper and red bramble fruit.

Body: Moderate.

Blended with: Usually with Cabernet Sauvignon and/or Cabernet Franc.

Other: Increasingly being sold as a varietal wine even in the Old World. Diacetyl (a buttery flavor from malo-lactic fermentation) and vanillic acid (vanilla flavor from oak aging) are common and often noticable in Merlot produced in the US.

Pinot Noir

Old world: Burgundy. Also Germany and Switzerland.

New world: California and Oregon, New Zealand.

Color: Red, sometimes with a slight hint of blue. Very translucent.

Aroma: Cherries and linden (a flower that to some has a 'Band-aid' smell).

Body: Light to medium.

Blended with: Rarely blended, except with Chardonnay in Champagne.

Other: The hardest of all wines to make, and often the most rewarding when it is successful.

Syrah

Old world: Rhône, France.

New world: Australia (called Shiraz), California.

Color: Deep red with a good deal of blue.

Aroma: Violets and sometimes black pepper. Some hints of tar in the heavier versions.

Body: Medium to heavy.

Blended with: Grenache, and in the region of Châteauneuf-du-Pape up to 11 other grapes. The white grape Viognier is used occasionally in the Côte Rôtie (Rhône). In Australia Syrah (Shiraz) is a very important grape and is often blended with Cabernet Sauvignon.

Other: The Syrah of Australia is an older clone than in the Rhône. The clone was taken before phylloxera. Petite Sirah is no relation at all.

Cabernet Franc

Old world: The Loire, and as a blending grape in Bordeaux, both in France.

New world: Anywhere Cabernet Sauvignon and Merlot is grown.

Color: Light to medium, bright red.

Aroma: Raspberry and/or dry hay.
Body: Light to medium.

Blended with: Very commonly blended with Merlot and Cabernet Sauvignon.

Other: Just starting to catch on as a single varietal wine in the US.

Grenache

Old world: Rhône and Southern France. Rioja, Spain.

New world: Some plantings in the US.

Color: Light red to orange.

Aroma: Spicy black pepper. Light red fruits.

Body: Light to heavy, usually medium.

Blended with: Extensively with Syrah in the Rhône and a countless other grapes in the south of France. In Rioja it is blended with Tempranillo. In the US Grenache is often blended with Zinfandel.

Other: Also used in France to make the excellent rosés of Tavel and Lirac, and exceptional fortified dessert wines of Roussillon.

Nebbiolo

Old world: Piedmont, Italy.

New world: Small amounts in US.

Color: Solid red. Very translucent.

Aroma: Light red fruit.

Body: Medium to heavy.

Blended with: Rarely.

Other: The grape of Barolo and Barberesco. A difficult grape that is often overlooked outside of the region.

Sangiovese

Old world: Tuscany, Italy.

New world: Rare, but increasing in California.

Color: Usually a translucent solid red with very little blue even in youth.

Aroma: Dark red fruits, dark cherries.

Body: From very light to very heavy, depending on the wine.

Blended with: In the Chianti section of Tuscany it is blended with the white grape Trebbianno (sometimes to a fault). In the "Super-Tuscans" it is blended with Cabernet Sauvignon.

Other: There are huge differences in the various clones of this grape. There is the Grosso clone which is the more common, and the Piccolo clone which is smaller in size and plantings. The Brunello clone may be the finest example of Sangiovese, and many would argue that it is almost a distinct grape of its own.

Zinfandel

Old world: Possibly the Primativo of Italy, but it is now rare (it has recently been suggested that Primativo came from Zin, and not the other way around).

New world: The only Vinifera grape that is exclusive to California.
Color: Deep purple, often inky.

Aroma: Bramble berries and jammy dark fruit.

Body: Light to moderate. Zinfandel lends itself to many styles, but usually has very little tannin.

Blended with: Any number of things, but Petite Syrah and Grenache are the most common. Some of the finest examples are field blends with many other grapes.

Other: Often made into a rosé, this exceptional grape has earned an undeserved reputation based on these insipid pink wines.

White wine grapes

Chardonnay

Old world: Burgundy, France and some plantings in Italy.

New world: Pervasive.

Color: Almost always tends toward light golden hues. The longer it has aged in oak, the more golden it will be.

Aroma: Tropical fruits, melons, mineral qualities, citrus and even green apple are all comon.

Body: Medium to heavy with oak aging.

Blended with: Rarely blended with anything, but occasionally with Sémillon.

Other: Increasingly being planted in Italy where it only recently received official status.

Riesling

Old world: Germany and Alsace, France.

New world: US, New Zealand.

Color: Almost always clear, becoming golden with age in the sweeter styles.

Aroma: Flowery with a distinct aroma often called "petrol" or "diesel."

Body: Light to medium, often made in a sweet style.

Blended with: With Ruländer (Pinot Gris) but never in quality wines.

Other: A great grape that doesn't get the respect it deserves. Many examples, either dry or sweet, are among the finest, most complex wines in the world.

Sémillon

Old world: Bordeaux.

New world: Australia primarily. Can be found in small plantings around the world.

Color: Clear to very light golden.

Aroma: Figs and/or orange marmalade are the traditional answers. I tend to find a rubbery smell on occasion.

Body: Moderate, often made into a dessert wine.

Blended with: Usually with Sauvignon Blanc, especially in the sweet styles.

Other: Widely planted, but rarely respected.

Sauvignon Blanc

Old world: Bordeaux and the Loire.

New world: Common in California and New Zealand. Some plantings may be found almost everywhere.

Color: Usually clear or with a slight green tint.

Aroma: Fresh cut grass is most common. Grapefruit is another style.

Body: Light to medium when oak aged or made in a sweet style.

Blended with: In Bordeaux almost always with Sémillon.

Other: Very common variety. Can be an excellent food wine.

Chenin Blanc

Old world: Loire (Anjou in particular).

New world: US and South Africa.

Color: Almost always clear.

Aroma: Green apples. Honey in the sweet examples.

Body: Light.

Blended with: Almost never, except in bulk wines, when it is blended with other bulk varieties..

Other: By far, the most misunderstood white variety. In the Anjou region of the Loire in France, it makes remarkable wines, the best of which (Coteaux du Layon) are lightly sweet and among the most long lived of any wine, red or white. The French also use it in the Loire to make sparkling wines of decent quality. In the rest of the world it is mostly used for cheap whites and jug wine.

Pinot Gris

Old world: Germany (Ruländer), Alsace, France (Tokay d'Alsace), Italy (Pinot Grigioh), Eastern Europe.

New world: Increasing being planted in Oregon.

Color: Clear, occasionally it has a pink tinge.

Aroma: Somewhat nondescript tart fruit.

Body: Light.

Blended with: Rarely blended.

Other: A degenerative clone of Pinot Noir.

Pinot Blanc

Old world: Alsace, Burgundy (disapearing rapidly) and Germany.

New world: Oregon, some in California.

Color: Clear to light golden.

Aroma: Crisp and clean, with little aroma.

Body: Light to medium.

Blended with: Rarely, although occasionally with Chardonnay.

Other: Descended from Pinot Noir (black), which became Pinot Gris (grey) and finally Pinot Blanc (white).

Gewürztraminer

Old world: Alsace, France and Germany.

New world: Mostly California.

Color: Clear.

Aroma: An intense flowery aroma, referred to as spicy (since the gewürz part of the grape name means "spicy").

Body: Light to Medium, often made in a slightly, or even intensely sweet style.

Blended with: I know of no blends ever being made.

Other: A wonderfully intense wine. The best examples are by far and away from Alsace where they are dry and full of flavor.

Viognier

Old world: Northern Rhône.

New world: Increasingly in California.

Color: Clear to yellow straw.

Aroma: Orange blossom and peaches. Always intense.

Body: From very light to medium for the sweet styles.

Blended with: Syrah, the red grape, to make Côte Rôtie in France.

Other: One of my favorite white grapes. It has become popular in the last decade.

Trebianno / Ugni Blanc

Old world: Ubiquitous in Italy. Used to make Cognac in France (where it is called St-Emilion).

New world: Increasing, especially in Australia.

Color: Clear.

Aroma: Almost nonexistent.

Body: Light.

Blended with: Used in some red wines in Italy, especially in Chianti. Blended with Malvasia and other white grapes throughout Italy.

Other: The "world's most prolific wine producer," more wine is made from this grape than any other. Few wines of note are made from Trebianno.

Malvasia

Old world: Italy, Spain, and Madeira (Malmsey).

New world: I do not know of any plantings.

Color: Clear to dark brown, as the grape oxidizes easily, and is often used to make fortified wines.

Aroma: Rich dried fruit, sometimes nutty.

Body: Light to medium in some fortified examples.

Blended with: In Chianti and Rioja, with red varieties. Often with Trebbiano in Italy.

Other: An ancient grape with a long heritage. It is being pushed out of Italy by Trebbiano and out of Spain by Viura. It is at its best when it is the base of oxidized dessert wines such as Vino Santo in Italy or Malmsey in Madeira.

Muscat de Frontignan

Old world: Very widespread.

New world: Surprisingly widespread.

Color: Light golden.

Aroma: Intensely fruity. Lychee nut and musk (the word musk comes from this grape).

Body: Light to medium.

Blended with: Rare.

Other: Muscat is an entire family of grapes, with this strain being recognized as the best. There is evidence that this was the first Vinifera grape, and that all the other Vinifera grapes (the primary wine grapes) have evolved from Muscat. This particular grape is known to mutate from light colored to very dark berries, sometimes even on the same vine. In the Asti region of Italy, this grape is often made sparkling. While Asti Spumante is well known, the version imported into the U.S. is best avoided, while the drier versions in Italy are worth looking for. Muscato d'Asti is the finest expression of the grape in Asti. In Australia and Portugal the grape is used to make fortified wines that are inexpensive and quite good. In most other wine regions of the world the wine is slightly sweet to very sweet, but not sparkling or fortified.

Palomino

Old world: Spain.

New world: Rare, but used for Sherry style wines, especially in South Africa.

Color: Light to brown in fortified wines.

Aroma: Not overly aromatic.

Body: Usually medium and fortified.

Blended with: Rare, but with Chenin Blanc for Sherry style wines in South Africa.

Other: While I could easily have left this one out, it is the grape of Sherry, a world class wine.

Roussanne

Old world: Rhône region of France.

New world: Some plantings in the U.S. but rare.

Color: Clear to light yellow.

Aroma: Rich and earthy.

Body: Medium to very heavy, at least as dry white wines go.

Blended with: Often with Marsanne. In Châteauneuf-du-Pape it is also allowed in the blend of both the white and red wines.

Other: Greatly underrated. The wines of St. Péray and the whites of Châteauneuf-du-Pape are begging to be discovered. An old vine Roussanne from Châteauneuf-du-Pape is certainly one of the world's great white wines.

Marsanne

Old world: Rhône region of France. Some in the Valais in Switzerland.

New world: Some plantings in the U.S. but rare.

Color: Light to medium amber, almost brown.

Aroma: Earthy with a characteristic "glue" smell.

Body: Light to medium.

Blended with: Often with Roussanne. The main grape in the White Rhônes of Hermitage, Crozes-Hermitage and St-Péray.

Other: Much more widely planted than Roussanne, but without its potential for greatness. Chosen more for its great economy, than for its great wines.

Other white grapes of note

<u>Cortese</u>

Old world: Piedmont in Italy.

New world: None.

Color: Clear.

Aroma: Almost none.

Body: Light and crisp.

Blended with: Never.

Other: Included because it is responsible for the Gavi wines of Italy. Gavi dei Gavi being considered by many to be the finest example, it is unquestionably Italy's most expensive white wine.

<u>Vernaccia di San Gimignano</u>

Old world: Tuscany, Italy.

New world: A few plantings in the U.S. but very rare.

Color: Clear.

Aroma: Often can smell like the "varnish" the name implies.

Body: Light to medium.

Blended with: None.

Other: There are several Vernaccias in Italy, but this is the most important one. The wine Vernaccia di San Gimignano was Italy's first D.O.C. (controlled place name).

Macabeo (Viura)

Old world: Rioja, Spain. Pyrenées Orientals, France.

New world: None.

Color: Clear.

Aroma: Flowery, perfumey.

Body: Light to medium.

Blended with: Tempranillo, and occasionally Malvasia.

Other: Macabeo has overtaken Malvasia as the chief white variety in Rioja. Malvasia tended to oxidize making a heavy and heady White Rioja. Many lament the demise of Malvasia in Rioja. I for one welcome Viura. While I enjoy Malvasia in other regions, I find the new modern Riojas to be more marketable and easier to drink than the older style. In France it is the 9th most planted variety, almost exclusively in the Pyrenées Orientals where it is responsible for Roussillon Blanc.

Garnacha Blanca

Old world: Spain and France (Grenache Blanc).

New world: Some in Australia.

Color: Clear.

Aroma: Light, white pepper.

Body: Heavy and alcoholic.

Blended with: One of the White Châteauneuf-du-Pape grapes.

Other: I use the Spanish name because there is more planted in Spain than in France, and yet it is France's third most planted white variety and only Spain's ninth. Used throughout both countries it is most important in Navarra, Spain.

Regions of the world

It is likely that wine began its long journey in that cradle of civilization, Mesopotamia. As people spread out from this point, so to did wine. Not all climates are ideal for growing grapes. Some are too hot, and some too cold. When the perfect climate is found, wine production flourishes.

Europe in general is such a climate. Far to the north it is too cold for grapes, but there is no part of Europe that is too hot. Italy and Spain are covered with vines. It seems that there is hardly a plantable acre that does not contain grape vines. While the wines of these countries are wonderful, and often legendary, there is a single country in Europe that is best known for its wines. France.

The climate, the soil, the history, and even the temperament of the people, have all shaped France to become the premier center of wine. Because of this tradition, the vocabulary of wine is dotted with French terms. The names of the grapes we usually use are the French names. And most importantly, the grapes and styles of wines we are most familiar with, all have an origin somewhere in France.

Learning about the French regions is critical for anyone that wishes to learn all they can about wine. Not only will these wines dominate wine lists, and the shelves of many wine stores, they are in many ways the benchmark wines that all others are compared to.

France is not the only region worth learning about; Germany, with its complex, but highly organized system of name places is the home of white wines, from very dry to very sweet, and more than a few red and sparkling wines as well. Italy and Spain are seas of wines. Italy is known for its many regions, and they will be covered here, but Spanish wines are often sold in bulk around Europe, and only those few regions that you are likely to encounter will be covered.

The New World too is awash with wine regions. The best known areas of the US, Australia, and New Zealand will be covered, but for these regions knowing the grapes in the previous section is critical.

One of the greatest joys in wine is exploring the incredible variety around the world. Many more regions exist than are covered in this book, and a trip to a wine store is like a trip around the world. Use these guides to help you as you explore all that wine has to offer.

Who drinks the most wine

Top 10

Luxembourg	93
France	81
Italy	73
Slovenia	65
Croatia	64
Portugal	63
Switzerland	55
Argentina	53
Spain	51
Uruguay	47
US (23rd)	11

Bottom 5

Turkey	.50
China	.40
Mexico	.21
Egypt	.03
Latvia	.01

In bottles per person per year.

Who has the most vineyards

Top 15

Spain	4556
France	3529
Italy	3471
Russia	3042
Turkey*	2324
US	1405
Iran*	1042
Portugal	1004
Romania	977
Argentina	811
China*	749
Chile*	556
Hungary	506
Greece	498
South Africa	429

In square miles.

Most of the grapes are used for something other than wine.

Who makes the most wine

Top 20

Italy	602
France	585
Spain	337
US	227
Russia	168
Argentina	141
Germany	120
South Africa	91
Australia	82
Uruguay	47
Chile	61
Romania	56
Hungary	46
Yugoslavia	45
Greece	43
Portugal	40
China	39
Bulgaria	37
Brazil	31
Austria	30

In millions of cases (12 bottles to a case).

France

Because of the importance of France in learning about wine, this country will be presented in more detail than the others. The section that follows is based on materials I use for my wine school.

Several maps are included to help you locate the regions. The maps are designed to give you a good idea, without confusing details. A wine atlas is always a good idea if you want to know more.

Figure 2.1 Wine map of France

Burgundy

Overview

A funny thing happened to the name of this region (and its subregion Chablis) in the United States. It was used to connote generic jug wines, and too many people still associate the name with low quality wines. The truth is quite the opposite, this is one of the greatest regions in France.

Burgundy has a deserved reputation as well: It is difficult to learn. The many vineyards and subtle distinctions can make even the most confident wine lover weak in the knees. It is expensive, almost always, and worth the price only occasionally, and great only rarely. When it is great though, Burgundy is my favorite wine in the world.

Cool with a long growing region, this difficult region is home to the equally difficult red wine grape Pinot Noir. The wines from Burgundy range from very rich and intense reds in the north, to lighter reds and heavy whites in the middle and light whites and few reds in the south.

Grapes

Pinot Noir for quality reds. Gamay for Beaujolais, and blended with Pinot for Passe-Tout-Grains, and Bourgogne Mousseux.

Chardonnay for quality whites. Aligoté for simple whites. Pinot Blanc and Pinot Gris allowed but rare. Melon de Bourgogne allowed but there are no plantings.

Subregions

In the north we have the region of Côte d'Or and the south the Maconnaise. There is also the exceptional white wine region of Chablis far to the north west, and unattached to the rest of Burgundy.

The Côte d'Or is further divided into the northern Côte de Nuits, primarily reds, and the Côte de Beaune with its famous whites and lighter reds.

It is important to know the names of the villages of the Côte d'Or. That way you can have an idea of the style and quality of the wine.

From North to South here are the villages of the Côte d'Or:

Côte de Nuits

Fixin - Light Reds, not well known. No Grand Crus.

Gevrey-Chambertin The largest number of Grand Cru reds. Rich, long lived wines.

The Grand Cru Vineyards:
Chambertin
Chambertin-Clos de Beze
Chapelle-Chambertin, Charmes (or Mazoyeres)-Chambertin
Griotte-Chambertin
Latricieres-Chambertin
Mazis-Chambertin
Ruchottes-Chambertin

Morey St. Denis - Meaty, rich reds.

The Grand Cru Vineyards:
Clos Saint-Denis
Clos de la Roche
Clos des Lambrays
Clos de Tart

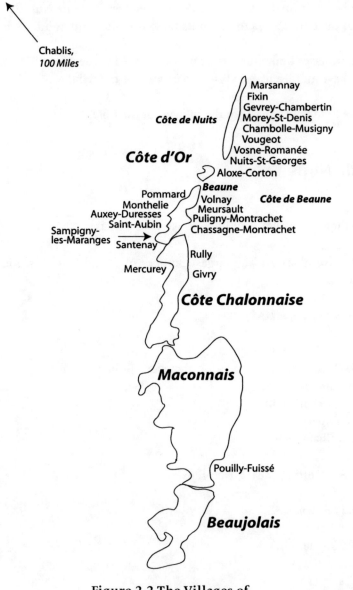

Chablis,
100 Miles

Marsannay
Fixin
Gevrey-Chambertin
Morey-St-Denis
Côte de Nuits   Chambolle-Musigny
Vougeot
Vosne-Romanée
Nuits-St-Georges

Côte d'Or   Aloxe-Corton

Beaune
Pommard   Volnay   *Côte de Beaune*
Monthelie   Meursault
Auxey-Duresses   Puligny-Montrachet
Saint-Aubin   Chassagne-Montrachet
Sampigny-
les-Maranges   Santenay

Rully

Mercurey   Givry

Côte Chalonnaise

Maconnais

Pouilly-Fuissé

Beaujolais

Figure 2.2 The Villages of
Burgundy

Chambolle-Musigny - Elegant reds and 1 great white Musigny Blanc.

The Grand Cru Vineyards:
Musigny (red and white)
Bonnes Mares

Vougeot - The most famous vineyard, Clos de Vougeot has so many different producers it is very difficult to buy.

The Grand Cru Vineyard:
Clos de Vougeot

Flagey-Echézeaux - Grouped with Vosne-Romanee.

The Grand Cru Vineyards:
Echézeaux
Grands Echézeaux

Vosne-Romanée- Some of the World's most expensive Red Wines.

The Grand Cru Vineyards:
Romanée
Romanée Conti
Romanée Saint-Vivant
Richbourg
La Tache
Clos des Reas

Nuits-St.Georges - Lighter, often well priced Reds. No Grand Crus, but many Premier Cru.

Côte de Beaune

Premeaux-Prissey
Comblanchien
Corgoloin - These wines are all sold under the name Côte de Nuits-Village.

Ladoix-Serrigny
Pernand-Vergelesses - The best wines of these villages are sold as Aloxe-Corton. The lowest quality wines are sold as Côte de Beaune-Villages.

The Grand Cru Vineyards:
Corton (red)
Corton-Charlemagne (white)

Aloxe-Corton - A rarity, Grand Cru Reds and Whites from the same village.

The Grand Cru Vineyards:
Corton (red)
Corton-Charlemagne (white)
Charlemagne (white)
Savigny-lès-Beaune
Chorey-lès-Beaune - Lesser known, often sold as Côte de Beaune-Villages.

Beaune - The unofficial wine capital of Burgundy. A great deal of wine is made here, some of it better than others. No Grand Crus; however, I personally feel that Clos des Mouches (for white particularly) could be elevated to Grand Cru.

Pommard
Volnay - The great reds of the south.

Monthélie
Saint-Romain - Sold as Côtes de Beaune-Village, almost always.

Auxey-Duresses - Except for the Premier Crus, almost always sold as Côtes de Beaune-Village.

Meursault - The first of the great white wine villages.

Blagny - Grouped with Meursault, but almost all red wines.

Puligny-Montrachet - With its neighbor Chassagne, this is the greatest white wine region for many people.

The Grand Cru Vineyards:
Montrachet
Chevalier-Montrachet
Bâtard-Montrachet
Bienvenues-Bâtard-Montrachet

Chassagne-Montrachet - Since the great vineyard Montrachet is in both Puligny and Chassagne, it is appended to both of their names.

The Grand Cru Vineyards:
Montrachet
Bâtard-Montrachet
Criots-Bâtard-Montrachet

Saint-Aubin
Cheilly-lès-Maranges
Dezize-lès-Maranges
Sampigny-lès-Maranges - All sold as Côtes de Beaune-Village.

Santenay
Remigny - Santenay reds are some of the best kept secrets in the region.

Chablis - Actually far to the north, but not connected to any other part of Burgundy. These Chardonnay based white wines are rich and often steely in character.

The Grand Cru Vineyards:
Bougros
Les Preuses
Vaudesir
Grenouilles
Valmur
Les Clos
Blanchots

South of the Côte d'Or are the regions of the Chalonnais and the Mâconnaise. While there are no Grand Cru vineyards in these regions, the villages of Mercurey and Givry in the Chalonnais and Pouilly-Fuisse in the Maconnaise are well known.

Beaujolais is often grouped with Burgundy. It is famous for very light red wines made from the grape Gamay. The simplest wines are just called Beaujolais. Those with a bit more complexity are Beaujolais-Villages. The nine villages that are considered Grand Cru Beaujolais are:

Moulin-a-Vent
Chenas, Fleurie
Chiroubles
Morgan
Brouilly
Côte de Brouilly
St-Amor and Julienas

Label info

Reading a Burgundy label is no easy task. Knowing the villages above is the first step.

A wine that does not come from a designated vineyard is referred to as an AC Class wine. It will have the name of the Village on it, or Côte-de-something-Villages.

Next step up is a single vineyard designate. Almost always this wine will be a Premier Cru (1er Cru) Class wine. It will have the name of the Village and the name of the vineyard on it.

Grand Cru Classe is the top rung. A single vineyard of such distinction, the name of the village does not even appear on the label. With the exception of the Chablis Grand Cru, the Grand Cru vineyards are always bottled separately. Price will be your biggest hint here. It is not likely that you will find a Grand Cru for under $50 or so.

> **Note:** An all too common and costly mistake is to ask for Montrachet, which is a Grand Cru vineyard, when you mean Puligny-Montrachet or Chassagne-Montrachet which are AC Class wines. This mistake can cost you hundreds of dollars, be specific.

Bordeaux

Overview

When most people think of Bordeaux they think of the famous wines of the Haut-Medoc that bear such names as Ch. Margaux (Ch. is the abbreviation for Chateau), Ch. Lafite Rothschild, Ch. Mouton Rothschild, Ch. Lafite, Ch. Latour, and Ch. Haut-Brion. These 5 wineries, often referred to as the Big 5, are so famous that it is tempting to forget about the other several thousand Chateaux in the region. In fact, Bordeaux is so rich in wine that it accounts for 34% of the total value of all French wine exports. It is a huge business in the area, with 1 in 6 people involved somehow in the various aspects of the trade.

Grapes

The undisputed red wine grape champion of Bordeaux is Cabernet Sauvignon. Almost always blended with Merlot and to varying degrees Cabernet Franc, Malbec and Petite Verdot.

For white, the grape of quality is Semillon sometimes blended with Sauvignon Blanc, or Sauvignon Blanc on its own.

There are a host of other grapes in the region, but these are the primary grapes and almost always used for the base of the wine.

Subregions

The **Haut Medoc** is the most famous subregion, it is further divided into (South to North and generally increasingly heavier in style):

Margaux - 1 Premier Cru, Ch. Margaux.

St-Julien - No Premier Cru, but several "Super Seconds."

Pauillac - 3 Premiers Cru, Chs. Lafite, Latour and Mouton.

St-Estephe - No Premier Cru.

Graves (not in the Haut Medoc at all but grouped with it because of the quality) - 1 Premier Cru, Ch. Haut-Brion. Graves is also well known for its whites.

The Haut Medoc is primarily Cabernet Sauvignon based wines with some Merlot.

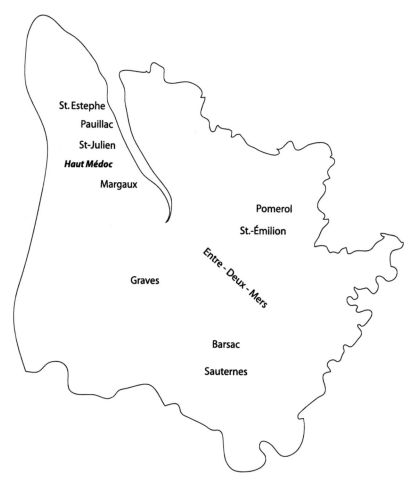

Figure 2.3 The Wine Areas of Bordeaux

Across the Gironde River are the regions of:

St-Emilion - 12 Premiers Grand Cru and most of the rest fall into Grand Cru Classes.

The surrounding areas are often referred to as the **Satellite Villages.**

There are 12 villages that can either use St-Emilion's name or add it to their own. Here (and in Pomerol) Merlot is often used alone or with increasing amounts of Cabernet Franc as the price of the wine goes down.

Pomerol - No official ratings (the only major region in France without a rating system) - Ch. Petrus is considered the best (and for many the best there is). Overall very high quality wines. Strangely there is no real town of Pomerol.

The unbelievably wonderful sweet white wines of **Sauternes and Barsac** are farther east (inland). There is 1 Premier Grand Cru (in all of Bordeaux) Ch. d'Yquem, as well as 11 Premiers Cru, 13 Second Growths and many more Minor Growths .

Entre-Deux-Mers (between 2 seas - the Gironde and Dordogne rivers) has been called a sea of white wines. Indeed much quantity, and some quality is made in this region.

Label info

There are more classification in Bordeaux than some regions have vineyards. Most well known is the classification of 1855 that created the 5 classes of Cru Classe wines of the Haut Medoc. Wines that did not fall into any of the first 5 Growths are rated (in descending order):

Cru Exceptionnel
Cru Bourgeois Superieur

In St. Emilion the order goes Premier Grand Cru Classe and then just Grand Cru Classe.

Bordeaux or Graves Superieur both mean a wine with at least 1 degree of alcohol higher than the minimum allowed.

Champagne

Overview

The word Champagne refers to chalky soil, and so you will find the word champagne not only associated with the great sparkling wine, but with the region of Cognac as well.

Champagne is a process as well as a wine, here is an over simplification of the process:

• The grapes are pressed, with the reds pressed especially gently to keep any color out of the wine.
• The wine is fermented, more or less the same as all white wines.
• The wine is placed in a bottle with some sugar and yeast, and then capped tightly.
• A secondary fermentation takes place from the added yeast and sugar which results in carbonation from the Carbon Dioxide mixing with the wine in the closed bottle.
• Either time and skilled labor, or a machine, coax the sediment caused by the dead yeast towards the neck of the bottle.
• The neck of the bottle is plunged into a salt water solution that causes ice to form in the bottle.
• The cap is removed, and the plug of ice, along with the sediment are removed.
• The lost wine is replaced and a little sweetener is added to the wine (this determines how sweet the style of the Champagne is).
• The finished Champagne has a special cork added to the bottle, and it is now ready to drink.

Grapes

Chardonnay and the red wine grape, Pinot Noir are the main grapes. Pinot Meunier is also used regularly, but it is considered a poor cousin of Pinot Noir.

Subregions

The villages of Champagne are host to a most unique and in many ways, a fitting form of economic rating. Every year an official price is set for a measure of grapes. Each village has a rating based on what percentage of this official price they can charge. Thus the finest grapes come from towns that rate 99% or more, and high average is 90% - 98%. Below 90% are not quality grapes, and are mostly used for rounding out the non vintage house styles of the numerous smaller Champagne houses that are almost never seen.

Only a few of the finest Champagnes are village designated, and it is hotly debated if this is marketing or if a distinct character can be found. Among these well known villages are Cramant, Avize and Le Mesnil.

Within the area of Champagne are also the larger sub regions of the Montagne de Reims, home of quality Pinot Noir, the Vallee de la Marne with its vineyards full of Pinot Noir and Pinot Meunier and the Côte des Blancs covered throughout with Chardonnay.

Label info

Demi-Sec (literally half dry) - Is the sweetest.

Extra Dry - Is the next driest, but is still slightly sweet.
Brut (literally raw or unrefined) - Traditionally the driest, but Natural with no added sweetness is sometimes found.

Rosé - Rosé Champagne is like Rosé Wine, slightly red to pink, and fun and easy to enjoy. The best are dry and serious with just a taste of the red wine (which is often added at the end).

Vintage vs. Non-Vintage - Almost every Champagne producer releases a vintage wine when the conditions merit. These vintage dated offerings represent a higher quality than the house style non-vintage wines, but the non-vintage wines have the advantage of consistency.

Tête du Cuvée - Not usually found on the label, but the term refers to the best of the lot. These wines have benefited from extended contact with the sediment and have a richer more expressive flavor. These are the expensive wines.

Crémant - This is a dessert style Champagne with less bubbles and usually a sweet style. It is becoming rare.

The Loire Valley

Overview

Winding along with the Loire River, the Loire Valley is peppered with magnificent castles. A reminder of a time long gone.

Most of the wines from this region, red and white, are light and crisp, and easy to enjoy. Bubbly wines from this region are considered by some to be the great value in Sparkling Wines.

Grapes

Sauvignon Blanc and Chenin Blanc are the predominant white grapes, with the notable exception being the Muscadet grape of the wine of the same name.

The Red and Rose wines are almost always made from Cabernet Franc.

Subregions

To the far east we have the Sauvignon Blanc based white wines of **Sancerre** and **Pouilly-Fume**. Grassy and rich, these are great wines with most foods.

To the far west we have **Muscadet**, crisp and simple, perfect with the local seafood that would over power many other wines.

In the middle we have the Chenin Blanc based wines, some of which can be sweet (Coteaux du Layon from the **Anjou** - is one of my favorite wines). The dry **Vouvray** wines of the region are crisp with a decided green apple quality.

In the town of **Chinon** and its environs we find the main source for the light, almost raspberry styled red wines based on Cabernet Franc. **Anjou** when it is not making sweet wines, is likely to make some nice, simple rosés.

The Loire is a huge region with many distinct areas. I recommend you visit for yourself, in many ways it is representative of the best of France.

Label info

Learn the major areas I mention above, and you may have a prayer. The large number of areas, and the varying labeling habits make it hard to pin down rules for this region.

The usual rules apply, but the only hint of quality is the price and reputation of the producer.

The Rhône Valley

Overview

This region of France was only known by the most serious wine lovers until the early 1980s. An explosion of popularity led to enormous price increases as demand grew. Unquestionably wines of great quality originate in this region; however of late, too many poor examples seem to be available.

Warm to hot in the South, the Northern Rhône is cooled by the Rhône River and the steep hillside vineyards. None steeper or more spectacular than those of the Côte Rôtie.

Grapes

In the North, Syrah rules, sometimes tempered by the fragrant white grape Viognier. Further to the south, as the temperature rises, Grenache takes on an increasing importance.

The White grapes are primarily Marsanne, along with Roussanne in the better wines.

Chateauneuf-du-Pape allows 13 varieties, reds and whites, to be blended to make this often exquisite wine. Chief among these are the important grapes listed above and the red wine grape Mouvedre.

Subregions

The Rhône Valley is long and wide. To even touch briefly on each village would be too much for this primer, so I will try to pick out the more important areas North to South.

Côte Rôtie - This northern-most region is made from Syrah with the occasional touch of Viognier for elegance. There are 2 parts of the Côte Rôtie, the Côtes Blonde and Brune. It is said that they are named after 2 daughters, and that the slopes retain the characteristics of these daughters. All poetry aside, it is common for the two slopes to be blended together as Blonde et Brune.

Condrieu - Home of Viognier. The white wines from this area on the next hill down river from Côte Rôtie can, at their best, be full of perfume and tart complexity. At their worst (too often Ch. Grillet, the most famous Condrieu) they are oxidized and lacking any flavor or charm, but selling for outrageous prices.

St-Joseph - Syrah with a touch of the white grape Marsanne on occasion, this wine is often as good (bad?) as its kin Crozes-Hermitage. Oddly this wine is made from a group of noncontiguous vineyards running for miles down the valley. A small amount of decent white wine is also made.

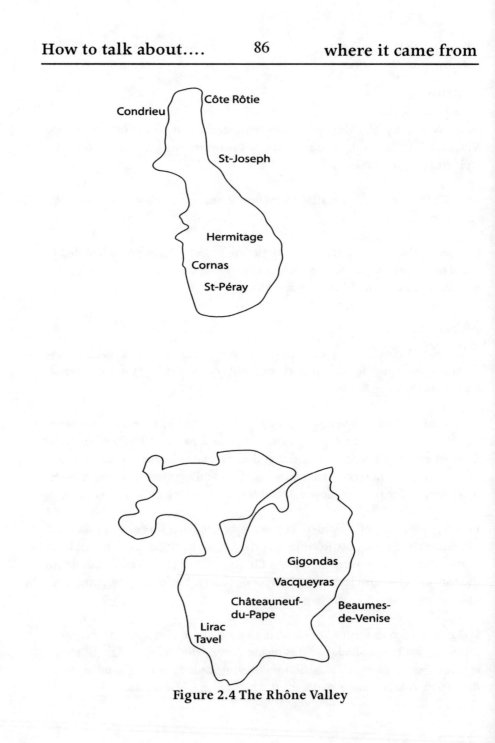

Figure 2.4 The Rhône Valley

Hermitage - In the running with Côte Rôtie as the best red wines of the Rhône. The Syrah grape as usual may have a small amount of white wine added to it. Rich and flavorful this is everything a great Syrah can be. Prices are often better than Côte Rôtie, but it is wise to look for an older vintage when you can. The Whites can be exceptional and again are made from Marsanne and with luck a percentage of Roussanne as well.

Crozes-Hermitage - A huge area on the hills that surround Hermitage. Referred to as the poor man's Hermitage, this is a disfavor to Hermitage. The wines of Crozes, and the similar wines of St-Joseph are too often light, almost beaujolais in style. When made with more traditional methods, the Syrah of the region can be elegant and flavorful, while easy to enjoy while still young.

Cornas - Richer and almost always better than Crozes or St-Joseph, this is the wine to look for if you want Syrah without the cost of Hermitage or Côte Rôtie. Given proper time to age, this wine can yield remarkable results.

Saint-Peray - Great white wines when you can find them.

Châteauneuf-du-Pape - One of the most famous wine names in France. Due in large part because of the wine labeling revolution that started here and later became the basis of the Appellation Contrôlée system. CdP still leads in the labeling front, allowing only Estate Grown wines to bear the glass embossed seal of the town on their bottles. High in alcohol and easy to enjoy, this remains the best known of the Rhône wines.

Tavel/Lirac - The great Grenache based Rosé wines that so few other Rosés have ever matched. Never expensive and best enjoyed as young as possible.

Gigondas - Grenache with a minimum of 15% Syrah and/or Mouvedre as well as a little of the 11 other allowed Côtes du Rhône varieties. Considered a 'Super Côtes du Rhône' it was the first of the Côtes du Rhône Villages to be elevated to AC status. Some good to very good, but never great red wines can be found from this village.

Côtes du Rhône / Côtes du Rhône-Village - Primarily made from Grenache, these wines are almost always blended. Not only blended from the other 13 allowed grape varieties, but blended between lots from different villages as well. Of varying quality, they are best when made by the traditional barrel fermented techniques and not the newer carbonic maceration technique (which is how Beaujolais is made, and why everything made this way tastes like Beaujolais).

Label info

Armed with the above regions and an idea of the price, you can get a good idea of where it came from. Price as always is the determining factor. Beaujolaised wines (made in the style of Beaujolais - my own term) are the cheapest and the most common. The white wines, being more rare than many of the reds, often fetch the highest prices.

Alsace

Overview

Alsace is so close to Germany that it keeps going back and forth from Germany to France, depending on the outcome of the last war. The wines are similarly inspired by the Germans, but with the important difference that Alsatian wines are vinified dry.

Even the late harvest wines (Vendage Tardive) that would be sweet anywhere else in the world are dry when made in Alsace. Dry, but unbelievably rich.

Grapes

Riesling is king, with Gewurztraminer a close second. Pinot Blanc, Pinot Gris and Muscat are all found here.

Subregions

There are no real subregions in Alsace, as far as the scope of this primer is concerned.

Label info

Cuvée, means blend, an important and common practice in Alsace.

Grand Vin means a decent quality wine with at least 11% alcohol, rarely is anything else exported.

Grand Cru, like Burgundy this means the best vineyards, it also, in this case, means the grapes can only be Riesling, Gewurztraminer, Muscat or Pinot Gris (in Alsace it is usually called Tokay d'Alsace).

Vendage Tardive, literally late harvested. Richer, and within the limits of Alsatian style, sweeter wines.

Sélection des Grains Nobles, wines made from hand sorted bunches. Only the very best grapes go into this wine. the German term is Beerenauslese; but unlike the German version, these wines are dry, or nearly so.

Cognac

Overview

I don't want to get too far into the intricacies of Cognac. I just wanted to point out that Brandy made in the region is referred to as Cognac. Brandy is a distilled wine product.

The word Champagne (Grande Champagne, Petite Champagne, Grande Fine Champagne) on the occasional Cognac label refers to the chalky soil area in the middle of the region. It is in no way related to the sparkling wine, other than Champagne means chalky soil area in both places.

Grapes

The Ugni Blanc, called St. Emilion here, and known in Italy as Trebbiano is distilled to make the local brandy, Cognac.

Subregions

See the Champagne explanation above.

Label info

Contrary to popular belief there is only one French Cognac law that refers to its age: Most Cognac sold is Three Star, the youngest.
V.S.O.P. (Very Superior Old Pale) must be at least 4 years old.
X.O., Extra or Cordon Bleu are all older by some unspecified amount than V.S.O.P.

Vintage dating is rare, and in fact by US law must refer to the bottling, not the vintage date.

Languedoc and Roussillon

Overview

A huge area that is lumped together for the sake of ease. Until a decade ago no one ever heard of this region, now it is one of the most popular for well valued wines.

There is a huge rush on to plant well known grape varieties in the region, and then to sell the wines with the name of the grape to the U.S. and other markets where varietal labeling is the norm.

Grapes

You name it, it is planted here. Grenache was once the most important, and it is still widely planted.

Subregions

There are more every time you look, but not as distinct as Burgundy. While the AC areas below may fetch a higher price, it is the simple wines of the region that have made it famous.

Label info

Every style of label can be found here, from the simple varietal label, to the more confusing regional labels. Chances are that you will only find wines labeled with the above AC names, or with the name of the grape. The more esoteric wines rarely leave France.

Provence

Overview

A land of sun and surf. These wines were made famous by visitors to the Riviera. They tend to be coarse and simple. Rosé wines were until recently the staple of the region.

Grapes

Until recently Grenache and Carignan were chief, now with a newfound market for the wines, Syrah, and even Cabernet Sauvignon are starting to be planted.

Subregions

The best known wine regions of the area are **Cassis** (no relation to the Crème de Cassis syrup) for whites and **Bandol** for reds. In fact Bandol Rouge has a cult following due in most part to the importer Kermit Lynch.

Label info

Pretty straight forward for a change. The name of the region is prominent, and the producer is also well displayed.

Italy

From fertile valleys to rocky mountain tops, it seems as if every inch of Italy is planted with grape vines. Some of the wines are considered along with the world's best, others are less distinguished.

Only a decade or two ago the general consensus for Italian wines was that they represented great value. A revolution in wine making has elevated the quality, and by extension, the prices of almost all Italian wines. The wines of Italy today are as likely to be destined for tables around the world, as they are to be enjoyed locally. A large percentage of the wines made in Italy are simple, and are made for local consumption, and this is the case for wine regions the world over. It is the exceptional wines that have raised the standards, and these are increasingly being made by a new generation which has learned to embrace all things technical.

As with any wine region, the trick to Italy is to learn as much as you can about the regions. Many of those that are listed here will not be found on your local wine shelves, but that still leaves a dizzying array of wines from all over the country.

The regions

Basilicata *(bah-zee-lee-cah'-tah)* A wine region in Southern Italy. Most of the wines are simple, and are best enjoyed locally.

Calabria *(cah-lah'-bree-ah)* If Italy is shaped like a boot, then Calabria is the wine region at the toe. Mountainous country, the wines from this region are not well known elsewhere.

Campania *(cahm-pah'-nyah)* A wine region in southern Italy, around the town of Naples. The wines are not well known outside of the region, but visitors to the active volcano, Mount Vesuvius, usually run across some examples in the local eateries.

Colli ... *(coh-lee)* No less than 7 wine regions thoughout Italy begin with the word Colli. The quality and style of the seven wine regions are not in anyway related, but few are exported to the US.

Colli Albani *(ahl-bah'-nee)*
Colli Berici *(beh-ree-t'chee)*
Colli Bolognesi *(boh-loh-n'yay'-zee)*
Colli Euganei *(eh-yoo-gah'-neh)*
Colli Lanuvini *(lah-noo-vee'-nee)*
Colli Orientali del Fruili *(oh-ree-en-tah'lee del free-oo'-lee)*
Colli Paicentini *(p'yah-t'chen-tee-nee)*

Emilia-Romagna *(eh-meel'-yah ro-mah'-n yah)* The Italian region north of Tuscany that is situated around the city of Bologna. Many visitors to Italy ignore this region because of the great deal of industry that is evident. What they do not realize is that this is the center of gastronomy for Italy. Parmesan cheese and Proscuitto Crudo both hale from nearby Parma, and Bologna is the cross roads for food from all over Italy. The most famous wine of the region is Lambrusco, a light, sometimes sparkling wine. Lambrusco is often overlooked as well, because the overly commercial Riunite is technically a Lambrusco.

Friuli-Venezia Giulia *(free-oo'-lee veh-net'-zee-ah joo'-lee-ah)* The wine region in the northeastern corner of Italy. The wines tend to be high quality, and the labels are usually marked with the name of the grape. This makes the wines friendly and easy to buy for most Americans. Merlot and Pinot Grigio (Pinot Gris) are among the best known red and white grapes grown here.

Latium *(lah'-tyum)* The wine region in Italy around Rome. Most of the wine made here is white from the ubiquitous Trebbiano grape.

Liguria *(lee-goo'-ree-ah)* A wine producing region of Italy that stretches along the Mediterranean from the French border down to Tuscany. The region is also unofficially known as the Italian Riviera and is dotted with famous resort towns.

Figure 2.5 The Regions of Italy

Lombardy *(lom-bar-dee)* A principal wine producing region of Northern Italy.

Marche *(mahr'-kay)* The Marches, as it is known in English, is an south eastern Italian region along the Adriatic Sea. This is the home of the well known white wine Verdicchio (which is both the wine and the grape name).

Piedmont / Piemonte *(peed-mont / p'yay-mon'-the)* One of the most important wine producing regions in Italy, it is situated in the northwestern corner of the country, up against the Alps. This is the home of the intense red wines Barolo and Barberesco, as well as the refreshingly light sparkling wine Moscato d'Asti and the well known sparkler Asti Spumante. Piemonte is the Italian name for the region.

Puglia *(poo'-lyah)* A southeastern Italian wine producing region. Every country has a region that excels in making bulk wines, and this is Italy's.

Sardinia *(sar-din'-ia)* A large island off the coast of Italy. For generations the wines here were coarse reds, or almost "sherry-like" whites. Modern wine making has allowed the producers of this area to discover an entirely new direction, with lighter, fresher tastes.

Sicily *(sis-ill-ee)* This island is not only the largest in the Mediterranean, it is also one of Italy's largest producers of wine. Marsala has long been the best known wine of Sicily. The oxidized white wine, that so many know for cooking, typified the wines made here until only a few years ago. New plantings on cooler hillsides and modern techniques have allowed the new generation of Sicilian wine maker to produce lighter, fruitier wines.

Trentino-Alto Adige *(tren-tee'-no ahl'-to ah'-dee-jay)* The northernmost of Italy's wine producing regions. A large amount of red wine is made here as well as whites, and even sparkling wines. This is a huge region with a great many wines and a great many grape varieties.

Tuscany *(tuss-can-ee)* A wine region in central Italy that extends from the city of Florence to the south. Some of the best known Italian wines come from this region. Notable are the Chianti wines, and Brunello di Montepulciano. The rising trend to create Cabernet Sauvignon based, or blended wines, has led to the unofficial designation "Super Tuscans" for these expensive and much sought after wines. Sangiovese (or Brunello as one of the clones is called) is the important red wine grape of the region. Malvasia is the important white for quality, and Trebbiano for quantity.

Umbria *(oom'-bree-ah)* The central Italian region that is home to the well known white wine Orvieto.

Valle d' Aosta *(vah'-leh dah-aw'ss-tah)* The smallest wine producing region in Italy. Skiers know the area for the famed Courmayeur ski resort, which is just on the other side of Mount Blanc from France's famed ski town, Chamonix. The crisp, dry white wines of the region are enjoyed by skiers, but rarely seen elsewhere.

Veneto *(veh'-neh-toe)* A large Italian wine region that includes the cities of Venice and Verona. Nearly a fifth of all the DOC wines of Italy come from this region. Soave and Valpolicella are two of the best known wines that are produced here.

Some well known Italian wines

Barolo *(bah-roh'-loh)* One of the top Italian wines. Made from the Nebbiolo grape in the Piedmont. It is often long lived and heavy when young.

Brachetto *(bra-keh'-toe)* A slightly sweet and sparkling red wine from the Piedmont region of Italy. This is my vote for the best pizza wine.

Chianti *(k'yahn-tee)* One of the most famous of the Italian red wines. Made from the Sangiovese grape, although a small amount of the white grapes, Trebbiano or Malvasia, may be added for finesse. The Chianti region encompasses much of the hills of Tuscany with the higher quality Chianti Classico region being a smaller and more defined "classic" region for producing the wine. In times gone past, Chianti was often sold in a straw covered bottle called a "fiasco." This has mostly given way to modern bottles.

Dolcetto *(dohl-chet'-oh)* One of the principal grapes of Northwestern Italy. The best known wines made from this variety bear its name.

Est! Est! Est!!! Other than the name, this is a rather forgetable Italian white wine. The name is an example of marketing that has withstood the ages. The story goes that a German Bishop in the 1100s sent a servant ahead to Rome with instructions to chalk Est ("it is" in Latin) on the side of every tavern with decent wine between the Bishop's home and Rome. That way the Bishop would not have to suffer through poor wine on his trip to visit the Pope. In the town of Montefiacone the servant was so enamoured of the wine that he scrawled the now famous epitaph. The Bishop, upon arriving in the town, was said to have agreed with his servant's taste to such an extent, that the Bishop never ventured on, living out his life drinking the wine he loved. Perhaps it was a different wine than what is sold today.

Gavi *(gah'-vee)* One of Italy's best known white wines. Made from the Cortese grape around the town of Gavi, in the northwestern part of the country, the Piedmont.

Lambrusco *(lam-broos'-coh)* A lightly sparkling wine, made from the grape of the same name. It is from the Emilia-Romagna region of Italy. Produced both in a dry or slightly sweet style, it is best know in the US as the brand Riunite (which is one of the sweetest examples made). In Italy, it is easier to find the drier styles, and they are a great match for the rich foods of the region. Lambrusco is made just west of Bologna, which is considered to be the capital of Italian gastronomy.

Marsala *(mar-sah'-lah)* Often relegated to the kitchen, this is the best known fortified wine of Sicily, Italy. While still popular as a cooking ingredient, it is not usually a favorite among lovers of fortified wines. The wine itself is vinified dry, and a sweeting agent "mosto cotto" (cooked must) is added to give it the distinctive brown color and flavor.

Moscato d'Asti *(moss-cah'-to dah'ss-tee)* One of my favorite wines, it is often overlooked in the US. Lightly sparkling, lightly sweet, and light in alcohol, this wine is light in everything, except flavor. Made from the Muscat (Moscatoh) grape in the town of Asti, in the Piedmont region of northern Italy. Only the finest grapes go into the production of Moscato d'Asti, with the bulk of them being utilized to make the better known, and fully sparkling, Asti Spumante.

Orvieto *(ohr-v'yay'-toh)* A well known Italian white wine made from the Trebbianno grape in the Umbria region.

Prosecco *(pro-seh-coh)* A white wine grape of Italy. In the US it is best known as a sparkling wine made from the same grape. In Italy the wine may be sparkling, lightly sparkling, or even still.

Rosso di Montalcino *(ross-oh dee mon-tahl-t'chee'-noh)* The lighter version of the Italian wine Brunello di Montalcino, made from the same grapes, in the same vineyards, but without oak (or in fact any) aging.

Sassicaia *(sah-see-cah'-yah)* A Cabernet Sauvignon based red wine from the coast of the Tuscany region in Italy. The wine is very consciously based on the wines of the Haut-Médoc in Bordeaux, France, and indeed even the grape cuttings originate from there. This wine forever changed the landscape of Italian wines. Even though it had no official classification, it was one of the most expensive and critically acclaimed wines of Italy. It was at the forefront of a class of wines that have been called "Super Tuscans" each based on Cabernet Sauvignon, even though, at the time, Cab was not an allowed grape anywhere in the Tuscany region. Because of the great popularity of these wines a new DOC designation was created in the region of Bolgheri for these wines, and a DOC Bolgheri Sassicaia was created for this wine alone. So popular is this wine, that counterfeiting has recently become a problem.

Soave *(s'wah'-veh)* The best known Italian white wine, it comes from the Verona region in the northeastern portion of the country. Made from the Garganega grape, with the ubiquitous Trebbiano sometimes used in the blend. Most Soave is uninspiring, made to fill the world wide demand for the name, with little regard to quality. There are exceptions among the smaller producers who struggle to provide a wine of interest for the discriminating consumer. Soave Classico comes from the smaller, more defined, and original, Soave region.

Tignanello *(tee-n'ya-nell'-oh)* An Italian wine made in the Chianti region by the well known Antinori firm. Since its inception in 1971, this wine has broken tradition with the Chianti region and produced a wine of character that does not follow the rules. The wine tends to be mostly Sangiovese, as is

Chianti, but without the white wine in the blend that softens Chianti. The addition of Cabernet Sauvignon takes this wine even further from its Chianti roots.

Valpolicella *(vahl-poh-lee-t'chell-ah)* One of the best known red wines of Italy. The name which means "valley of many cellars" is a testament to the region, north of Verona where it is made. When the vintage permits, a portion of the grapes are brought from the vineyard to be dried on straw mats. The sweet version of the wine, which is hard to find in the US is called Recioto della Valpolicella and the better known dry version is Recioto della Valpolicella Amarone, or simply Amarone.

Verdicchio *(vair-deek'-ee-oh)* An Italian white wine made from the grape of the same in the Marche region. There are several versions made, but the best known in the US comes in a curved bottle, reminiscent of the clay amphora that stored wine in ancient times.

Verduzzo *(vair-doot-soh)* An Italian white wine and grape. Many of the best examples are somewhat sweet.

Vernaccia di San Gimignano *(vair-nah'-t'chah dee san-d'jee-mee-n'yah'-noh)* A well known Italian dry white wine and grape. San Gimignano itself is a quaint tourist town, not far from Florence. It is famous for its towers, and visitors often come home with a taste for the local wine.

Vin Santo *(veen sahn'-toe)* An Italian white wine from the Tuscany region. Made from Trebbiano and Malvasia grapes that have been dried before making the wine. The very sweet grapes are then fermented in small barrels that have some air in them, allowing the wine to maderize (oxidize). The result is a slightly brown wine that is either sweet, or very dry and alcoholic.

Vino Nobile di Montepulciano *(veen-no noh'-bee-leh dee mon-teh-pool-t'cha'-noh)* An Italian red wine from the Tuscany region. Made from the Sangiovese grape in and around the town of Montepulciano. The region neighbors the southern Chianti area, and many examples are similar in style to Chianti.

Terms you may find on Italian Wine Labels

Denominazione do Origine Controllata *(deh-noh-mee-nah-t'zee-oh'-neh dee oh-ree-jeen-eh con-troh-lah'-tah)* The Italian term for their appellation laws, established in 1963. Abbreviated DOC.

Denominazione do Origine Controllata e Garantita *((deh-noh-mee-nah-t'zee-oh'-neh dee oh-ree-jeen-eh con-troh-lah'-tah eh gah-rahn-tee-tah)* The highest level of the Italian DOC laws. The wines must not only be typical of their region, but must pass a blind tasting. The first wines that began using this designation went on sale in the mid 1980s. Abbreviated DOCG.

Imbottigliato *(im-boh-tee-l'yah'-toe)* Italian for "bottled." "Imbottigliato all'origine" is the term for estate bottled.

Indicazione Geographica Tipica *(in-dee-katz-ee-oe-nee jee-oe-graf-ee-ca tee-pee-cah)* A relatively new quality designation for Italian wines. It is used for wines that are typical of what is being made in the region, but may not be made with the official grapes or in a traditional style. Many of these wines are simple, but some are the most expensive wines in Italy. Usually abbreviated to IGT.

Liquoroso *(lee-kwoh-roh'-soh)* An Italian term for a dessert wine that is made sweet by adding spirits to stop the fermentation process while there is still sugar left unfermented. The English term is "Fortified Wine."

Riserva *(ree-zair-vah)* In Italian wine laws this term can only be used for wines that have been aged for a period before release. The length of time varies by region. It is three years for Chianti Riserva, but five for Barolo or Brunello Riserva. Unlike the similar Spanish term, Italian wines do not necessarily have to be aged in barrel to qualify for Riserva.

Rosso *(ross'-oh)* Italian for red and used as part of the name for some red Italian wines.

Secco *(seck'-oh)* The Italian term for dry (meaning a wine without any residual sugar).

Tenuta *(teh-new-ta)* A holding or estate. Similar to the word Château in French.

Vino *(veen-noh)* Italian for wine.

Vino da Tavola *(vee-no dah tah'-voh-lah)* The Italian term for "table wine." As with other European countries, this is the lowest designation for wines. Since some of Italy's greatest wines are made in a style or grape variety inconsistent with their regions, this lowly designation has appeared on the label of some of the most popular and expensive Italian wines. To help reduce confusion, Italy created a new designation for the best of these wines called Indicazione Geographica Tipica.

Spain

Spain produces a huge amount of wine. Until recently much of it was of the bulk variety. With Spain's entry into the EU, everything is changing. Modern wine making, better communication in the industry, and worldwide attention have all helped to increase the quality of wine throughout Spain.

No doubt the next edition of this book will contain updated information about the latest and greatest Spain has to offer. In the mean time, here are the regions and wines that helped to get Spain noticed, and are helping to propel Spain into the 21st century.

The regions

Navarra *(na-var)* A wine making region in northern Spain, once only known for its rosé wines. Increasingly, red wines of note have been coming out of this region.

Penedès *(peh-neh-dess')* A wine producing region in Spain, just west of Barcelona. Most of Spain's sparkling wine, Cava, is produced here. There has been an explosion of red wines produced in the area, many from the Cabernet Sauvignon grape. The well known producer Torres is one of the leaders in the region, as well as Jean Leon who helped to made Spanish Cabernet popular in the US.

Ribera del Duero *(ree-bair'ah del doo-eh-roh)* While this wine region in Spain is not well known among many wine lovers, it is the home of two of Spain's greatest producers, Vega Sicilia and the Alejandro Fernandex, maker of Pasquera. The region is in the north of Spain at 2600 feet, along the Duero River, the same river that will become the Douro in Portugal on who's banks the grapes for Port are grown. The red wine grape here is the Tempranillo, which is also responsible for the high quality of Spain's most famous red wine, Rioja. Tempranillo is known locally as Tinta del Pais. The incredible quality of Vega Sicilia has in the last few decades prompted more producers and consumers to pay attention to this high altitude treasure.

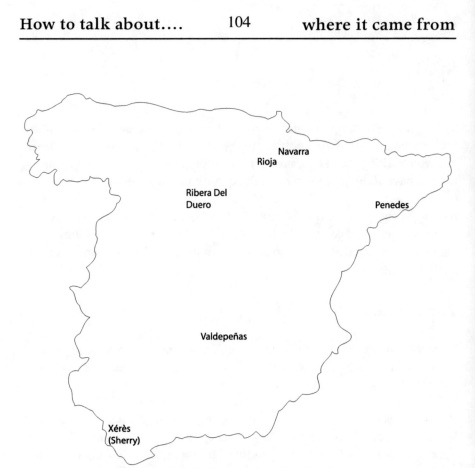

Figure 2.6 The Spanish Wine Regions

Rioja *(ree-oh-ha)* One of the best known wine production regions in Spain. Red wines are made from Tempranillo and Grenacha (the Grenache of France). Whites are primarily made from Viura. The region is proud of its heritage, which dates back to the 19th century when groups of wine makers from the Bordeaux region of France settled here, trying to escape phylloxera. The insect finally made its way south of the border to Spain, but not before the Bordelais had made their mark. Because of the hot weather the wines can suffer from being baked before and during vinification. This led to inconsistent quality, and damaged the reputation of the region. Enter modern wine making techniques, along with temperature controlled vats, and Rioja is undergoing a renaissance of sorts. This is doubly true for the white wines which were once brown and maderized, but are now fresh and fruity.

Valdepeñas *(val-deh-pay'-n'yahss)* A wine producing district in central Spain, known for its light reds.

Xérès *(sair-ress)* The old name for the town of Jerez de la Frontera in Spain, where Sherry is produced. It was the mispronunciation of this word that led to the name of Sherry.

The wines of Spain

Fino *(fee-noh)* A dry type of Sherry (a fortified wine from Spain). It is one of the styles of Sherry which is created by the presence of flor (A type of yeast found on some wine).

Manzanilla *(mahn-thah-nee'-yah)* One of the styles of Sherry. Very dry, and some say, almost salty.

Oloroso *(o-lo-ro'-soh)* A Sherry that has not been aged in the presence of "flor." Dry, as is all Sherry when aging in a barrel, this is the Sherry that is often sweetened and sold as Cream Sherry.

Sangria *(sahn-gree'-ah)* An iced red wine and fruit mixture from Spain. The concept of adding fruit and/or sweetening agents to wine is of ancient origin. Originally used to hide the fact that the wine has gone bad, today it is a delightfully cool drink for a hot day. Similar products (e.g. wine coolers) make the rounds every generation in the US, but it can not compare to the carefully crafted Sangria of Spain. One of the secret ingredients in my personal recipe is the addition of Spanish brandy, which is slightly sweet.

Sherry *(share-ee)* A fortified wine made in the Sherry district in southern Spain around the city of Jerez de la Frontera. The wine is made primarily from the grape Palomino. The grapes are brought into the winery and pressed. The first pressed juice (that of the highest quality) is reserved to make the "Fino" styles. The remaining "press wine" will be used for the "Olorosos" style. The wine is vinified in the traditional manner, until dry. That wine which is to become Fino is placed into a partially filled barrel, so that the special yeast called "flor" can develop. The Olorosos wine is placed in completely filled barrels and fortified to 18% alcohol to prevent spoilage or the accidental introduction of flor. Once the Fino wine has developed flor, it is first fortified (to 17%) to prevent the further growth of flor and then allowed to continue to age, and oxidize, developing a rich dark brown color and nutty flavor. If the bodega (warehouse) is near the ocean town of Sanlucar de Barrameda, the fino will be allowed to develop into the very dry Manzanilla style. Some claim to be able to taste the salt of the ocean breezes in this wine. This is where the Solera system comes into play. Six or more barrels are stacked up. Each of the barrels contains wine of different ages, in different proportions. Wine is drawn from the oldest barrel, and replaced with the next oldest, and so on. The theory is that in this way you "train" the younger wines. The final solera barrel may contain a fraction of wine that is fifty years old or even more. The Sherry that is brought to market is a blend of the wine from these barrels. Sherry, like Champagne, is sweetened just before bottling to determine its final style. The sweetening agent is often concentrated grape juice from the Pedro Ximenez grape (PX is also increasingly being used on its own to make very sweet styled Sherrys). A final fortification is also performed before bottling to bring the final product up to 19% alcohol. The Olorosso style Sherry that did not benefit from the introduction of the flor yeast is usually sweetened heavily and ends up as Cream Sherry.

Vega Sicilia *(vay'-gah see-see'-l'yah)* A Spanish wine that is very famous, among a select few. The producer's top label, Vega Sicilia Unico, is often aged for decades before bottling, and sells for prices that rival the finest Bordeaux or Burgundies.

Terms found on Spanish Wine Labels

Bodega *(boh-day'-gah)* The Spanish term for a winery or above the ground wine storage.

Cava *(cah-vah)* The Spanish term for "cellar" it is also refers to Spanish sparking wine.

Crianza *(cree-ahn-zah)* The Spanish term for oak aging. The terms "con crianza" or "vino de crianza" on the label require that the wine has been aged for at least one year in oak. Similarly "sin crianza" means that the wine was never aged in oak before bottling.

Denominación de Origen *(deh-noh-mee-nah-th'yon' deh oh-ree-hen')* The Spanish term for their appellation laws. Established first for the wine growing region of Rioja in 1926. Often abbreviated DO.

Denominazíone do Origine Controllata *(deh-noh-mee-nah-t'zee-oh'-neh dee oh-ree-jeen-eh con-troh-lah'-tah)* The Italian term for their appellation laws, established in 1963. Abbreviated DOC.

Gran Reserva *(grahn reh-zehr-vah)* A Spanish term for a red wine that has been aged for a minimum of five years (with at least two in wood) before being released. For whites and rosé, it is four years before release and six months in wood.

Reserva *(reh-zehr'-vah)* A Spanish term that is regulated by law to mean a red wine that has been aged for at least three years before release, at least one of which must have been in a barrel. For rosé and white wines it is two years before release and six months in wood.

Germany

Germany is a northernly country. In fact, it is the northern-most wine growing region in the world. This means that the vineyards are often growing in areas that are marginally too cold, especially in a cold year. This has led to steeply terraced hillsides with warming southern exposures, especially in the quality growing areas.

The cool climate also means that white wine grapes, which ripen earlier than red wine grapes, are the norm. There is a public perception that all German wines are sweet and white. Some red wine is made, mostly from the Pinot Noir grape (which also thrives in the cool northern French regions of Burgundy and Champagne). While some of the greatest sweeter and even very sweet wines are made in Germany, there are also many great (and some not so great) dry white wines made as well.

Germany is noted for being orderly, and so it is with their vineyards and wine labels. It can be daunting to try to figure out what kind of German wine you are holding, doubly so if the label uses the ornate old German script. The good news is that with a little effort, it is possible to decipher that label, and enjoy some of the finest wines the world has to offer.

The regions

Ahr *(ahr)* A tiny wine region in Germany. It is unusual for Germany in that most of the wine made is red. The main grape is Pinot Noir which is known locally as Spätburgunder.

Baden *(bah-d'n)* One of the larger German wine regions. It is bordered by France on the West, and Switzerland in the South. The grapes tend to be planted along the foothills of the Black Forest. This is where you can find most of the German plantings of the red wine grape Pinot Noir which is known locally as Spätburgunder. Müller-Thurgau and Ruländer (Pinot Gris) are the main white wine grapes.

Bernkastel *(bairn'-cast'l)* One of the world's greatest "cute little wine towns." This one is situated on the Mosel River in Germany, in the Mosel-Saar-Ruwer region. The most famous wines of Germany, Bernkastler Doctor, are grown on the steep hillsides overlooking the river. The Doctor vineyard has the perfect southern exposure. Important in these chilly northern vineyards.

Franken *(frahn'-ken)* A large German wine region that specializes in dry white wines made from the grape Silvaner. While many German wine regions produce flowery and somewhat sweet wines, the wines of Franken tend to be clean and crisp. This has earned them a following, especially among those who are looking for dry German wines to drink with food. The region is sometimes known as Franconia in English language texts.

Hessische Bergstrasse *(heh-see-shuh bairg-strah-suh)* A tiny German region that primarily produces white wines from the Riesling grape. Most of the wine is consumed locally.

Hochheim *(hawk-heim)* An important German wine making town. It overlooks the Main river, but it is considered part of the Rheingau.

Johannisberg *(yo-hahn'iss-bairg)* One of the most famous German wine towns. It is situated in the middle of the Rheingau region. Because of the fame of this village, the word "Johannisberg" is sometimes (in the US only) added to the Riesling grape, Riesling being the principal grape of this region in Germany. "Johannisberg Riesling" was adopted in the US to distinguish it from the now rare Franken Riesling (which is actually the grape Sylvaner).

Mittelrhein *(mit' l-rine)* A tiny and very picturesque wine region in Germany along the Rhine River. Most of the wine is white and made from the Riesling grape. It is rarely exported.

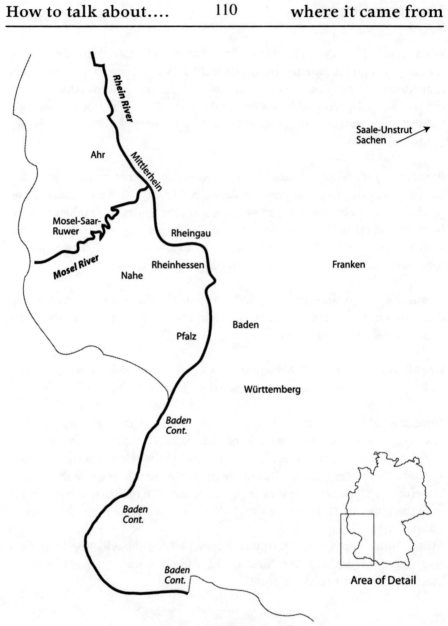

Figure 2.7 Regions of Germany

Mosel / Moselle *(mo'-zl / mo-zell')* The river that runs through part of the Mosel-Saar-Ruwer wine region in Germany. Moselle is the English spelling. Many of the very best vineyards in Germany can be found along the banks of this river as it winds it way through the region.

Mosel-Saar-Ruwer *(mo'z'l sahr roo'-ver)* One of the highest quality wine regions in Germany. It includes two of the tributaries to the Moselle River, the Saar and the Ruwer. The finest vineyards are found on steeply terraced hills, overlooking the rivers. The best wines are made from Riesling, but increasing amounts of Müller-Thurgau, Elbling and Kerner are being planted. Some of the best known wine growing regions in Germany can be found here: Zeller Schwarze Katz, Piesporter and the Bernkastler vineyards. The Bernkastler Doctor vineyard in particular is heralded by many as the source of their favorite German wine.

Nahe *(nah'-huh)* One of the major wine growing areas of Germany, and for many, as high a quality as the Mosel, and the Rheingau. A visit to Bad Kreuznach, the wine capital of the region, will not only yield exceptional Rieslings, but you may soak in the therapeutic baths and gamble your nights away in the casino.

Nierstein *(neer'-sh'tine)* The leading wine village in the Rheinhessen region of Germany.

Phalz / Rheinpfalz *(fahl'tz / rine'-fal'tz)* One of the Anbaugebiete (specified wine regions) of Germany, and the most up and coming. Also referred to as the Rheinpfalz, and sometimes known in English speaking circles as the "Palatinate." Stretching for 50 miles, just north of Alsace from the French-German border, the Phalz produces red and white wines of distinction. Pinot Noir, known as Spatburgunder in German, is the red wine grape of the region, where it produces a very light styled wine. Riesling is king here, but Müller-Thurgau is a close second, with a variety of other grapes constituting 60% of the vineyards. While the second largest German region by size, it may be the largest by volume of wine produced. The words Phalz and Palatinate both derive from the Latin "palatium", meaning palace. The Roman emperors constructed their imperial residences on a hill in the region 2000 years ago, and the name still sticks.

Rheingau *(rine'-gaoh)* Historically one of the highest quality German wine producing regions. The Rhine River flows primarily northwest through Germany, except for here, where it takes a southwest course for about 20 miles. It is the direction of the river that allows the vineyards to have a south facing view, critical for ripening the grapes in this cold growing region. Here you will find Johannsberg, a region that for the US is literally synonymous with Riesling. The influx of faster maturing and easier to grow grapes has not reached this part of Germany, as it has in so much of the country. Instead, Riesling continues to be the primary grape of the region, which in no small way helps to define the quality of the wines. Critics charge that the wines of the region have been declining in quality as producers rush to meet the demand for their wines. In 2000 the German government made a stab at correcting the problem by assigning a new vineyard classification system, not unlike that used in the Burgundy region of France. Critics now point out that the system is less than effective as it gave 33% of the vineyards the superior rating (as compared to Burgundy where 3% of the vineyards are Grand Cru and 11% Premiers Cru).

Rheinhessen *(rine-hess'-en)* The largest of Germany's wine regions. You will find very little Riesling here, with the wines being made primarily of Müller-Thurgau and/or Sylvaner. As with so many large growing regions around the world, the emphasis here is on quantity over quality.

Rüdesheim *(roo-dess-heim)* A small wine producing town in the Rheingau region of Germany. The Rieslings from the area are popular with tourists who flock to the picturesque town, which in turn goes out of its way to accommodate the throngs.

Ruwer *(roo-ver')* A tributary of the Moselle River, and part of the Mosel-Saar-Ruwer region. Little wine is produced here, although it can be of very high quality, and the river is not much more than a stream.

Saale-Unstrut *(zahl' oon-shtrut)* A tiny, and northerly German wine region. In what was once considered East Germany, this region produces dry white wines near the city of Leipzig.

Saar *(sahr)* A tributary of the Moselle River, and part of the Mosel-Saar-Ruwer region. The region is so cold that the Riesling grape only gets ripe enough to make fine wines a few years out of a decade. The rest of the time the wines go to make Sekt, the German sparkling wine, which like all sparkling wines starts with an acidic base. As with all cold growing regions, the emphasis here is on ripening and finding a southern exposure for the grapes. Since the Saar runs north through the wine producing area, its banks are not lined with vineyards, as are so many other German rivers. Instead it is the side valleys, with their south facing slopes that are home to the vines. The wines in a great year are unsurpassed, and unforgettable. It is this potential alone that keeps this region under vine.

Saar-Ruwer *(sahr-roover)* A Bereich (group of villages and vineyards) in the Mosel-Saar-Ruwer region.

Sachsen *(zahkh'-zuhn)* The smallest of the German wine regions. It is centered around the city of Dresden in what was once East Germany. The region produces dry white wines.

Württemberg *(vur'-tem-bairg)* A good sized German wine region. It is situated around the well known German city of Stuttgart, home of the German automobile industry. The red wines made in the region are of the greatest interest. Besides the usual red wine grape Spätburgunder (Pinot Noir) here you will also find local varieties such as Trollinger, Lemberger and Schwarzriesling (which is not a black riesling at all, rather it is the Pinot Meunier grape which is also found in the Champagne region of France).

The German wine label

Auslese *(ouse'-lay-zuh)* A German term for "Select Harvest." Wines with this designation are slightly sweet and lucious. Don't be afraid of these wines, they are often great with food, and rarely expensive.

Beerenauslese *(bear'-en-ouse'-lay-zuh)* Literally "Select Berry Picking" in German. The English term is "Individual Berry Select." Tiny scissors are used to cut just the most perfectly ripe berries (grapes) from the cluster.

The grapes must have no less than 125 degrees Oeschsle (about 30%) sugar. The resulting wine usually is somewhat sweet (average of about 6% residual sugar) with great flavors and amazing complexity. This is one of the world's finest styles of wine. It is a great match for spicy foods of all sorts.

Bereich *(beh-rye'sh)* The German term for a wine producing subregion as defined by the 1971 German wine laws. A bereich contains many villages and vineyards in its scope.

Domäne *(doe-may'-nuh)* A rarely used German term for "Estate." Mostly reserved for state-owned vineyards.

Einzellage *(ay'n-t sel-lah-guh)* The German term for a single vineyard worthy of being mentioned on a label. Any German wine that carries a vineyard name may be considered a wine of quality. The name of the town usually comes first on the label as in the case of Piesporter Goldtröpfchen.

Erzeugerabfüllung *(air'-t zoo-gher-ahb'-foo-lung)* This rather imposing German word is found on labels of wines that have been Estate Bottled.

Grosslage *(gross'-lah-guh)* German for "large vineyard." In German wine law, it is a collection of individual vineyards (Einzellagen) that share common traits. This allows the wines to be marketed under either their vineyard name, or the often better known Grosslage name.

Halbtrocken *(hahlb-trock-en)* German for "half-dry." Wines with this designation may contain no more than 1.8% residual sugar.

Kabinett *(kah-bee-net')* The entry level designation for quality German wines (QmP). Drier than other wines of the class, a Kabinett must be made from grapes with at least 16 percent sugar at harvest. The result is a drier (although not necessarily dry), lighter styled wine that is low in alcohol. The term comes from the practice of the wine producers reserving some wine for their own use, by locking it away in a cabinet.

Keller *(kel-ler)* The German word for cellar.

Lage *(lah'-guh)* German for vineyard. Hence "einzellage" and "grosslage."

Originalabfüllung *(o-reeg'-ee-nahl-ahh'-foo-lung)* The older German term for "Estate Bottled." It was largely replaced in 1971 by the term "Erzeugurabfüllung."

QbA The complete phrase is "Qualitätswein bestimmter Anbaugebiete" which is almost always abbreviated to QbA in the US and on the wine label. It means "quality wine from a specified region." It is a legal designation under the 1971 German wine laws. A QbA wine must have a minimum sugar level at harvest, but may be chaptalized (have sugar added). It must come from one of the 11 specific growing regions of Germany, and the name of the region must be on the label.

QmP "Qualitätswein mit Prädikat" which translates from German to quality wine with distinction. Almost always abbreviated in the US, and on the wine label. A legal designation under the German wine laws of 1971. As well as this phrase the label must identify the wine as belonging to one of these six classés from driest to sweetest: Kabinett, Spätlese, Auslese, Beerenauslese, Eiswein or Trokenbeeranauslese (see each listed individually). The rules for QmP are similar to those of QbA, except that the wine may not be chaptalized (have sugar added). These are the highest quality wines made in Germany.

Rotwein *(rot-vine)* The German term for red wine.

Schloss *(sh'loss)* The German word for castle. Often used in the same way the French use "chateau," to mean the vineyard, the wine and the property.

Spätlese *(sh'pay't-lay-zuh)* The German term for late picked. It is a QmP (quality wine without sugar added) designation. Most wines of this level are only slightly sweet.

Tafelwein *(tah'-fel-vine)* German for Table Wine.

Troken *(traw'-ken)* The German word for dry. Legally it means a wine that has less than 1% residual sugar. The Germans have been experimenting more with drier wines, to give them more universal appeal, and to match more cuisines. Halbtroken, meaning "half-dry" has also become popular.

Trokenbeeranauslese *(Traw'-ken-bear'-en-ouse'-lay-zuh)* The top German wine. Sweeter and more expensive than any other of the QmP class. The English language term would be "Individual Berry Special Select Late Harvest." The grapes must not only be late harvested, but they must be dried (troken) to an almost raisin state before picking. This intense dessert wine, which is usually abbreviated to TBA, is only made in very special vintages, often less than once a decade. It ages unbelievably well. I have tasted 40 year old examples that still seemed to be quite young.

Wein *(vine)* The German word for wine.

Weingut *(vine'-goot)* The German term for a vineyard estate. If it appears on a bottle the grapes must come entirely from vineyards the producer owns.

Weinkellerei *(vine-kel'-er-rye)* The German term for a wine cellar. If you see this on the label, it may be an off hand way of telling you that the grapes for this wine do not come from the producers own vineyards.

Portugal

Port, not to anyone's surprise comes from Portugal. As does Madeira (the wine is made on an island of the same name off the coast of Portugal). These, along with Sherry from neighboring Spain, are the best known fortified wines. Wines that have been left sweet, to varying degrees, by the addition of a neutral grape spirit (like a rather raw brandy). Adding the spirit before the yeast finish fermenting all of the sugars ensures not only that the wine will be sweeter than not, but that the fermentation process will not restart.

Portugal makes many wines that are not fortified, though few find their way to the US. It is then these fortified wines that define Portugal in the minds of most wine drinkers. If you are ever presented with a chance to explore the real Portugal, to delight in its fresh and simple wines, and to meet the generous people, you will not be disappointed. For many, the closest you will come is to sip a little Port on a cold winters night, or to enjoy a glass of rare and ancient Madeira over a creamy soup. Explore these fine wines, if not the country itself.

The wines of Portugal

Bual [or Boal] *(boh-ahl)* A grape variety used in Madeira. Increasingly it is used to indicate a medium sweet style of Madeira, regardless of the grape.

Late Bottled Vintage Port A style of Port created originally for restaurants. Since Vintage Port throws a great deal of sediment, it can be difficult for a restaurant to deal with. The solution was to age the Vintage Port in barrels for four to six years, before bottling. This allows the wine to be ready to drink when released as opposed to Vintage Port which may require decades of aging before it is at its best. With an LBV there is little to no sediment so decanting is not necessary. This style of wine is delightful, but is no substitute for actual Vintage Port. Often abbreviated as LBV.

Port A sweet red wine that is made by adding neutral grape spirit (brandy) to the unfinished wine. This is the process known as "fortification." Port is made in several styles. Vintage Port is made in years that are exceptional. It is bottled young, and ages in the bottle for decades. An aged Vintage Port throws a good deal of sediment and must be decanted before serving. Late Bottled Vintage Port is aged for several years in a barrel before it is bottled. It is a short cut method that allows the wine to be served with a minimum of fuss. It never will have the complexity of a fine Vintage Port, nor the price. Character Port is a house style that is not vintage dated. It is a simple, inexpensive style that will not improve with age. The label will not say "Character Port," it will have a brand name instead. Tawny Port has been aged in a barrel for a number of years (usually listed on the label). As the Port throws sediment, it is racked into a new barrel, leaving the sediment behind, as well as the coloring agent. The result is a lightly brown (tawny) colored wine that is nutty and complex. 10, 20 and 40 year old Tawnies are common. There is also a White Port made from white wine grapes. It is a drier, aperitif style. It is rarely seen in the US. Outside of the European Economic Community, which controls the legal use of the term Port, there are several Port style wines made in a similar fashion. Australia and the US are both producers of these Port styled wines.

Rainwater Once a trademark for a particular Madeira, it is now a generic term for a lighter, not too sweet, style.

Ruby Port A wood port, meaning it has aged in a barrel for some time, usually three years. The term Ruby Port is rarely used anymore, and when it is, it may mean a blend of red and white ports served as an aperitif in the cafés of Europe.

Sercial *(sair-s'yahl)* The driest style of Madeira.

Setúbal *(shtoo'-bahl)* A fortified Muscat wine from Portugal. It is made in the rancio style, meaning that it is brown like a Sherry or Tawny Port. This type of wine is made in many parts of the world, but Setubal is one of the very finest, and worth looking for.

Tawny Port A Port that has been aged in a barrel instead of a bottle. The process allows the wine to take on a nutty aroma, and to lose its red color over time (turning a tawny brown). The best examples are usually labeled in decades, such as a 10-year-old, 20-year-old or 40-year-old. Inexpensive tawny ports may be a blend of red and white port, and do not resemble the real thing in any way. The US and Australia make fortified wines that they continue to label "Port" and the tawny versions of some of these are a relative bargain.

Vinho Verde *(veen'-yoh vair'-day)* This Portuguese "green wine" may be red or white, and is often slightly sparkling. Green in this case refers to the youth of the wine, rather than its color. The wine is produced far up the Douro river, almost to the border of Spain.

Vintage Port The most expensive, and longest lived style of Port. These wines are only made in years of exceptional quality, usually only a few times a decade. They are bottled when they are young, but are intended to age for 20 years or more before they are consumed. As they age, Vintage Ports will throw sediment and will need to be decanted before serving. This is the best wine to buy to celebrate the life of a child, as the wine will age in much the same way as a person. First the parent, and then the offspring can celebrate 12 milestones in their life with a case of Vintage Port. In its youth the Vintage Port is but a hint of what it will be. As it reaches its teens, it starts to develop character, but remains fiery. By the time it is 21 years old, it is fully mature, but without the character further age will bring. By the time it is 40 years old, it has mellowed from a hot plum-like flavor, to a soft nutty taste, full of complexity. As the port continues to age, it starts to lose some of its strength and intensity, but gains complexity and character. 60 to 80 years is often the upper limit of a Vintage Port, and few have the opportunity to taste them this mature, but few forget the experience. Only the greatest Port Vintages make it to the 100 year mark, while lesser years have faded long before this. While I eschew anthropomorphism in wine jargon, for Vintage Port it seems appropriate to make this connection to a human life span.

The United States

The history of wine making in the US starts as far back as the 16th century when missionaries planted grapes and made wine in what is now New Mexico. By the early 19th century commercial wine making ventures had begun in the eastern states, propelled by the interest of Thomas Jefferson and others. The eastern states proved to be too cool for quality wine making, and growers started to look further west for ideal climates. As the population moved west, so did the wine. The discovery of gold in California brought thousands of settlers. Some hoped to strike it rich by pulling wealth out of the ground, and others hoped that the way to riches lay in planting in the ground. Spain controlled California then, and it was the Spanish governor that commissioned Agoston Haraszthy to travel to Europe with the express intent of bringing back vine cuttings to jump start the wine industry. Spain and the gold are gone, but the vines remain. Throughout the state, anywhere the climate is cool enough to accommodate grapes, you will find vines planted.

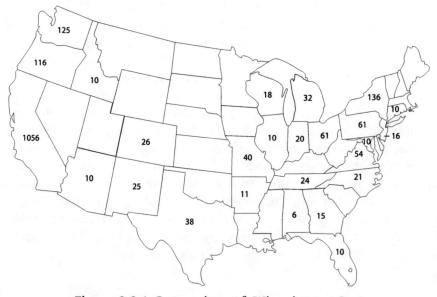

Figure 2.8 A Comparison of Wineries per State

California is not the only place that wine is made in the US. The Pacific Northwest states of Oregon and Washington, as well as the eastern state of New York all have thriving wine industries. In fact, it may surprise many people to learn that most states have wineries, and vineyards. The US is far behind Europe in both production and consumption of wine, but thanks to research and modern techniques, many of which originated in the US, the quality of American wines rival that of the rest of the world.

California

This is the best known wine producing State in the US. With a tradition going back to the early 19th century, California has some of the oldest continuing vineyards in the country. The well known Napa and Sonoma Valleys are just two of the many growing regions around the state. The same warm sunny days that attracted so many people to live in this state, help to create a grape grower's paradise. Vintage variation is often less of an issue with California wines than anywhere else in the world. The blisteringly hot Central Valley of California is a huge growing area that produces food of all types. It is also where much wine, of little note, is made. The intense sun and heat can easily overwhelm the vines, so most of the quality growing regions are cooled either by proximity to the ocean, or by being planted at altitude. There is a huge variety of grapes planted throughout California, as growers either attempt to match climate to grape, or simply continue the tradition of planting started by their great grandparents. Some of the largest wineries in the world are found in California, as well as many hundreds of producers that are so tiny only a handful of people ever get to try their wines.

Subregions

Carneros A California wine producing region. Situated where the Napa and Sonoma valleys meet in the south, and just north of the Bay. The proximity to the Bay makes the region cooler than its neighbors and as such, many sparkling wine producers have elected to grow here. The region has also proven itself as ideal for Pinot Noir (Pinot is also one of the grapes in most sparkling wines).

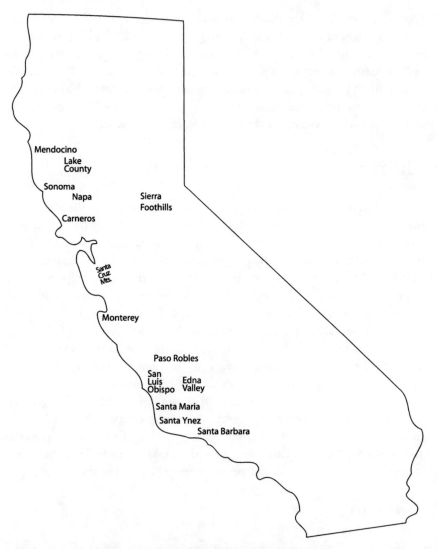

Mendocino
Lake
County
Sonoma
Napa
Sierra
Foothills
Carneros
Santa
Cruz
Mts.
Monterey
Paso Robles
San
Luis
Obispo
Edna
Valley
Santa Maria
Santa Ynez
Santa Barbara

Figure 2.9 California Wine Regions

Edna Valley An American Viticultural Area south of San Luis Obispo in California (an area broadly referred to as the Central Coast). One of the few transverse valleys in the US (meaning it points to the sea). This makes the region much cooler than surrounding growing regions and is ideal for Chardonnay and Pinot Noir.

Lake County North of Napa and east of Sonoma in California, Lake County does not have proximity to the ocean or altitude to cool the vineyards. The warmer growing climate has been a boon for Zinfandel, and has led to some very popular, although slightly sweet, Chardonnay. While it has a long history, it is only recently that the quality of Lake County's wines have become recognized.

Mendocino County The northernmost wine region in California's North Coast. The quality of the wines from the region have improved greatly in the last few decades, and some exceptional sparkling wine has started to be produced.

Monterey County Until recently this county in California was better known as the setting for Steinbeck novels than for wine. In the early 1960s large concerns began to make wine of varying quality from the region. The wine improved, and so the number of wineries increased. Today Monterey County is still home to some of the best values in California wines, as well as a few well known, but pricier producers.

Napa Valley Easily the best known wine region in the US, this area of California has been making wine for generations. Some of the best known names in California wines can be found here, and certainly some of the most expensive. Cabernet Sauvignon based wines have proven to be the most successful, although Chardonnay and many other grapes continue to be planted. The valley floor can be very hot. Too hot for some varieties, and so the hills that overlook the Napa River valley are dotted with vineyards. The legal term Napa Valley also includes several neighboring valleys and mountain sides.

Paso Robles A wine growing region in California, south of the bay, and south of Monterey as well. Look for Cabernet Sauvignon and Zinfandel from this region.

San Luis Obispo A California wine region that is south of Paso Robles (although technically part of Paso Robles is in San Luis Obispo County) and continues south to Santa Barbara County. This is a wide and general area that has many types of wine, and producers of varying quality. Since the cost of land in Napa and Sonoma Counties has surpassed the budget of many would be grape growers, San Luis Obispo has been growing at an amazing rate.

Santa Barbara Directly south of San Luis Obispo in California, the city and county of Santa Barbara is a hidden jewel. Two of the main growing regions in Santa Barbara County are the Santa Maria and Santa Ynez valleys. Both of these valleys directly face the ocean, capturing the breezes that make these some of the coolest growing regions in California. For this reason Pinot Noir, and Chardonnay have done very well here. Syrah from the region has also been impressive and Viognier and Riesling, more lovers of cool climates, thrive here as well.

Santa Cruz Mountains Just South of the Bay and overlooking the famed Silicon Valley of San Jose, the Santa Cruz Mountains are home to a few hearty wine makers who's names are near and dear to all California wine lovers. One of California's longest lived and most respected Cabernet Sauvignon comes from here. The intensity of this cab is due in no small measure to the infertile soils of the region.

Santa Maria Valley One of the coolest growing regions in California, this valley is located in Santa Barbara County, far to the south of the better known Napa and Sonoma Valleys. California is warm, and it can be too warm for quality grape growing in many regions. Generally, the further south in California you go, the warmer it gets. Santa Maria Valley is efficiently cooled by the ocean breezes making it ideal for the cool loving Pinot Noir and Chardonnay grapes.

Santa Ynez Valley The charming Danish town of Solvang used to be the main attraction to this valley. Located in Santa Barbara County, California. Tourist now are just as likely to come for wine tasting. The cool ocean breezes keep this valley temperate enough to grow world class Pinot Noir, Chardonnay and Syrah. The wineries here are not as numerous as those way to the north in Napa, and the tourist are not anywhere near as common. For those who intrepidly explore, either in person or by popping a cork, this is a region not to miss.

Sierra Foothills Far to the east of the Pacific Ocean, further even than the great farming expanse of the Central Valley of California, the foothills of the Sierra Mountains begin to rise. Here, where gold was once found and miners clamored for refreshment, a wine industry sprang up in the 19th century. More than a century later, a growing number of wineries have made these foothills their home. Here the venerable Zinfandel vine was planted many generations ago, and now has matured to offer some of the most intense juice anyone has made wine from. Zinfandel reigns here, but new grape varieties are slowly being planted as the region expands.

Sonoma Valley / County The Russian River has carved a wide and fertile valley for this Northern California wine region. West of Napa, and closer to the ocean, Sonoma is a collection of micro-climates that range from hot and dry, to foggy and cool. Almost every type of wine grape known can be found somewhere in this sprawling region. Some of this may be due to the long tradition of grape growing in the region. In Sonoma, a near legendary figure named Haraszthy planted some of the earliest European grape varieties in California. Generations of immigrants and wine makers followed, giving the region a tradition of wine making that still permeates every nook and cranny of the valley.

The Pacific Northwest

As vineyard prices in California started to move out of most people's range, many set eyes further north, up the coast. Oregon, and Washington State turned out to be ideal places to grow grapes. The inevitable learning curve meant that early wines produced in the regions were not always consistent. Time has passed, and the vineyards and winemakers have matured.

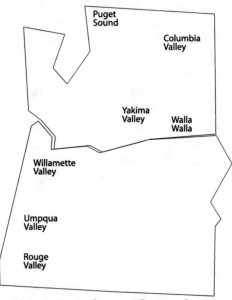

Figure 2.10 The Pacific Northwest
Oregon and Washington State

Oregon

This Pacific Northwestern state is well known for its Pinot Noir wines. The climate has proven that it can produce remarkable wines; however, as is the case with so many of the finest cool regions, the vintages can be variable. Riesling, Chardonnay and Pinot Gris are white varieties that have been successfully planted in Oregon.

Rouge Valley The southernmost wine growing region in the State of Oregon.

Umpqua Valley A wine region in western Oregon, just south of the Willamette Valley.

Willamette Valley *(will-am'-it)* The main growing region in Oregon, and planted primarily in Pinot Noir. Vintages here can be variable, but when the conditions are right, Pinot Noir thrives, and a growing number of wineries are attempting to make their mark with this difficult grape. Even those with concerns in the Mecca of Pinot Noir, Burgundy, France, have thrown in their lots with those gambling on the suitability of Oregon to produce world class wines. While there have been some disappointments, the general trend is promising, and the wines just keep getting better.

Washington

Along with Oregon, Washington State is often referred to as the Pacific Northwest. The mild climate, and the relatively low cost of land has drawn an increasing number of wine makers to this state. Most of the grapes are grown in the Columbia River basin, in the southeastern corner of the state. Here, shielded from the ocean by the Cascade mountains, an arid plain has been redefined thanks to irrigation and tenacity. Cabernet Sauvignon and Merlot have done well here, as has Riesling.

Columbia Valley A wine producing region in Washington State in the US. Following the mighty Columbia river as it winds down the eastern portion of the state, the Columbia Valley runs nearly the entire length of Washington into Oregon.

Puget Sound A small wine region in western Washington that is centered around the city of Seattle. While most of the wine boom in the state has been in the eastern regions, this area is one of the oldest in the state, and is home to some of the better known wineries.

Walla Walla Walla Walla, Washington. The name rolls off the tongue, and for many it is known only as a near nonsense word used by Bugs Bunny. Some of the State's finest grapes are grown here, or near here (Washington State is not a stickler for precise geographic designations).

Yakima Valley This region in Washington State is a tiny subsection of the Columbia River Valley.

New York

Second only to California in wine production, New York has been producing wines since the earliest days of the US. Few US wine lovers think of New York in the same regard as they would California. This is changing as small wineries have begun planting Vinifera (European grape varieties such as Cabernet and Chardonnay) in place of the more traditional Hybrids and native American grapes. You are now more likely to be offered a New York Riesling than the once ubiquitous White Concord. The Concord, a native American grape, is now relegated to making juice, which it does best. Sparkling wines continue to be produced in New York, in response to the cool climate (crisp tart grapes are required for sparkling wine). New York has a ways to go before it can lose the stigma it gained from centuries of indifferent wines, but it is moving in the right direction.

Finger Lakes The main wine producing area in New York state. The region, which is about 300 miles northwest of New York City is dotted with lakes. These help to keep the ground from freezing in winter, and so help improve the conditions for vines. While wine has been made here since the early 19th century, the results had always been spotty. Once planted almost exclusively to French Hybrids (crosses between native American grapes and the European wine grapes) the Finger Lakes are now as likely to produce the better known white wines, Chardonnay and Riesling.

Long Island The maritime climate of this region has led many to compare it to Bordeaux. While the wines have been steadily improving over the years, no wine from Long Island has gained a world wide reputation. Cabernet Sauvignon and Merlot are the most common red grapes. Chardonnay is the main white grape.

Figure 2.11 New York State

Wine and label terms in the US

American Viticultural Area Often abbreviated AVA. This is the set of US laws which regulate the use of place names on wine labels. Unlike similar laws in Europe, there are no restrictions on grape variety, yield or wine making practices. AVAs seem to be created more as a response to politics, then as a form of consumer protection. There are over 140 AVAs at this time.

Estate Bottled - Estate Bottling Wine that was bottled by the vineyard owner. Many wines are still bottled and produced from grapes that are purchased on the open market, often for the lowest price. This designation assures that the winery had control over the grapes from beginning to end so that they could produce a high quality wine. In the US the vineyard need not belong to the winery, if there is a long term exclusive contract for the grapes of the vineyard (which also must be in the same geographic location as the winery). See also Domaine for the French equivalent of this designation.

Ice Wine This is an intense dessert wine that has been made from very ripe grapes (without Botrytis) that were frozen on the vine. The frozen water is removed during pressing, leaving a very sweet must. In German it is known as "eiswein." A modern technique called cryoextraction utilizes a freezer in place of mother nature.

Jug Wine A term used for low quality wines that are sold in large bottles, or jugs. While this type of wine is rarely written about, it is important to remember that most of the wine made in the world is in fact, of jug wine quality.

Late Harvest By harvesting later, the grapes are riper, and sweeter. This is appropriate for making sweet, dessert style wines. Some Late Harvest wines are almost dry, opting for increased alcohol and intensity rather than sweetness, as in the Alsatian "vendange tardive" (French for late harvest). In the US the term usually refers to a lightly sweet wine. Select Late Harvest refers to a sweeter wine, and Special Select Late Harvest to a very sweet wine. This is consistent with the German terms Aulese, Beerenauslese, and Trokenbeerenauslese.

Reserve In the US, the term reserve has no legal meaning. It implies that the wine is from the better part of the production; however, it is often used on the label of very cheap wines that have not been reserved from anything. Since this term has meaning in Spain and Italy, it is confusing for the consumer.

Rhine Wine It would seem obvious that this phrase relates to those wines made in the Rhine Valley of Germany; however, in a never ending attempt to confuse consumers and to belittle the place names of Europe, under US law a Rhine Wine can be any white wine with less than 14% alcohol.

Table Wine A US legal term that encompasses all wines that are between 7% and 14% alcohol. The term is used in Europe to mean a wine that was not made under the rules of any specific controlled area. Winemakers who are interested in pushing the boundaries of wine production in their area often can only bottle their wines as the local equivalent of table wine. Some of these wines are of very high quality, and can command higher prices than the usual wines from the region. As such, it can be a very confusing term.

Table Wine can be either:
most wines (as in the US),
a wine of lower quality or distinction,
or a wine of distinction that does not conform to a standard.

Varietal Wine Any wine that takes its name from the predominant grape variety. This is very common in the US and the rest of the New World, but in Europe, wines are usually labeled with the place name. In the US there must be 75% of the named grape. Elsewhere the percentage varies, but is rarely, if ever, lower.

Wine Cooler A mix of wine and fruit juices (or lime flavored soda). The practice of disguising bad wine with sweetened juice is as old as wine itself. The name has developed a negative connotation for many wine lovers, since the prepackaged, sweetened and carbonated version is little more than soda pop with a touch of alcohol.

Australia

The history of wine in Australia goes back almost as far as it does in the US. Australia's wine industry had a slower start, since the country did not have the waves of European immigrants that the US did in the 19th century. None the less, Australia was settled by the British who have long been lovers and merchants of wine, but due to the climate, had never been able to produce their own. Australia then was a dream come true for many of English descent, who had always longed for a place to plant grapes and produce wine.

While Australia did not have the head start of the US, it also did not have that bump in US wine history, Prohibition. Able to produce wine throughout the 20th century, Australia's vineyards matured, as did their wine making. The last part of the 20th century saw technical breakthroughs in wine making, and grape growing. One of the most important contributors to the revolution in modern grape growing is an Australian, Dr. Richard Smart, and this helped Australia (and New Zealand) to jump ahead of the rest of the world in the critical area of vineyard management.

The center of Australia is largely dessert, with the population and arable land scattered along the coasts. This limits the growth of the wine industry, and new growing areas are rare.

The regions

Coonawarra One of the most notable red wine regions of Australia. Situated in the state of South Australia, it is primarily planted to Shiraz and Cabernet Sauvignon.

Hunter Valley The oldest vineyard region in Australia. About 100 miles northwest of Sydney. Traditionally Shiraz (the Syrah grape of the Rhône Valley, in France) is king here, with Sémillon being the white grape of choice. Bowing to international tastes, Cabernet Sauvignon and Chardonnay are now almost 50% of the total vines planted.

Margret River An up and coming wine region in Western Australia. The cool climate has proved to be one of the most successful in Australia, and there is every reason to believe the production of quality wines from the region has just begun.

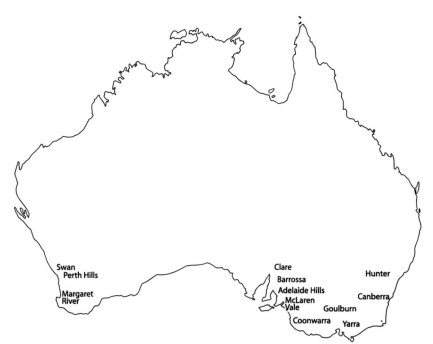

Figure 2.12 The wine regions of Australia are primarily concentrated around the coast in the cooler regions of the south

McLaren Vale A quality wine growing region in the Southern Vales region of Australia.

Adelaide Hills One of the oldest wine producing regions in Australia. Situated in the south-central part of the country, around the city of Adelaide.

Barossa Valley One of the South Australia wine regions. North of the city of Adelaide, Barossa was one of the first areas to become popular outside of Australia. Because the region was planted earlier than most, the vines tend to have a greater average age, and this helps to maintain high quality.

Canberra A wine region in Australia. Situated near the east coast, approximately halfway between Melbourne and Sydney.

Clare Valley One of the wine producing regions of South Australia that are clustered near the city of Adelaide. A long history of winemaking here, and a long slow ripening season, have produced some very hearty red wines.

Goulburn Once a prominent wine region in Australia, it would have faded into obscurity if not for the single winery Tahbilk (they used to have Château in front of their name, but recently dropped it). Tahbilk can trace its roots back to 1860 when it was the original wine producer in the region. History has gone full circle and Tahbilk has stood the test of time.

Perth Hills A tiny wine growing region in Western Australia that is east of the city of Perth. This is one of the newest wine regions in the country. By planting at altitude, the grape growers here are able to escape the heat that plagues the neighboring Swan Valley.

Swan District This is the original wine district in Western Australia. Just north of the city of Perth, this is a very warm region that seems best suited for the fortified dessert wines that are found here. As interest in producing wine in the Perth region grows, it is the cooler hillsides that are being cultivated, while the Swan District continues to fall out of favor.

Yarra Valley Situated just north of the Australian city of Melbourne, this may be the area's best known wine region. Close enough to the city for a leisurely drive, the Yarra Valley is dotted with picturesque wineries that are well prepared for tours and entertaining.

Australian wine labels

For the most part, the wine labels of Australia are the same as those in the US. Most wines are labeled by the grape variety, rather than the place name.

New Zealand

Like its neighbor Australia, New Zealand was settled in a large part by the English. Here too, wine making was an early goal and vines were planted all around the North and South Islands.

The climate in New Zealand can be cool, and even cold in places. This may have influenced the early grape growers to choose varieties more at home in cooler regions, than New Zealand turned out to be. It takes time for people, much less an entire industry, to learn it has made a mistake, and to adapt.

In the 1980s too many wines from New Zealand had a flavor that can only be described as canned asparagus. This was true for red and white wines, and it was hampering the forward progress of the industry. Around this time the new Australian vineyard management techniques started to catch on in New Zealand, perhaps faster than even in Australia. This new way of looking at growing grapes, as well as the general attention that was being paid to New Zealand wines, paid off.

The wines of New Zealand today rarely exhibit the problems of the past, and new regions are yielding exciting wines to explore. As with so many other parts of the world, New Zealand is undergoing a wine revolution, and early indications are promising.

The regions

Auckland The wine region in New Zealand's north island, centered around the city of the same name.

Bay of Plenty A wine producing region on New Zealand's north island.

Canterbury A large wine region on the south island of New Zealand. The region is almost too large and varied to make general comments about, but it is certainly a region that is still looking for its identity. Many of the vineyards are planted to white varieties, notably Riesling and Chardonnay, in an attempt to make the best of what may be too cool of a climate. The cold temperatures mean that some vineyards in this region may have problems ripening in certain vintages.

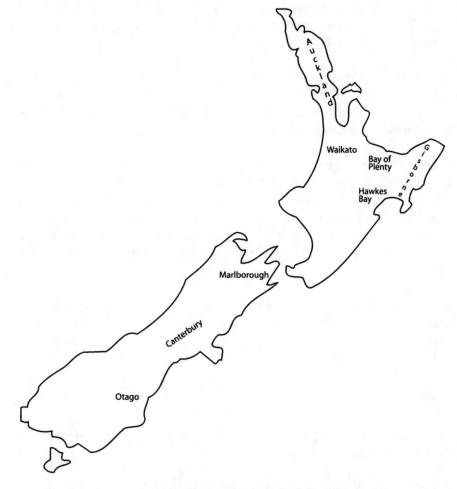

Figure 2.12 New Zealand

Gisborne A wine region on the north island of New Zealand. Situated on the east coast, this region is one of the largest by volume. Many of the grapes are used by the large producers, and as such there are not many wineries here. Chardonnay is the main grape of the region.

Hawkes Bay Sometimes referred to in the press as the "Bordeaux of New Zealand." The inference is not only due to the Cabernet and Merlot based wines from the region, but as well to the variability of vintages that plagues Hawkes Bay. Chardonnay and rich, oak aged Sauvignon Blanc are the whites of the region.

Marlborough Possibly New Zealands finest wine region. Located on the northern end of the southern island, Marlborough is a cool growing region with long dry autumns. This is important since the grapes would not have a chance to ripen fully if the region had rain around the time of the harvest. Sauvignon Blanc made the region well known, but it is Pinot Noir that may ultimately make its mark on Marlborough.

Otago The southernmost wine region in New Zealand. In fact, the southernmost wine region in the World. Nestled in the mountains, the climate is different than almost anywhere else in New Zealand. Vineyards, reminiscent of those in Germany's Mosel (one of the northernmost growing regions) are perched on hillsides with an exposure designed to eke out every bit of solar radiation possible. Pinot Noir is being planted here, as is Riesling. These grapes too are found in the cool climates of Germany, and the comparison is inevitable. Time will tell how this region does, as most of the plantings are fairly recent, but there are high hopes.

Waikato A wine region in New Zealand's northern island.

New Zealand wine labels

For the most part, the wine labels of NZ are the same as those in the US. Most wines are labeled by the grape variety, rather than the place name.

How to talk about
How it was made

The tech of wine

I love all things technical. From computers and the Internet, to growing grapes and making wine. I love to taste wine, and try to determine how it was made, and where. It is like being a great detective. Over the years I have actually learned to do what I call "reading" a wine. I look for the tell-tale signs that can lead me to determine exactly what I am tasting, and how it got there. Sometimes I hit it perfectly, sometimes I miss. What is important to know is that anyone can learn this skill. I teach it twice a year at my wine school in Aspen. For all this, it has nothing to do with simply enjoying wine.

For those who share my love of how it was made, or for those that push their wine knowledge beyond the basic, I offer this chapter. It is far beyond the scope of this book to teach anyone how to make wine, or to grow grapes. Instead these few pages will illustrate what the general process looks like, and define the vocabulary associated with raising grapes and turning it into wine.

A year in the life of a winemaker

This is a look at the average winemaker's schedule for an average year in the northern hemisphere.

January

Vineyard: Vines are being pruned.

Winery: The wine is aging in barrels or vats. Previous vintages are being prepared for sale. Equipment maintenance, etc.

February

Vineyard: Late pruning. New grafts are prepared. Equipment maintenance, etc.

Winery: Racking (moving wine into clean barrels) begins. Some wineries add barrels of wine together to assemble the first blend. Since the wine has to be moved out of the barrels, and barrels are expensive, assembling the blend also allows the wine to be stored in a large vat while the barrels are cleaned for reuse.

March

Vineyard: Final pruning. Sap begins to rise. Soil is worked to aerate and uncover base of vines.

Winery: Racking should be close to complete. Topping off continues. As the weather warms malo-lactic fermentation may start or be induced. End of previous vintage bottling, etc.

April

Vineyard: General vineyard maintenance. You often see cuttings burning in the vineyards.

Winery: General maintenance. Time to finish anything that may not have gotten done earlier.

May

Vineyard: Frost watch. Smudge pots are burning at night and everyone is praying. Soil is worked again to turn under weeds. First spraying against mold and mildew. Remove suckers.

Winery: Shipping of previous vintage and preparing for next racking.

June

Vineyard: The vines flower. This is another critical time, so everyone is still anxious. Much of the quantity of the vintage will be determined at this stage. Shoots are thinned and tied. Second spraying.

Winery: Second racking. Older wines are racked. As weather warms, barrel maintenance becomes crucial.

July

Vineyard: Tiny grapes begin to develop. Vines sprayed with Bordeaux mixture. Turn the weeds into the soil again. Keep shoots trimmed.

Winery: Winery is closed down in times of heat. Steps are taken to prevent bacterial growth in winery.

August

Vineyard: Color begins to change in black grapes. Trimming and weeding keep everyone busy. Preparation is made for harvest.

Winery: Everything is cleaned and inspected for the coming harvest.

September

Vineyard: Final harvest preparations made. Earliest harvesting begins.

Winery: Double check everything. Make sure all vats and barrels are water tight.

October

Vineyard: Most vintages start late September and continue into early October. Once the grapes are picked and the whites are pressed, the grape skins are spread on the vineyard and turned into the soil in preparation of the winter.

Winery: Stemming, crushing and in some cases, pressing, fill the hours. The new wine begins to ferment. Last year's wine is racked and moved to the aging cellar.

November

Vineyard: Shoots are cut and collected to burn (or sell as firewood in some cases). Vineyard is plowed and soil heaped on the base of the vines.

Winery: Young wines are now finished with fining and filtering, and are then bottled. Older vintages may also be bottled. Wines that will be aged are still fermenting in contact with their skins.

December

Vineyard: Some vineyards the soil needs to be replaced after rains. Pruning starts about halfway through the month.

Winery: The end of fermentation for the hearty reds. Bottling of young and older wines is completed. Wines for aging are moved from vat to barrel after fining and possible filtering.

Words from the vineyard

Bordeaux Mixture A fungicide made from copper sulfate and slaked lime. Used widely in Europe to prevent mildew. It is recognizable by its distinctive blue-green color.

Botrytis Cinerea *(bo-trie'-tiss sin-eh-ray'-ah)* The special mold that is responsible for many of the world's greatest dessert wines. It creates micro lesions in the skin of the grape, and then removes the water from inside the grape. The result is fruit with a much higher ratio of sugar, suitable for creating sweet wines. The mold can also be harmful when it attacks dry wine vineyards (it is usually called Gray Rot when it is a pest). The French call Botrytis "Pourriture Noble" - the noble rot.

Cépage *(seh-pahj)* The French term that refers to the variety of grapevine. Cabernet Sauvignon is a popular cépage in the US. The term is also used to indicate the blend of grapes in a wine.

Climat *(clee-mah)* The French term for climate, although it is often used to refer to a region or vineyard that has a unifying characteristic. The English term would be "microclimate."

Clone A plant produced by graphing or cutting, so that it retains the identical genetic characteristics of the host. Each grape variety has many different subvarieties, or clones (much in the way that roses and other domesticated flowers doh). For example there are dozens of clones of Pinot Noir or Cabernet, each excelling in a specific characteristic or resistance to disease.

Coulure *(coo-loo'r)* A condition in the vineyard that results from rainy or cold weather that keeps the flowers from being pollinated and therefore from turning into grapes. If the effect is not too widespread the result can be an intense, but small harvest. Widespread, coulure can spell disaster for grape growing, resulting in a very small harvest.

Cultivar A cultivated grape variety. Some use this as a more precise term than "grape variety."

Degree Days Also known as the "heat summation method." A scale created by the University of California at Davis in the 1930s to determine the suitability for vineyards in any given climate. Modern instrumentation has largely supplanted this scale. The total accumulative number of degrees above 50F during the growing season. If the temperature for any given day rises to 70F that day would add 20 points to the summation. Over the 200 days of the

California growing season the total would range from less than 2,500 degrees days for the coolest areas, classified as Region I, to region V with more than 4,000 degree days.

Hectare The metric unit for measuring land area. It is 10,000 square meters. One hectare = 2.471 acres.

Microclimate In meteorological terms this is the effect of geography on weather on a very small scale. In wine tasting, this term, like the French term Terrioir (see goût de terrior) has been expanded to include the geology as well as geography of any given area. In total, it refers to the different conditions any individual vineyard may face. The vineyards of Burgundy, France are a living example of this effect. While many of the vineyards are tiny, they each have a taste characteristic that is noticeably different from their neighbor.

Mildew The same fungus that plagues home owners can be found in the vineyard, with the same undesirable results. There are two types in the vineyard, "downy" and "powdery." It is the powdery type that is known as Oidium and devistated the vineyards of Europe in the late 19th century. It is now controlled by the careful use of powdered sulfur or copper sulfate in the vineyard.

Noble Rot A term for Botrytis Cinerea. The special mold that is responsible for many of the world's greatest dessert wines. It creates micro lesions in the skin of the grape, and then removes the water from inside the grape. The result is fruit with a much higher ratio of sugar, suitable for creating sweet wines. The mold can also be harmful when it attacks dry wine vineyards (it is usually called Gray Rot when it is a pest). The French call Botrytis "Pourriture Noble" - noble rot.

Oechsle *(uh'k-sleh)* The German scale of measuring the sugar content of must (in the US we use the Brix Scale). The aim of such scales is to determine the potential alcohol content of the finished wine. This is a critical measure of when to harvest.

Oidium *(oh-ee'-d'yum)* The powdery mildew fungus that devastated the vineyards of Europe in the mid-nineteenth century. Like the phylloxera plague that would follow, Oidium was brought from America. It is now controlled in the vineyard by spraying.

Phylloxera *(fil-lox'-er-ra)* A small insect that was responsible for the most devastating plague in wine history. A native of North America, the phylloxera louse is happy to live off the leaves of the native North American grapes. It was accidently exported to Europe where it found a new type of grape to live off of (Vinifera). Instead of the leaves, it found that the roots of this new type of grape was a delicacy. It so liked the roots of Vinifera that it changed its life cycle to exclude males and the winged form of the insect, learning to specialize as a female only, root eating monster. This made phylloxera much harder to detect, and to destroy. The late 19th century saw this insect spread throughout Europe, and even to the wine making regions of the New World, where it nearly wiped out the wine making industry. Many solutions were tried, but it was the grafting of native North American root stock (which is resistant to the bug) to the Vinifera grape vines that was finally found to be effective. This technique is used world over to this day. Phylloxera is mostly controlled except in areas where through greed, ignorance or accident, root stock that is not resistant is used. Such was the case in California in the 80s and 90s where phylloxera was found to be rampant in the famous vineyards of Napa Valley and elsewhere, primarily due to the wrong choice of root stock.

Pourriture Noble *(poor-rit-ch'yer no-bluh)* French for "Noble Rot" a term for Botrytis Cinerea, the special mold that is responsible for many of the world's greatest dessert wines. Botrytis creates micro lesions in the skin of the grape, and then removes the water from inside the grape. The result is fruit with a much higher ratio of sugar, suitable for creating sweet wines. The mold can also be harmful when it attacks dry wine vineyards (it is usually called Gray Rot when it is a pest).

Pruning One of the most important steps in vineyard management. Conducted during the dormant period in the vineyard. The goal is to shape the vine for the coming growing season, with a specific goal in mind. The goal may be to increase or decrease the amount of grapes to be produced, or to

make the grapes easier to harvest by machine, or a host of other considerations.

Pulp The center of the grape which contains the juice. It is surrounded by
the skin of the grape, where tannin, and in the case of red wines, the coloring agents are found. The pulp in turn surrounds the seed, or pip, which is
also a source of tannin.

Rebe *(reh'-buh)* The German word for vine. Hence the name of the grape
Sheurebe which was created by a man named Sheu.

Riperia The most common species of native North American grape vine.
Because it is highly resistant to phylloxera, it is often used to create new
crosses of root stock.

Roses Many a traveler has photos of roses planted at the end of a row of
vines. The usual explanation is that these flowers are decorative and traditional. The truth is that roses are the canary of the wine world. Roses are
very susceptible to oidium (powdery mildew) and when they exhibit signs
of this fungus, the grapes are sprayed to stave off infestation.

Skin The outer layer of the grape, usually called hulls or husks in scientific
circles. This is where most of the color comes from in red wines, and a great
deal of the tannin. Many grapes have light colored pulp, and if were not
left in contact with the skins would have very little color; this is how rosé
wines are made. Different grape varieties have different skin characteristics.
Some are thick with a fair amount of tannin, such as Cabernet Sauvignon,
which yields dark, tannic wines. Others, such as Nebbiolo, have thin skins
and even more tannin, yielding lighter colored wines that are heavy in their
youth. Others still, such as Pinot Noir, have thin skins and low tannins, making for crisp, fruity wines that are more approachable when young.

T-Budding A vineyard management term. The root of a vine takes decades
to grow and can be very extensive. If a vine is in place, but no longer a desirable varietal, for whatever reason, just the top can be replaced, and the
roots left intact by a grafting process known as T-Budding. The old vine is
removed just above the soil line. The new graft is inserted into a T shaped

incision made into the remains of the old vine. The process is quick and successful.

Veraison *(veh-ray-zohn)* A viticultural term originally from the French. Young grapes are tiny, hard and green. As they swell and ripen they take on the color they will be when they are harvested. Veraison is the point where the grapes just start to turn color.

Vigne *(veen-yuh)* The French word for vine. Related words are "cep de vigne" which refers to the actual grape vine and cépage which means grape variety.

Vineyard A group of grape vines. The boundaries of a vineyard may be determined by ownership or by geological / geographical considerations.

Vinifera *(vin-if'-er-ah)* There are over 40 species of grape, each belonging to the genus Vitis. Vinifera is the species responsible for almost all wine. The original Vinifera is often thought to be the Muscat grape, but the use of these grapes goes back long before written history. Cabernet Sauvignon, Chardonnay, and indeed almost any grape variety you can name, are all Vitis Vinifera.

Vitis That genus of plants to which all grapes belong.

Yield When related to wine this term refers to the amount of fruit any given vine or vineyard produces. As with so many things in wine, this is a balancing act. You want to get enough fruit to remain profitable; however, by reducing the yield you attain more flavorful fruit. In Europe the relative yield of a vineyard or vine is often regulated by law. This ensures quality wines. Modern vineyard techniques have managed to increase yields while still maintaining quality. The laws and the world of wine remain in flux as the perfect balance of the number of vines per area and the yield per vine are sought.

A quick look at wine making

The following charts show the order of the steps for red and white wine making. Since red wine needs to be in contact with the skins to gain color, and white wine avoids the skins in order to retain fruit, the two processes diverge at the very beginning, even if they end up at the same place.

While sparkling wines, and fortified wines differ from the steps listed here, these basic procedures relate to some extent to all wines.

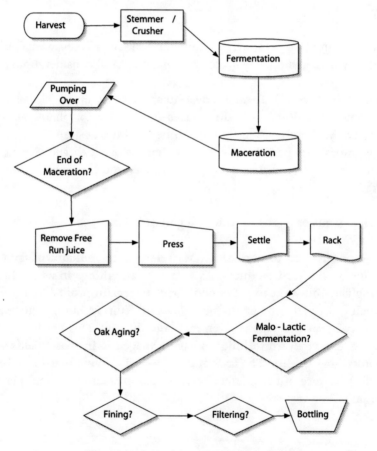

Figure 3.1 Basic Red Wine making

Understanding the order of the process, and familiarizing yourself with the words that are related to making wine, will go a long way to helping you feel more comfortable when you talk about wine tech. If you wish to learn more than I offer here, there are a great many books available for those who want to delve into the chemistry and science of wine.

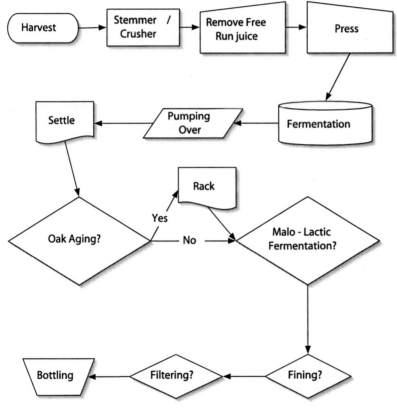

Figure 3.2 Making White Wine

The words of wine making

Blending Blending is perhaps the most important tool of the wine maker. While chemistry and science often have a hand in the final blend of a wine, more often than not it is a tasting that determines the final ratios. Like a chef seasoning a sauce, the winemaker adds a little of this, and a little of that, until the wine resembles that winemaker's idea of perfection. There are several types of blending: Some wines, like Châteauneuf de Pape, Côte Rôtie, Chianti, and Champagne, can be made from a blend of red and white grapes. Similarly Rosé Champagne is often given that nice pink color, with the additition of red wine (Pinot Noir). [Note: Rosé, or "Blush" wines are made pink by pressing red grapes very carefully and ending up with a pink wine.] Other wines, such as those from Bordeaux are blends of the same color grapes. In the case of Bordeaux, the grape variety Cabernet Sauvignon and Merlot (primarily) are blended, in order to add the character of each grape to the final wine. Even wines of a single variety are (or should be) blended. In this last case, wines that have been vinified seperately (refered to as 'lots') are blended together. This blending may come from the simple necessity of having more grapes to vinify than can fit into a single tank or barrel, or the blending may be carried out in order to create a specific style of wine. At the highest quality level, individual vineyards are vinified seperately, each adding their own character to the final blend, with the remaining wine declassified and sold as a lesser wine.

Blush Wine A term that is sometimes used to indicate a wine made in a white wine style from red wine grapes. "Blush" is actually a registered trademark. These light pink wines are also called "Rosé" or in some cases "White (Name of red wine grape here)."

Bodega *(boh-day'-gah)* The Spanish term for a winery or above the ground wine storage.

Brix *(briks)* A scale used to measure the ripeness of a grape. The predicted alcohol level of the wine can be expressed as brix x .55 = alc%. A grape picked at 22 brix will yield a wine with approximately 12% alcohol and no residual sugar. A dessert wine grape may be picked at 30 degrees brix and the resulting wine would have about 12% alcohol and 8% residual sugar.

Calcium Alginate Beads (also called encapsulated yeast) For the technically minded out there, and lovers of Champagne. This is a technique of encapsulating the yeast used for making sparkling wines sparkle. Normally the yeast must be removed by a process that can take months or years to complete. Encapsulated yeast just rolls out of the bottle instantly. Developed by Moët & Chandon, this may be the wave of the future.

Cap The solid parts of the grape - skins, seeds, and stems, which rise to the top of the must (partially fermented juice and solids) during red wine making. The cap needs to be broken up regularly so that these elements may impart characteristics to the wines.

Carbonic Maceration (also known as whole berry fermentation, or CM) The fermentation method used in Beaujolais and other regions to produce a very light and fruity red wine. By fermenting in an enclosed tank that is filled with carbon dioxide the process takes place inside the berry. As the weight of the grapes on top crushes the grapes on the bottom, the juice is removed and fermentation of the juice proceeds normally.

Chaptalization *(shap-it-al-iz'-ae-shun)* The practice of adding sugar to the juice prior to fermentation to increase the potential alcohol and quality of the wine. Chaptalization is illegal in many regions, and tightly controlled in others. In some cooler wine regions it would not be possible to make wine in some years without chapitalizing.

Concentrate Just like orange juice, grape juice is sometimes sold as a concentrate. Not only to make juice, but to make wines. In California and Italy, where adding sugar is forbidden, the addition of grape juice concentrate is often allowed as a way of bolstering a weak vintage.

Cooked A fault found in wine that has been exposed to heat, especially in the presence of air. Grapes that are vinefied too warm may exhibit this characteristic, as well as wines that have been shipped badly.

Cooperage Any and everything to do with wooden casks and barrels. A barrel maker is a cooper, hence the term.

Cooperative A central processing facility where vineyard owners can take their grapes to be made into wine and/or bottled. Usually owned by the members, it is a way to reduce the cost of wine making for the smaller producer. Many fine wines are made in cooperatives, as it is the only way that the vineyard owners could afford the most up-to-date equipment.

Cork The stopper for most wine bottles. Whether made from the bark of the cork tree or from plastic, cork must be flexible, durable, and able to create an air tight seal in the neck of the bottle. Corks can be a natural product of the cork oak, or increasingly, a conglomerate of cork and/or synthetic materials. This is due to the diminishing number of cork oaks, and the ever increasing need for more cork.

Crianza *(cree-ahn-zah)* The Spanish term for oak aging. The terms "con crianza" or "vino de crianza" on the label require that the wine has been aged for at least one year in oak. Similarly "sin crianza" means that the wine was never aged in oak before bottling.

Crush The English language term (especially in California) for the harvest.

Cuvaison *(coo-veh-zohn)* The French term for maceration. The practice of leaving the skins in contact with the juice during fermentation to extract color, tannin, and aroma. The period of time the wine is left macerating is referred to as the "Cuvage." There is also a winery by this name in Napa Valley in California.

Cuvée *(coo-vay)* From the French term "cuve" meaning a vat or tank. It now usually refers to a specific lot or batch of wine. The term is sometimes used on a wine label to signify that the wine comes from a special batch of wine. It also refers to a blend of wines.

Demi-Sec *(deh-mee seck)* Literally this French term means "half-dry." In practice it refers to the sweetest style of Champagne a house will make.

Disgorging The process of removing the sediment from sparkling wine as the final step of the "methode champenoise." All of the sediment that has been building up in the bottle over the years has ended up in the neck of the bottle. The bottle is plunged into a freezing brine solution and ice forms in the bottle. The top is removed and the "plug" of ice is forced out by the pressure in the bottle. A small amount of wine is lost, and is replaced by other wine that has been mixed with sugar. This "dose" of sugar (or in French "dosage") determines how sweet the final sparkling wine will be. The French term is "dégorgement."

Dosage *(doh-saj)* The addition of sugar and wine to sparkling wine after disgorging. The amount of sugar added determines the style of the sparkling wine.

Dry Extract A technical wine tasting term. If you place wine in a centrifuge and remove all of the water, the powder that is left will be the dry extract. The amount of flavor that a wine has can be directly attributed to the dry extract. The body of the wine is also a function of dry extract.

Edelfäule *(eh-dell-foy-luh)* Literally noble rot in German. This term refers to the mold Botrytis Cinerea. The French also call it noble rot (pourriture noble). This mold is responsible for reducing the water ratio in grapes, making them very sweet and useful as dessert wines.

Enology - also Oenology The science of wine production.

Esters A scientific term. It relates to components in wine formed by the combination of acids and alcohol. They contribute the fruity, perfume-like smell to wine. In wine the most important esther is ethyl acetate.

Extract - Dry Extract A scientific term often used in wine tasting. It literally refers to what would be left in a centerfuge once you have removed the liquid. In wine, the term is used to indicate that a wine has a lot of flavor, especially when the wine would indeed be shown in a laboratory to have a greater amount of dry extract. The terms "heavy", "intense", and "big" are related to the amount of extract in the wine.

Fermentation The process that turns grapes into wine. Specifically the metabolization of the sugars by the yeast, into alcohol, carbon dioxide and heat.

Filtering A wine making technique used to ensure clarity and sterility in wine. Careful use of precise filtering pads and agents allow the winemaker to target specific foreign substances to remove, based on their size. Some winemakers feel that filtering reduces the quality of wine. Emile Peynaud, the preeminent University of Bordeaux enologist (enology being the science of wine) had this to say about the filtering debate: "Resistance to the practice of filtering arose from the reproach made that it tended to thin down and emaciate the wines. Nevertheless, if every precaution is taken... it may be stated that the mechanical action of filtering has never had a negative influence on quality. To suggest the contrary would mean conceding that the foreign substances... which filtration is precisely designed to remove, have a favorable taste function." From "Knowing and Making Wine."

Fining The method for clarifying wine. Depending on the cause of the cloudiness, different agents can be used. Most, like gelatin, and egg whites, are proteins, while another is Bentonite, a form of clay. The general concept is to add a substance to the wine that the cloudy particles will stick to, and fall to the bottom. The winemaker then draws the clear wine off the top.

Flor *(flore)* A special type of yeast found on the surface of wine. In the Sherry district of Spain, the flor yeast help to make the finest Sherries. On other wines it is a pest and must be controlled. It is also the Spanish word for flower.

Fortified Wine A class of wines that have been made sweet by interrupting the fermentation process with the addition of a neutral distilled spirit. The spirit kills the yeast before they have finished converting all of the sugar. Port and Sherry are both fortified wines.

Free Run In wine making, it is the juice that appears after crushing, but before pressing. It is the highest quality juice for wine making.

Glycerol One of the alcohols found in wine as a result of fermentation. Sometimes referred to as glycerin, this can be misleading. Glycerin is marketed as a sweet, and syrupy liquid, used for soap making and adding viscosity to some liquors. The amount of glycerol found in wine is too small to make the wine thick (in fact, dry wines are slightly less viscous than water). It can contribute to the sweetening effect of the alcohol, since glycerol is much sweeter than most sugars, but again, it is only found in very small amounts (less than 1/10 of the alcohol found in wine). It has nothing to do with the formation or quantity of tears or legs found on a glass of swirled wine.

Hectoliter The metric unit for measuring volume. It is 100 liters. One hectoliter = 26.42 gallons (US) = 133 bottles of wine (11 cases).

Lees The sediment from young wines while still in the barrel, tank or vat. Racking is the process of removing the wine and leaving the lees behind. Some white wines, such as Chardonnay, are often aged in contact with the lees in order to give the wine more flavor (see "sur lie").

Liqueur A sweet, flavored, alcohol based drink. Used in the world of wine to mean something completely different. In the champagne method of making sparking wines "liqueur de tirage" is the mix of sugar solution and yeast added to the wine, to create the secondary fermentation, which will in turn produce bubbles. Again in sparkling wine production, the term is also used as "liqueur d'expédition" which is the sweeting agent added to the finished sparkling wine, which will determine the final style (from Extra-Dry, which is sweet to Brut, which is dry). Liqueur is also used in Sauternes, the dessert wine making region of Bordeaux, France, to refer to the sweetness of the wine. Finally, also from France, there is the occasionally used term "vin de liqueur," which refers to a wine made sweet by adding spirits to stop the fermentation process. This type of wine is more often called "Vin Doux Naturel."

Malolactic Fermentation A secondary fermentation that changes the tart malic acid (found in green apples) into the softer lactic acid, found in milk. Common in red wine, but used almost exclusively in Chardonnay for white. One of the byproducts of this process is a chemical called "diacetyl" which is responsible for the buttery taste of some wines. Often abbreviated ML.

Marc *(mar)* The French word for pomace (the solids left after making wine). Also a brandy distilled from pomace (eau-de-vie de marc). In Italy the brandy is known as Grappa.

Méthode Champenoise *(meh-toh'd shahm-peh-n'wahz)* First a dry, still wine is made. It is then bottled. A small amount of sugar and yeast is added to the bottle, which is then sealed. The yeast turns the sugar into carbon dioxide, heat and alcohol. The carbon dioxide dissolves in the wine, making the wine bubbly. Once the process has finished, the bottle of wine still contains the sediment from the yeast. Through a process known as riddling, the bottles are slowly turned upside down (over a period of weeks or months) until the sediment is in the neck of the bottle. The neck is then plunged into a very cold salt water solution, which freezes a bit of the wine around the sediment. The bottle is opened and the chunk of ice, complete with all of the sediment, is removed. The bottle then needs to be refilled to replace the lost wine. At this point, some Champagne is added, along with a solution of sugar, which will determine the final sweetness and style of the wine.

Must The crushed grapes and juice that will be fermented into wine.

Oak Used to make containers for storing and aging wine, specific types of oak are used for small barrels to impart flavor and tannins to the wine. The newer the barrel, the more flavor it imparts. Oak is critical for making long-lived red wines, and some whites. It can sometimes be over used to hide flavors or to make up for lackluster crops. Oak in wine should always be subtle, and in balance. Beware of any wine where the oak is the defining character. In larger containers, and older barrels, the oak does not impart much if any flavor, and so less expensive oak is used. There is a certain amount of air exchanged through the pores of a small oak barrel that can help to develop the aromas of the young wine (secondary aromas). Again, this process is diminished in larger oak barrels because of the volume of wine they hold. On the average, oak barrels hold around 60 gallons (225 liters).

Passito *(pah-see'-toe)* An Italian wine making technique. The grapes are dried on mats until they turn to raisins. The result is a much higher sugar ratio in the grapes. Mostly used for dessert wines, but also used to make the dry red wine Reccioto della Valpolicella Amarone.

Pasteurization The process of sterilizing liquids by heating. Rarely used for fine wines, but occasionally used for simpler wines, especially if they contain residual sugar.

pH Wine makers, and wine writers often talk about the total acidity (TA) in a wine. It is only half the story. pH is the measure of how strong the acid is in wine. The lower the number, the stronger the acid. A wine with a low TA may still taste tart if the pH is low enough. To be confusing pH is essentially backwards when talking about acidity. The higher the number, the more alkaline (the opposite of acidity) a solution is. The technical answer is that pH is a measurement of the number of hydrogen ions a solution contains. In dry table wine the range, very generally, is around 3.1 - 3.6.

Plastering A confusing term. It means either the addition of substances such as calcium sulfate before fermentation in order to increase acidity, or calcium carbonate to reduce acidity. Since both of these are a white powder that is added to a liquid, as is plaster, it may explain the term, but not why it can mean two potentially opposite results.

Pomace All of the seeds, skins, pulp and stems left over after fermenting and pressing the red wine. The French call this "Marc" and distill it into a brandy by the same name. The Italians call this brandy "Grappa."

Press A piece of wine making equipment used to press the juice out of the grapes. In the case of red wine this is done after fermentation.

Press Wine When making wine, the juice that is extracted without pressing is of the highest quality, and is called "free run." In order to extract the rest of the juice, the grapes must be pressed. This is often done multiple times. Each succeeding press yields juice of a lower quality. The term "Press Wine" is mostly used to connote this lower quality juice. In order to make an inexpensive wine from expensive grapes, such as Cabernet Sauvignon, or Chardonnay, the grapes must be pressed many times in order to increase the quantity produced. In some cases, only this press wine is used, the free run juice being used for higher quality wine. Since this press wine is often bitter, it becomes necessary to leave a small amount of sugar in the wine to hide the bitterness.

Primeur *(pree-muh'r)* A French term for wines that are consumed shortly after harvest. The best known example is Beaujolais Nouveau.

Proof A method of expressing the alcohol content of spirits. Wine has the actual percentage listed. In the US proof is double the percentage of alcohol. So a 100 proof spirit, contains 50% alcohol. In Great Britian it would be 57.06% by volume. This is an important distiction, because Scotch Whiskey imported into the US will say 80 proof when it has 40% alcohol, but the same whiskey in Great Britain will only say 70 proof.

Punt The indentation in the bottom of a Champagne bottle. Originally designed to strengthen the bottle, so that it could withstand the internal pressure of the sparkling wine, it is now found on many wine bottles. It not only increases the strength, but it makes it easier for the bottle makers to stack the bottles on end.

Puttonyos *(poo'-tun-yosh)* In the production of Tokaji Aszu wine of Hungary, baskets of very ripe grapes, effected with botrytis, are added to the base wine to sweeten it. The baskets are themselves known as puttonyos, and the label of the wine will indicate how many puttonyos have been added. Three is common for the drier styles, with five being used in the sweetest. Six puttonyos wines exist, but are nearly legendary. There also exists an even more legendary wine, Essencia which is made entirely from the puttonyos grapes.

Racking An important step in wine making. The transfer of the young wine from one barrel, where it has thrown some sediment, to a new barrel, leaving behind the sediment. Not only does this help to clarify the wine, it is an opportunity for the wine to come into contact with air. A certain amount of oxygen is required at this stage of a wine's development, in order to produce necessary aromas (secondary aromas). Racking must be conducted carefully, as too much oxygen will be more harmful than beneficial for the wine. Heavy red wines may be racked three or four times. Lighter reds and whites may only be racked once or twice.

Ratafia *(rah-tah-fee'-ah)* Any of several aperitifs made by adding brandy to unfermented grape juice. The best known example may be the Pineau de Charentes of the Cognac region, although Ratafias are found in the Champagne and Burgundy regions of France as well.The name is said to come from the tradition of toasting the ratification of a new treaty with such a concoction.

Rémuage *(rem-you-ah'j)* The French term for "riddling." The practice of turning and inverting bottles of sparkling wine, made in the champagne method, over a period of a week or more, until the sediment has all collected in the neck of the bottle, for easy removal.

Riddling One of the steps to making sparkling wine in the champagne method. The practice of turning and inverting bottles over a period of a week or more, until the sediment has all collected in the neck of the bottle, this allows the sediment to be easily removed. Known in French as "rémuage." Once done exclusively by hand, it is now largely done by machine.

Rosé *(ro-zay)* The French word for "pink" and the wines that are close to that color. Rosé wines suffer from an image problem. It may be that white wine and red wine drinkers feel that rosé does not fit either niche, rather than being a bridge between them. It may also be that the sweet and simple rosé wines from the 60s and 70s made people think that all rosé wines are uninspiring. Certainly the "white zinfandel" and blush wines made in the US haven't helped the reputation any (even if they are rarely called rosé wines). In fact there are dry rosés such as the famed Tavel and Lirac of the Rhône Valley in France that deserve more recognition. Served well chilled, these wines are great for hot summer days or picnics where a heavier red or white wine would simply be too much. Many regions of the world produce rosé wines, and many of them are best enjoyed locally. Certainly there are many rosé wines that are easy to dismiss, but it is a shame to dismiss the entire class out of hand. Technically these wines are also known as blanc de noirs (white from black) or Vin Gris (grey wines).

Saccharomyces *(sac'eh-ro-mi'sez)* The genus of yeast responsible for the primary (sugar) fermentation in wine. They turn the grape sugars into alcohol, carbon dioxide, and heat.

Sekt *(zekt)* The German term for sparkling wine. About 25 million cases of Sekt are produced in Germany each year.

Solera *(soh-leh'-rah)* A system of blending wines used primarily for Sherry and Madeira. Basically it is a way to add older wines to the new wine, in order to maintain a consistent style. As a small portion of the old wine is removed from the cask, it is replaced with an equal portion of new wine. The old wine is then added to the new wine. In this way the high quality of the older wine is thought to improve the quality of the younger wine, while the younger wine replenishes the cask of older wine. Some Sherry, and especially Madeira will be labeled with the word "Solera" and a date. This is a marketing ploy. It simply means the year that the Solera was started, and the bottle may at best, contain trace amounts from that year.

Sparkling Wine   That class of wines which has been carbonated. The highest quality versions are carbonated through the action of yeast in a sealed bottle. This is the champagne method, and all Champagne is made this way. Another method is to start in the bottle, but then transfer all the wine to a tank and filter out the sediment. This is known as the transfer method. Less expensive sparkling wines are made in a tank, with the yeast again adding the carbon dioxide. These wines are then bottled. The final method is to add carbon dioxide to the finished wine, much as you would for a soda pop, no quality sparkling wine is made in this method. Champagne is a method and a region in France. Sparkling wines should only be called Champagne when they come from that region in France. This is the law in Europe, but the US and Australia still allow domestic sparkling wines to be labeled with the Champagne name.

Spumante / Spumanti   *(spoo-mahn'-teh / spoo-mahn'-tee)*   Italian for sparkling. Most Italian sparkling wines are made with the transfer method, although a growing number of quality wines are being made in the champagne method (called "metodo classico" in Italian). Asti Spumante is one of the best known Italian sparklers, with Prosecco being another. Spumanti is the plural version of the word.

Stabilizing   Any number of wine making procedures that make the wine more stable. The most common example is "cold stabilization" which is used to ensure that tartaric precipitants do not appear in white wine if it has been chilled and then warmed again. Filtering and fining are common examples of stabilization that are used to improve and maintain the clarity of wine. Pasteurization is sometimes (but not often) used to reduce the chance of bacterial spoilage, and/or to reduce the effect of shipping.

Stemmer A piece of wine making equipment used to remove the stems from the grape bunches before the grapes are pressed and fermented. The stems can leave a bitter flavor, and are rarely used in white wine. Some red wines benefit from the tannins that the stems impart, and so are added back in. Stemmer machines are often combined with a crusher and are known as "Stemmer Crushers."

Still Any wine that is not sparkling.

Stuck A wine making term. "Stuck fermentation" and "stuck wine" are the same thing. A wine sticks during fermentation when the yeast can no longer metabolize the sugar, or there are not enough viable yeast left to do the job. Heat and/or the lack of oxygen are the two most common reasons for a stuck fermentation. This is a very bad situation as it can be difficult, or even impossible, to get the fermentation restarted.

Sugaring The practice of adding sugar (grape sugar ideally) to the unfermented grapes (must). This is done when the grapes are not ripe enough on their own to produce enough alcohol. Common for lesser quality wines in cool growing regions such as Germany, it is illegal in many other parts of the world. Another term is Chaptalization.

Sulfites / Sulfur A much maligned element of wine making. While it can be overused and ruin the flavor of the wine if not used carefully, it is an integral part of most wine making. Sulfur Dioxide, the gas form of sulfur, is sprayed on the vines to control fungus. Barrels are treated with sulfites (sulfur combined with another element, usually metallic) to kill unwanted bacteria. Sulfites are also added to the juice prior to fermentation to prevent browning and to control the yeast that come in from the fields with the grapes. It is also used to stop fermentation on some sweet wines, so that residual sugar can be left in the wine. Sulfur adds control to the wine making process, and those few wines that are made without it tend to be very poor. The amount of sulfur that can be in wine is controlled by law. Because the smell and taste of sulfur in wine can be ruinous, the sulfur is almost always very carefully applied and is used in amounts well below the legal limits and in amounts too small to cause health considerations for most people.

Sur Lie *(soo'r lee)* The French term for "on the lees." Wines that have been aged in contact with these dead yeast cells gain some measure of complexity.

Tank A large container for making or storing wine. Wood was a traditional material for centuries, but that was replaced by cement tanks which in turn have largely been replaced by stainless steel, with modern temperature controls. Some wine, such as Pinot Noir, can still benefit from the proper use of classic wooden, open topped tanks. Also called a vat.

Tartar Tartaric acid is the main acid in wine. Some of it can crystalize in a chilled wine. Since the crystals are unsightly, and can cause concern for the consumer, some white wines in particular are cold stabilized to remove the crystals before the wine is released. The crystals are flavorless and harmless.

Tête de Cuvée *(tet duh coo-vay)* Literally, French for "head blend." The term is unofficial, but is often used to mean the top of the line from any Champagne house. For example Dom Pérignon is the tête du cuvée from Moët.

Thief A glass or metal tube used to extract wine from a barrel. The French call it a "pipette."

Topping The winery practice of replacing evaporated wine in the barrel. This "head space" is also called "ullage." This is an important step to reduce the oxidation of the wine, and to ensure quality.

Transfer Method One of the more economical (and common) ways to make a sparkling wine. The wine is placed in a closed bottle, to allow yeast to make the bubbles, as in the champagne method, but then the bottles are opened, and all "transferred" into a tank to be blended. This blend is then filtered (as opposed to riddling in the champagne method) and rebottled. A key phrase on the bottle may be "Fermented in the bottle" as opposed to "Fermented in this bottle" which can only be said of wine made in the higher quality champagne method. Champagne from the Champagne region can not be made via the transfer method.

Treading This is the classic image of a group of people stomping on grapes. The technique (almost extinct now) was used to crush the grapes, to improve the color of the wine and to speed the start of fermentation, rather than to press the juice out of the grapes, as many people may think. It was particularly important for making Port, which is deeply colored, and benefited greatly from the technique. Some Port producers still hold to the tradition, but most opt for modern wine making techniques which yield similar results, with greater control.

Ullage *(oo-lehj)* The amount of air that results in a barrel or bottle due to evaporation. In the barrel the missing wine is replaced to keep the wine from becoming oxidized (topping). In theory the same could be done with old bottles of wine (this is called recorking). It is rare to see recorked bottles of wine, and if it is done, there needs to be a complete explanation of the process and a certificate from the company that performed the task. The amount of ullage in a bottle greatly influences the value of the wine at auction.

Vat Another name for a tank. A container for fermenting, storing and blending wine. Wood was a traditional material for centuries, but that was replaced by cement vats which in turn have largely been replaced by stainless steel, with modern temperature controls. Some wine, such as Pinot Noir, can still benefit from the proper use of classic wooden, open topped vats.

Vendage *(vahn-danj)* The French term for harvest or vintage. As with the Italian term "vendemmia" and the Spanish "vendima" vendage refers to the actual harvest, rather than the year (which is how vintage is commonly used in English). The French term for the year that appears on the label is "millésime."

Vendima *(ven-dee'-mee-ah)* The Spanish term for harvest or vintage. It refers to the actual harvest, rather than the year (which is how vintage is commonly used in English).

Vin Bourro *(van boo-rew)* The French term for a wine that has just been pressed. It is not uncommon for vineyard workers and others to consume this incredibly young wine. It is often still sweet, and full of carbon dioxide, since the wine is not altogether finished fermenting.

Vin de Paille *(van duh pah'y)* A wine made in the Jura region of France by first drying the grapes on straw mats. This is the French term, but the Italian Vin Santo is one of the best known examples of wines made in this style. This process increases the ratio of sugar to water in the grape. The result is a wine that either has more alcohol, or that is somewhat sweet, or both.

Vinification The process of yeast turning grape juice into wine.

Yeast The single cell organisms that are responsible for fermentation. This is as true in wine as it is in beer or even bread. In the case of wine, the primary yeast responsible for the first (alcohol) fermentation belong to the class "Sacharomyces." Not all yeast is good yeast, and some can lead to spoilage. Many types of yeast may be found in and around wineries, and due to the need to control the specific yeast in wine, sterility is extremely important in a winery.

Zymase The enzymes excreted by yeast that actually do the work of fermentation. While this is so technical that most books do not even bother to mention zymase, it has yet another claim to fame. It is the root of the word Zymurgy which ends nearly all English language dictionaries.

Zymurgy *(zi'-mer-gee)* The science and study of fermentation.

Of bottles and barrels

In the US when we think of wine, we think of a glass bottle, filled with wine, and stoppered with cork. Some wines come with screw tops, but these have unfairly suffered from the perception that cork is better. Modern screw caps can be every bit as good as cork.

In other parts of the world, the bottle itself may be optional. It is not uncommon for wine to come in any number of large containers (usually boxes or glass jugs in the US) or for people to bring their own containers to fill. This is because most of the wine in the world is simple, meant to be enjoyed young, and simply does not need a bottle.

The glass bottle is convenient to store, and to transport. It is cost effective for most wines, and it is ubiquitous, but it has not always been so. While glass has been used to store wine since the times of the Romans, it was the tight seal of the perfect cork that made the difference. Prior to the adoption of the cork around the late 18th century, glass bottles were often sealed with burlap and wax. The industrial revolution changed glass from a luxury into an every day item and bottles became a cheap easy way to not only store wine, but to age it as well.

When we look at a barrel today, we tend to think of wine, or perhaps whisky. We know that the right sized barrel made from the right kind of oak can improve wine and help it age. What many of us do not realize is that the barrel was until very recently much more than a way to age wine or soften spirits. The barrel was the universal shipping container the world used for thousands of years. Everything from nails to cloth were shipped in barrels. They are easy to move, easy to stack, and cheap to build. That they ended up synonymous with wine is an accident of history.

Wooden ships ruled the seas, and require vast forests to create and maintain. Several such forests in France were built just for such a purpose. These mighty oak forest built mighty ships, until the end of the Great Ships era. Suddenly these mighty oaks had no purpose, and instead of being the most expensive wood you could buy, they became redundant, and cheap. Barrels, still being the universal shipping container at this time, were an ideal use for this dense and strong wood. So it came to pass that wine was shipped in such a barrel, and it was learned that these barrels improved the wine in a way no barrel had before. And so, oak aging was born.

Bottles and barrels, and vats come in all sizes. Until quite recently it was a mater of regional tradition that determined the sizes of what collectively is called "cooperage." In this day and age much has been standardized, and the regional containers of years past are all but extinct. Most wine can now be found in standard sized bottles, which by tradition have been named after the kings and sons of the Bible.

Balthazar An oversized bottle that holds 12 liters, or 16 regular bottles of wine.

Barrel Once the most common way of shipping everything from nails to flour, these wooden containers have a long history. From the point of view of wine, this is the standard aging container in a winery. Usually a barrel holds about 60 gallons (225 liters). When made from oak, and before they have been used for too many years (less than 3 or 4 vintages) barrels impart flavor and tannin to the wine, helping it to age better. Older barrels, those that are much more than 60 gallons, or those made from a wood other than oak, do not impart anything to the wine, and are mostly used for storage.

Bottle Holding .75 liters, this is the standard glass container for wine. The glass bottle itself has been used since antiquity, but it was not until the cork closure and experiments on sizes and shapes in the late 19th century, that the bottle we know today started to come into existence. The single bottle is a good average size for two or three people, so it has remained the standard size, even though the Magnum at twice the size is even better suited to aging wine.

Demijohn Any very large bottle, usually around 10 gallons. Often used by amateur wine makers as a vat or storage container. May be covered in straw or rest in a wooden frame. From the French "Dame Jeanne" which has the same meaning.

Double Magnum A large wine bottle, which holds the same as four normal bottles (3 liters). This is one of the more common large format sizes, and is also referred to by its capacity as a Three Liter bottle.

Feuillette *(fuh-yet)* A small oak barrel. At 36 gallons (136L) it is slightly more than half the size of a regular barrel, which averages about 60 gallons (225L).

Fiasco *(fee-ask'-coh)* The straw covered bottle of Chianti fame. Like most regional bottles, this one has become rarer as bottles have become increasingly standardized.

Half Bottle A small bottle that holds .375L.

Imperial A large bottle (6 liters), equivalent to eight regular sized bottles.

Jeroboam A large bottle (4.5 liters), equivalent to to six regular sized bottles (four in Champagne - 3 liters).

Limousin *(lee-moo-zan)* A forest in central France that is a major source of oak for wooden barrels. The barrels made from this oak impart a stronger taste than oak from other French sources, and so Limousin oak has somewhat fallen out of favor around the world.

Magnum A large wine bottle, which holds the same as two normal bottles (1.5 liters). The larger the bottle, the slower the wine ages. A magnum is the perfect size for aging great red wines, as it ages the wine slowly, but not too slowly.

Methuselah / Methuselem An oversized bottle (6 liters) used for Champagne. It holds eight normal bottles.

Nebuchadnezzar The largest of the Champagne bottles. It holds 20 ordinary bottles (15 liters). They are very impressive, until you try to pour from one.

Pipe A large oak barrel that is tapered at the ends. At 522.5 liters or 138 gallons it is about twice the size of the average barrel. Used primarily for Port.

Rehoboam *(ree-o-boa-em)* An oversized bottle (4 1/2 liters) that holds six regular bottles of wine.

Salmanazar *(sahl-man'-a-zar)* An oversized wine bottle (9 liters) that holds 12 regular bottles.

Split The name for a quarter bottle of wine (.187 liters), especially Champagne.

Tonneau *(tuh-noh)* A measure of wine in Bordeaux, France equivalent to 100 cases (1200 bottles). The term is not used much any more, as most wine makers simply talk about cases or bottles.

What does that word mean?

A

Acidity The tart taste in wines. When there is too much acidity the wine can taste sour.

Adelaide Hills One of the oldest wine producing regions in Australia. Situated in the south-central part of the country, around the city of Adelaide.

Aftertaste The taste that stays in your mouth after swallowing the wine. It should be pleasant and in fine wines it should last a long time after the wine is gone.

Ahr *(ahr)* A tiny wine region in Germany. It is unusual for Germany in that most of the wine made is red. The main grape is Pinot Noir which is known locally as Spätburgunder.

Aloxe-Corton *(ah-loks cor-tawn)* A wine producing village in Burgundy, France that is famous for both great reds and whites. The Grand Cru reds are Corton (with or without additional names, e.g. Le Clos du Roi or Les Renardes) and the famous white wine is Corton-Charlemagne.

Alsace *(al-zass)* A French province that makes some of the finest dry white wines in the world. The wines are made from grapes that in other parts of the world would be used to make sweet wines, such as Riesling and Gewürztraminer.

American Viticultural Area Often abbreviated AVA. This is the set of US laws which regulate the use of place names on wine labels. Unlike similar laws in Europe, there are no restrictions on grape variety, yield, or wine making practices. AVAs seem to be created more as a response to politics, then as a form of consumer protection. There are over 140 AVAs at this time.

Appellation d'Origine Contrôlée *(ah-pel-ah-s'yawn daw-ree-jeen cawn-trohl-lay)* Often abbreviated AOC. The designation for wines of better quality from France. It is a set of laws which help the consumer to determine the origin and quality of a wine. These laws dictate the grape variety, the minimum alcohol and other quality factors, for any given wine from a specific region. Higher quality wines may come from a place as specific as a single vineyard, while other wines of the region may use a more generic place name. The rules for wines from a single vineyard tend to be more stringent than those for a general area.

Aroma The smell of a young wine. Different from bouquet, in that Aroma is the smell that comes from the grapes, and bouquet, which takes time to develop, is the smell that comes from the finished wine. Technically there are 3 forms of aroma. Primary aroma, which originates in the grape itself. Secondary aroma, those which are aerobic (happens in air) and are due to the wine making process (this includes barrel aging). Finally, tertiary aromas are those which develop in a reductive environment (without air) in the sealed bottle, over time, these are what is usually called "bouquet."

Astringent That mouth puckering feeling that some wines give you. Related to, and usually caused by tannins. The sensation is accentuated by the acid in wine.

Auckland The wine region in New Zealand's north island, centered around the city of the same name.

Auslese *(ouse'-lay-zuh)* A German term for select harvest. Wines with this designation are slightly sweet and lucious. Don't be afraid of these wines, they are often great with food, and rarely expensive.

Ausone, Ch. *(oh-zon)* One of the greatest French wines, it is made in the village of St.-Emilion in the region of Bordeaux. This wine is too often overlooked by some consumers for its better known peers from the Haut-Médoc, such as Latour, Margaux and the other First Growths. As with most wines of St.-Emilion, Ch. Ausone is made from Merlot and Cabernet Franc, and the resulting wine is more elegant than the Cabernet Sauvignon based wines from the Haut-Médoc, across the river.

B

Baden *(bah-d'n)* One of the larger German wine regions. It is bordered by France on the West, and Switzerland in the South. The grapes tend to be planted along the foothills of the Black Forest. This is where you can find most of the German plantings of the red wine grape Pinot Noir which is known locally as Spätburgunder. Müller-Thurgau and Ruländer (Pinot Gris) are the main white wine grapes.

Balance A much used, but rarely defined term in wine tasting. A wine is said to be balanced when no single component is overwhelming the wine, and the overall impression is pleasing.

Balthazar An oversized bottle that holds 12 liters, or 16 regular bottles of wine.

Barolo *(bah-roh'-loh)* One of the top Italian wines. Made from the Nebbiolo grape in the Piedmont. It is often long lived and heavy when young.

Barossa Valley One of the South Australia wine regions. North of the city of Adelaide, Barossa was one of the first areas to become popular outside of Australia. Because the region was planted earlier than most, the vines tend to have a greater average age, and this helps to maintain high quality.

Barrel Once the most common way of shipping everything from nails to flour, these wooden containers have a long history. From the point of view of wine, this is the standard aging container in a winery. Usually a barrel holds about 60 gallons (225 liters). When made from oak, and before they have been used for too many years (less than 3 or 4 vintages) barrels impart flavor and tannin to the wine, helping it to age better. Older barrels, those that are much more than 60 gallons, or those made from a wood other than oak, do not impart anything to the wine, and are mostly used for storage.

Barsac *(bar-sack)* One of the major towns of the Sauternes region, in Bordeaux, France. The quality of the sweet wines from this area, along with the pride of the producers, ensures that you will often see the name of this town on the label, while other towns in the region will only say Sauternes.

Basilicata *(bah-zee-lee-cah'-tah)* A wine region in Southern Italy. Most of the wines are simple, and are best enjoyed locally.

Bay of Plenty A wine producing region on New Zealand's north island.

Beaujolais *(bo-jo-lay)* A wine producing district just south of Burgundy, France. The red wines from the region are made from Gamay, and are typically light and fruity. Beaujolais Nouveau *(noo-voh)* is an early released style of this wine, that is sold with more fan fair and hoopla than the wine deserves, it is released the third Thursday of November.

Beaumes-de-Venise *(bohm duh veh-neez)* A town in the Southern Rhône region of France. Best known for its fortified Muscat based wine. In many ways this is the bench mark for the many lightly fortified Muscat wines found through out the New World.

Beaune *(bone)* This quaint little walled city is the unofficial capital of the Burgundy wine trade. The surrounding wine area, in fact the entire southern part of the Côte d'Or (Northern Burgundy), is referred to as the Côte de Beaune.

Beerenauslese *(bear'-en-ouse'-lay-zuh)* Literally select berry picking in German. The English term is "individual berry select." Tiny scissors are used to cut just the most perfectly ripe berries (grapes) from the cluster. The grapes must have no less than 125 degrees Oeschsle (about 30%) sugar. The resulting wine usually is somewhat sweet (average of about 6% residual sugar) with great flavors and amazing complexity. This is one of the world's finest styles of wine. It is a great match for spicy foods of all sorts.

Bereich *(beh-rye'sh)* The German term for a wine producing subregion as defined by the 1971 German wine laws. A bereich contains many villages and vineyards in its scope.

Bernkastel *(bairn'-cast'l)* One of the world's greatest "cute little wine towns." This one is situated on the Mosel River in Germany, in the Mosel-Saar-Ruwer region. The most famous wines of Germany, Bernkastler Doctor, are grown on the steep hillsides overlooking the river. The Doctor vineyard has the perfect southern exposure. Important in these chilly northern vineyards.

Beychevelle, Ch. *(bay'sh-vel)* A Fourth Growth Bordeaux, France wine from the commune of Saint-Julien. The exceptional quality of this producer has propelled its fame beyond its rank. Alas, the price is as high as its reputation.

Bitter Wine tasting term for the sensation in the finish of a wine. This is different than astringency (q.v.) which is a dry feeling in the mouth. Bitterness is very hard to spot, it is rare and undesireable in wine. As well, the taster gets used to the bitterness quickly, so the impression goes away after a few sips.

Blanc de Blanc *(blahn duh blahn)* White from white in French. The term is applied to white wines made from white grapes. Mainly used in Champagne to denote wines made entirely from Chardonnay.

Blanc de Noirs *(blahn duh n'wahr)* White from black in French. The term is applied to white wines made from red (black) grapes. Mainly used in Champagne to denote wines made entirely from Pinot Noir and Pinot Meunier.

Blending Blending is perhaps the most important tool of the wine maker. While chemistry and science often have a hand in the final blend of a wine, more often than not it is a tasting that determines the final ratios. Like a chef seasoning a sauce, the winemaker adds a little of this, and a little of that, until the wine resembles that winemaker's idea of perfection. There are several types of blending: Some wines, like Châteauneuf de Pape, Côte Rôtie, Chianti, and Champagne, can be made from a blend of red and white grapes. Similarly Rosé Champagne is often given that nice pink color, with the addition of red wine (Pinot Noir). [Note: Rosé, or "blush" wines are made pink by pressing red grapes very carefully and ending up with a pink wine.] Other wines, such as those from Bordeaux are blends of the same color grapes. In the case of Bordeaux, the grape variety Cabernet Sauvignon and Merlot (primarily) are blended, in order to add the character of each grape to the final wine. Even wines of a single variety are (or should be) blended. In this last case, wines that have been vinified seperately (refered to as 'lots') are blended together. This blending may come from the simple necessity of having more grapes to vinify than can fit into a single tank or barrel, or the blending may be carried out in order to create a specific style of wine. At the highest quality level, individual vineyards are vinified seperately, each adding their own character to the final blend, with the remaining wine declassified and sold as a lesser wine.

Blush Wine A term that is sometimes used to indicate a wine made in a white wine style from red wine grapes. Blush is actually a registered trademark. These light pink wines are also called "rosé" or in some cases "white (name of red wine grape here)."

Bodega *(boh-day'-gah)* The Spanish term for a winery or above the ground wine storage.

Body The overall mouth feel or weight of a wine. Some tasters incorrectly attribute it to glycerin or glycol in wine (there is not enough in wine to make wine thick). The term may be related to the amount of dry extract in a wine (what is left when you remove the water).

Bonnes Mares *(bon mar)* A Grand Cru red wine vineyard in the Côte d'Or in Burgundy, France. Located in the commune of Chambolle-Musigny.

Bordeaux *(bore-doe)* One of the largest cities in France, and a generic term for the sea of wine that is made around the region. This is the home of the Haut-Médoc and such famous wineries as Château Lafite-Rothschild, Ch. Haut-Brion and Ch. Pétrus. Sub regions include the Médoc, Sauternes (the great dessert wine of France), St. Emilion and Pomerol. With over 215,000 acres planted to vineyards, and an average 35 million cases produced annually, Bordeaux is one of the leading wine regions in the world in quality and quantity. The principal grapes are Cabernet Sauvignon and Merlo for reds and Sauvignon Blanc and Sémillon for whites.

Bordeaux Mixture A fungicide made from copper sulfate and slaked lime. Used widely in Europe to prevent mildew. It is recognizable by its distinctive blue-green color.

Botrytis Cinerea *(bo-trie'-tiss sin-eh-ray'-ah)* The special mold that is responsible for many of the world's greatest dessert wines. It creates micro lesions in the skin of the grape, and then removes the water from inside the grape. The result is fruit with a much higher ratio of sugar, suitable for creating sweet wines. The mold can also be harmful when it attacks dry wine vineyards (it is usually called Gray Rot when it is a pest). The French call Botrytis "pourriture noble" - the noble rot.

Bottle Holding .75 liters, this is the standard glass container for wine. The glass bottle itself has been used since antiquity, but it was not until the cork closure and experiments on sizes and shapes in the late 19th century, that the bottle we know today started to come into existence. The single bottle is a good average size for two or three people, so it has remained the standard size, even though the Magnum at twice the size is even better suited to aging wine.

Bouquet Used generically to indicate how a wine smells, or more specifically to indicate aromas associated with bottle aging. A more technical term for this later definition is "tertiary aromas."

Bourgogne *(boor-gon'-yah)* The French word for Burgundy. Used on a label to indicate that the origin of the grapes can be from anywhere in Burgundy. If red, the grape is likely Pinot Noir, or if white, Chardonnay.

Bourgogne Passe-tout-grains *(boor-gon'-yah pahss too gran)* A blend of Gamay and Pinot Noir (at least 33%) from southern Burgundy. Not often seen, but worth trying.

Bourguiel (boor-guh'y) A town and wine from the Loire region of France. Light and easy to enjoy, it is made from the Cabernet Franc grape.

Brachetto *(bra-keh'-toe)* A slightly sweet and sparkling red wine from the Piedmont region of Italy. This is my vote for the best pizza wine.

Breathing Allowing the wine to come in contact with air, either forcibly or by resting. Since most of the practices surrounding wine are one way or another designed to keep air from wine, breathing is a questionable practice. My own blind tastings have not shown a correlation between a recently opened bottle, and one that has been allowed to remain open (or decanted) for an hour. The phenomena of wine improving after time may be more accurately attributed to changes in your mouth and "getting used to" the taste of tannins and acids.

Brix *(briks)* A scale used to measure the ripeness of a grape. The predicted alcohol level of the wine can be expressed as brix x .55 = alc%. A grape picked at 22 brix will yield a wine with approximately 12% alcohol and no residual sugar. A dessert wine grape may be picked at 30 degrees brix and the resulting wine would have about 12% alcohol and 8% residual sugar.

Bual [or Boal] *(boh-ahl)* A grape variety used in Madeira. Increasingly it is used to indicate a medium sweet style of Madeira, regardless of the grape.

Burgundy One of the most important wine regions in France. The main red grape is Pinot Noir and the white grape is chiefly Chardonnay.

C

Cabernet Franc *(cab-air-nay frahn)* Often blended with Merlot and/or Cabernet Sauvignon, this is the "other" Cabernet grape. It stands on its own in the Loire region of France where it makes light red wines.

Cabernet Sauvignon *(cab-air-nay so-vee-n'yohn)* One of the best known red wine grapes. It is the base for many of the New World's finest wines, as well as the wines of Bordeaux, France. A rich grape, with sufficient tannins for making wines that age.

Calabria *(cah-lah'-bree-ah)* If Italy is shaped like a boot, then Calabria is the wine region at the toe. Mountainous country, the wines from this region are not well known elsewhere.

Calcium Alginate Beads (also called encapsulated yeast) For the technically minded out there, and lovers of Champagne. This is a technique of encapsulating the yeast used for making sparkling wines sparkle. Normally the yeast must be removed by a process that can take months or years to complete. Encapsulated yeast just rolls out of the bottle instantly. Developed by Moët & Chandon, this may be the wave of the future.

California This is the best known wine producing State in the US. With a tradition going back to the early 19th century, California has some of the oldest continuing vineyards in the country. The well known Napa and Sonoma Valleys are just two of the many growing regions around the state. The same warm sunny days that attracted so many people to live in this state, help to create a grape grower's paradise. Vintage variation is often less of an issue with California wines than anywhere else in the world. The blisteringly hot Central Valley of California is a huge growing area that produces food of all types. It is also where much wine, of little note, is made. All of the sun and heat can easily overwhelm the vines, so most of the quality growing regions are cooled either by proximity to the ocean, or by being planted at altitude. There is a huge variety of grapes planted throughout California, as growers either attempt to match climate to grape, or simply continue the tradition of planting started by their great grandparents. Some of the largest wineries in the world are found in California, as well as many hundreds of producers that are so tiny only a handful of people ever get to try their wines.

Calories In dry wine calories come from the alcohol. There are about 100 - 110 calories per glass.

Campania *(cahm-pah'-nyah)* A wine region in southern Italy, around the town of Naples. The wines are not well known outside of the region, but visitors to the active volcano, Mount Vesuvius, usually run across some examples in the local eateries.

Canada Most famous for the delicious ice wines and other dessert wines of the Niagra region, Canada is producing an increasing number of dry table wines of note.

Canberra A wine region in Australia. Situated near the east coast, approximately halfway between Melbourne and Sydney.

Canterbury A large wine region on the south island of New Zealand. The region is almost too large and varied to make general comments about, but it is certainly a region that is still looking for its identity. Many of the vineyards are planted to white varieties, notably Riesling and Chardonnay, in an attempt to make the best of what may be too cool of a climate. The cold temperatures mean that some vineyards in this region may have problems ripening in certain vintages.

Cantina *(cahn-tee'-nah)* Italian for cellar.

Cap The solid parts of the grape - skins, seeds, and stems, which rise to the top of the must (partially fermented juice and solids) during red wine making. The cap needs to be broken up regularly so that these elements may impart characteristics to the wines.

Carbonic Maceration (also known as whole berry fermentation, or CM) The fermentation method used in Beaujolais and other regions to produce a very light and fruity red wine. By fermenting in an enclosed tank that is filled with carbon dioxide the process takes place inside the berry. As the weight of the grapes on top crushes the grapes on the bottom, the juice is removed and fermentation of the juice proceeds normally.

Carneros A California wine producing region. Situated where the Napa and Sonoma valleys meet in the south, and just north of the Bay. The proximity to the Bay makes the region cooler than its neighbors and as such, many sparkling wine producers have elected to grow here. The region has also proven itself as ideal for Pinot Noir (Pinot is also one of the grapes in most sparkling wines).

Cava *(cah-vah)* The Spanish term for cellar, it is also refers to Spanish sparking wine.

Cave *(cah'v)* The French term for cellar.

Cellar A storage place for wine, and by extension, a winery.

Cépage *(seh-pahj)* The French term that refers to the variety of grapevine. Cabernet Sauvignon is a popular cépage in the US. The term is also used to indicate the blend of grapes in a wine.

Chablis (shah-blee) A small town in France that produces crisp dry Chardonnay. It is considered part of the Burgundy region due to similar soils and grape affinities, even though it is miles to the north west from the rest of Burgundy. The term has been unfairly bastardized in the US and Australia to mean any white wine of little note.

Chai *(shay)* The French term for above the ground wine storage.

Chambertin *(sham-bair-tan)* One of the top Grand Cru red wine vineyards of Burgundy, and one of my personal favorites. It is in the commune of Gevrey-Chambertin, which in the tradition of Burgundy, appended the name of this famous vineyard to its own.

Chambolle-Musigny *(shahm-bol moo-see-n'yee)* A wine village, or commune, in the Burgundy region of France. Situated to the north of the Côte d'Or it is the home of two red Grand Crus, and the only white Grand Cru of the north, Musigny Blanc.

Champagne Literally it means a white chalky plane. This region in France is famous for its sparkling wines, and the method to make them, méthode champenoise. "Fine Champagne" and "Grand Fine Champagne" on a bottle of Cognac refers to the white chalky plain found in the Cognac area, and not in any way to the sparkling wine region.

Chapelle-Chambertin *(shah-pel sham-bair-tan)* A Grand Cru vineyard for red wine in the northern section of Burgundy, France. Adjacent to the Chambertin vineyard, Chapelle is allowed to append the name of the more famous vineyard to its own.

Chaptalization *(shap-it-al-iz'-ae-shun)* The practice of adding sugar to the juice prior to fermentation to increase the potential alcohol and quality of the wine. Chaptalization is illegal in many regions, and tightly controlled in others. In some cooler wine regions it would not be possible to make wine in some years without chapitalizing.

Chardonnay *(shar-doh-nay)* One of the most popular white grapes in the world. It is at home in the Burgundy region of France, and found throughout the New World. When first aged in oak, Chardonnay is one of the few white wines that improve with bottle aging.

Charmes-Chambertin *(sharm sham-bair-tan)* One of the Grand Cru red wine vineyards of Gevry-Chambertin in Burgundy, France.

Chassagne-Montrachet *(shah-san'yuh mohn-rah-shay)* A white wine making village in the Côte de Beaune in Burgundy, France. The famed vineyard Montrachet straddles this town, and Puligny-Montrachet, both of which have appended the famous vineyard names to their own.

Château *(shah-toe)* In Bordeaux, France, this is the name of the winery and vineyards that produce the wine. While it specifically means a castle or mansion, few Châteaux (the plural form) still exist in Bordeaux in the literal sense. More often than not a modest winery or farm house is the only building on the property. It is common to use Ch. to abbreviate Château when used with a specific property.

Château Bottled The term in Bordeaux, France for estate bottled, meaning that the wine was bottled by the producer or owner of the vineyards.

Châteauneuf-du-Pape *(chah-toe-nuff doo pahp)* Literally the new castle of the Popes, this was the summer home of the Popes while the papacy resided in nearby Avignon, France in the 1300s. It is now one of the best known wine producing regions of the southern Rhône. With 13 grapes to choose from, and a higher minimum alcohol content than most wines, Châteauneuf-du-Pape is a wine worth exploring.

Chenin Blanc *(sheh-nan blahn)* One of the great white grapes, and all too often over looked in the US. Many of the finest wines of the Loire region in France are Chenin Blanc, including the incredible, and long lived dessert wine, Coteaux du Layon.

Chevalier-Motrachet *(shuh-vahl-yay mon-rah-shay)* A Grand Cru vineyard for white wine (Chardonnay) in Burgundy, France. The vineyard of Montrachet was broken up long ago and this section was said to have been given to the daughter. As is often the case, the myth reflects the nature of the wines; a softer, more subtle style of wine is produced from this vineyard, than from the other adjacent Montrachet vineyards.

Chianti *(k'yahn-tee)* One of the most famous of the Italian red wines. Made from the Sangiovese grape, although a small amount of the white grapes, Trebbiano or Malvasia, may be added for finesse. The Chianti region encompasses much of the hills of Tuscany with the higher quality Chianti Classico region being a smaller and more defined "classic" region for producing the wine. In times gone past, Chianti was often sold in a straw covered bottle called a "fiasco." This has mostly given way to modern bottles.

China The Chinese have been making wine as long as Europeans, perhaps longer. Historically, wine was considered medicinal in Europe, but it was also enjoyed as a beverage. In China, medicinal uses have always dominated wine production. Cough syrups and other alcohol based medicines are well known to Americans, but in China wine based medicines remain more common than wine as a beverage. As China enters the world market more traditional western style wines are being produced; largely due to cooperative efforts of the French. The quality varies greatly and grape growing has not been perfected, but there remains potential.

Chinon *(shee-nohn)* A picturesque village in the Loire Valley of France where light red wines are made from Cabernet Franc.

Cinsault A red wine grape used primarily for blending. One of the 13 grape varieties allowed in the French wine Châteauneuf-du-Pape.

Clare Valley One of the wine producing regions of South Australia that are clustered near the city of Adelaide. A long history of winemaking here, and a long slow ripening season, have produced some very hearty red wines.

Claret *(clare-eht)* A term without legal meaning. In some parts of the world in refers to a light red wine. In England, where the term is most widely used, it means a red wine of the Bordeaux, France region.

Clean In wine tasting this term refers to wines that do not have any noticeable unpleasant or out of the ordinary odors or flavors. Modern wine making has ensured that most wines today are clean. Some may complain that New World wines can be clean to a fault. The lack of faults as a fault in itself is an interesting argument, and one that implies that a few faults in wine give it "character."

Climat *(clee-mah)* The French term for climate, although it is often used to refer to a region or vineyard that has a unifying characteristic. The English term would be "microclimate."

Clone A plant produced by graphing or cutting, so that it retains the identical genetic characteristics of the host. Each grape variety has many different subvarieties, or clones (much in the way that roses or other domesticated flowers doh). For example there are dozens of clones of Pinot Noir or Cabernet, each excelling in a specific characteristic or resistance to disease.

Clos *(cloh)* A French term that originally meant walled vineyard. It is used more widely today, especially to give a New World wine an Old World name.

Clos de Bèze *(cloh duh bez)* Along with Chambertin, the main red Grand Cru vineyard of Gevry-Chambertin in Burgundy, France. Often has the name of Chambertin preceding it, an honor that places Clos de Bèze on a par with the top rated Chambertin. When pressed, I often cite this as my favorite vineyard.

Clos de la Roche *(cloh duh lah rosh)* Grand Cru red wine vineyard of Burgundy, France from the commune of Morey-Saint-Denis.

Clos de Tart *(cloh duh tar)* Grand Cru red wine vineyard of Burgundy from the commune of Morey-Saint-Denis.

Clos de Vougeot *(cloh duh voo-joh)* The largest Grand Cru red wine vineyard of Burgundy. Located near the town of Vosne-Romanée, this vineyard boasts over 60 different owners, each making wine of varying quality.

Clos des Mouches *(cloh deh moosh)* Literally French for walled vineyard of the flies. This Premier Cru vineyard outside Beaune in Burgundy, France, produces red and white wines; especially the white, that often rival the more costly and famous Grand Crus of the region. The wine company Drouhin is the largest owner and producer of Clos des Mouches.

Clos Saint-Denis *(cloh san deh-nee)* Grand Cru red wine vineyard of Burgundy, France from the commune of Morey-Saint-Denis and the namesake vineyard of the town.

Cloudy A wine with particles floating in it from the wine making process. Modern wine making has made this very rare; however, some wine makers skip the filtering process and their wines may exhibit this fault. Wine that has "thrown sediment" with age is not said to be cloudy.

Cloying Overly sweet, to the point of being faulty. Wine should be balanced. The sweet flavors should be balanced with the sour flavors of the acids (much as lemonade is).

Cold Duck This now rare wine was once the sweet sparkling wine of the the bargain minded. In theory it is a mix of Champagne and sparkling Burgundy (often red). More often than not it had a less noble birth. The term comes from the German kalte ente (cold duck) which in turn is a corruption of kalte ende (cold end) which refers to the practice of marrying all of the left over wine after a banquet. There is an urban myth that the wine was a mixture from the dump buckets after a tasting, but, this is yet another corruption of the origins.

Colli ... *(coh-lee)* No less than 7 wine regions thoughout Italy begin with the word Colli. All make simple wines.

Colli Albani *(ahl-bah'-nee)*
Colli Berici *(beh-ree-t'chee)*
Colli Bolognesi *(boh-loh-n'yay'-zee)*
Colli Euganei *(eh-yoo-gah'-neh)*
Colli Lanuvini *(lah-noo-vee'-nee)*
Colli Orientali del Fruili *(oh-ree-en-tah'lee del free-oo'-lee)*
Colli Paicentini *(p'yah-t'chen-tee-nee)*

Colombard A passably decent grape with high yields. It is the most widely planted grape in California. The wine is usually produced for the bulk market.

Color The color of wine tells us much about its origin and wine making. Deeper colors usually relate to longer wine making practices and higher quality wines. Red wines range from blue-red, through red and as they age towards orange red (or brick red). White wines range in color from clear to deep golden, with hints of greens common in lighter wines. As whites age they tend to turn towards brown.

Columbia Valley A wine producing region in Washington State in the US. Following the mighty Columbia river as it winds down the eastern portion of the state, the Columbia Valley runs nearly the entire length of Washington into Oregon.

Commune The French term for a town. Often used interchangeably with village *(vee-lahj)*. Commune is more accurate as it includes the surrounding area as well as the town itself.

Concentrate Just like orange juice, grape juice is sometimes sold as a concentrate. Not only to make juice, but to make wines. In California and Italy, where adding sugar is forbidden, the addition of grape juice concentrate is often allowed as a way of bolstering a weak vintage.

Concord A native American grape that is still widely planted for wine and table consumption. Very dark, this is the grape of Welch's grape juice and its use as a winemaking grape is limited to low quality wines.

Condrieu *(coh'n-dree-uh)* A tiny wine making commune in the northern Rhône Valley of France. The wine is made exclusively from the Viognier grape. The best can be exceptional; however, Viognier is also making a home for itself in the New World where the wines are much less pricey. Château Grillet is in Condrieu and in a stroke of masterful lobbying, has been given its own appellation.

Cooked A fault found in wine that has been exposed to heat, especially in the presence of air. Grapes that are vinefied too warm may exhibit this characteristic, as well as wines that have been shipped badly.

Coonawarra One of the most notable red wine regions of Australia. Situated in the state of South Australia, it is primarily planted to Shiraz and Cabernet Sauvignon.

Cooperage Any and everything to do with wooden casks and barrels. A barrel maker is a cooper, hence the term.

Cooperative A central processing facility where vineyard owners can take their grapes to be made into wine and/or bottled. Usually owned by the members, it is a way to reduce the cost of wine making for the smaller producer. Many fine wines are made in cooperatives, as it is the only way that the vineyard owners could afford the most up-to-date equipment.

Cork The stopper for most wine bottles. Whether made from the bark of the cork tree or from plastic, cork must be flexible, durable, and able to create an air tight seal in the neck of the bottle. Corks can be a natural product of the cork oak, or increasingly, a conglomerate of cork and/or synthetic materials. This is due to the diminishing number of cork oaks, and the ever increasing need for more cork.

Corkage The fee paid to a restaurant for the privilege of being allowed to bring in your own wine. Usually $5 - $20 a bottle depending on the restaurant. This fee pays for the rental of the glasses and the service you receive. Unless a restaurant does not serve any wine, you should always be prepared to pay a corkage fee since you are cutting into their expected profit margin. Always check with the restaurant before bringing in your own wines.

Corked / Corky The most common fault in wine and the reason for the tasting ritual at a restaurant. The characteristic smell is a moldy, wet cardboard aroma. The cause is bacteria from the cork that has reacted with the bleaching process. Synthetic corks are free of this defect and this is a leading reason for their increasing adoption.

Corkscrew One of any number of devices that are used to extract corks from bottles.

Cornas *(cor-nahss)* A tiny wine producing commune in the northern Rhône in France. The red wines from this town are made from the grape Syrah.

Cortese *(cor-teh'-zeh)* A high quality white wine grape of northern Italy. The best known examples are the Gavi wines.

Corton *(cor-tawn)* The only Grand Cru red wine of the Côte de Beaune in Burgundy, France. The name sake of the commune Aloxe-Corton. The name Corton may appear with or without additional vineyard names such as "Le Clos du Roi" or "Les Renardes."

Corton-Charlemagne *(cor-tawn shahr-luh-mahn'yuh)* The Grand Cru white wine from the same or adjoining vineyards as the Grand Cru red wine Corton. Among the longest lived of any dry whites.

Cot The local name of the grape Malbec in Bordeaux, France.

Côte Chalonnaise *(coat chah-loh-neh'z)* Just south of Côte de Beaune in Burgundy, France, and named after the industrial city of Chalon-sur-Saone east of the grape growing region. The most famous commune is Mercurey, which produces primarily red wines. The Challonaise produces light, but well priced reds and rather simple whites.

Côte d'Or *(coat dor)* The heart of Burgundy, France. Comprised of the Côte de Nuits in the north and the Côte de Beaune in the south. This may well be the highest quality growing region in the world. It is also one of the most likely to be disappointing. A complicated (but exact) classification system, combined with wide swings in vintage quality, make this one of the most difficult regions to find a well priced quality wine. When it is good, it is so good that it keeps us coming back to recapture that fleeting experience. Learning the vineyards, the producers and the vintages will go a long way to making Burgundy less of a hit or miss proposition.

Côte de Beaune *(coat duh bone)* The southern half of the Côte d'Or in Burgundy, France. While the northern vineyards are almost exclusively red, the vineyards of the Côte de Beaune produce both red and white. With the exception of Corton which borders on the Côte d'Or to the north, all of the Grand Cru wines of the Côte de Beaune are white. This is the home of the famous Montrachet vineyards and the communes of Meursault, Chassagne and Puligny.

Côte de Beaune-Villages *(coat duh bone vee-lahj)* Pinot Noir from the smaller growing areas in the Côte de Beaune region of Burgundy, France. It refers to the smaller regions in the northern section that rarely bottle under their own names.

Côte de Nuits *(coat duh n'wee)* The northern half of the Côte d'Or in Burgundy, France. Home of great red wines made from the Pinot Noir. In a few scant miles a visitor passes through many of the best known vineyards in the world. There is no better way to learn about this complicated region than to visit. The scale is so small it is hard to believe without seeing it that so many of the famous Burgundy reds come from such a tiny region.

Côte de Nuits-Villages *(coat duh n'wee vee-lahj)* The lesser communes of the Côte de Nuits are bottled under this name. While some may also bottle under their own name, using this appellation allows them to blend the tiny output of these towns together.

Côte des Blancs *(coat duh blahn)* A district of the Champagne region where only the white wine grape Chardonnay is planted, hence the name. Pinot Noir, a red wine grape is also used to make most Champagne.

Côte Rôtie *(coat roe-tee)* The northernmost growing region of the Northern Rhône in France. The wines are made from Syrah and a touch of the white grape Viognier is sometimes added. The growing area is divided into 2 slopes, the Côte Brune and Côte Blonde. Legends has it there were two daughters, one blond, one brunette. They each inherited one of the slopes, which then magically took on the characteristics of the daughters. The Brune was rich and intense, the Blonde lighter and more elegant. The truth has more to do with the color of the soils than any legend.

Coteaux Champenois *(coat-toe shah'm-pen-wah)* The still (not sparkling) wine from the Champagne region of France. Rare, and worth trying.

Coteaux d'Aix-en-Provence *(coat-toe deks ahn pro-vahn'ss)* One the most important parts of the Provence region in southern France. Light reds and dry rosés are made from Grenache and other Rhône varietals. Very little white wine is made.

Coteaux du Layon *(coat-toe doo lay-awn)* A region in the Loire Valley in France, specifically in the Anjou. The best wines are made from late harvested Chenin Blanc grapes and are unbelievably long lived. These sweet wines are best enjoyed before the meal rather than after. One of the best kept secrets of France, these wines deserve better recognition.

Côtes de Provence *(coat duh pro-vahn'ss)* A section of Provence, France that is better known for its beaches than its wines. Stretching from the sea to well inland, this large subset of the Provence region is dedicated primarily to light rosé wines that are popular with the tourists.

Côtes du Jura *(coat dew joo-rah)* The Jura Mountains are in the extreme eastern border of France. Light, fresh reds, whites, and rosés and even some sparkling wines are made in the region. Like its neighbor Switzerland's wines, those of the Jura are best enjoyed locally and are rarely found outside of the region.

Côtes-du-Rhône *(coat doo rone)* The general name for the wine growing region of the Rhône Valley of France. A wine that uses this name on the label may originate from anywhere in the Rhône Valley. Occasionally a bargain can be found in this appellation, as a Rhône producer declassifies its lesser vineyards or lots. While declassification used to be common, it is now scarce. More likely a Côte-du-Rone will be red, very light, and made in the carbonic maceration style, much like Beaujolais. The whites may be the last bargain in Côtes-du-Rhône as they occasionally still contain decent wine.

Coulant *(coo-lahn)* A rather poetic French wine tasting term that literally means flowing. It is used for wines that are easy to drink. In the US we may say "quaffable."

Coulure *(coo-loo'r)* A condition in the vineyard that results from rainy or cold weather that keeps the flowers from being pollinated and therefore from turning into grapes. If the effect is not too widespread the result can be an intense, but small harvest. Widespread, coulure can spell disaster for grape growing, resulting in a very small harvest.

Crackling The English language term for a wine that is slightly sparkling, or bubbly, due to dissolved carbon dioxide. The French use the term "pétillant" and the Italians use the term I prefer "frizzante." The slight sparkle in crackling wines is intended to add freshness, and these types of wine are not uncommon in Italy. Some wines that exhibit this slight sparkling character do so less from intent than by accident. Dissolved carbon dioxide that may be unnoticeable at sea level is quite distinct at the high altitude of our offices (almost 9000 feet or 3000 meters). Wine makers are often surprised to find this in their wines when they visit.

Cramant *(crah-mahn)* A wine producing village in the Champagne region of France that is so highly regarded, it is one of the few village names that sometimes appears on the label.

Crémant *(creh-mahn)* The French term for sparkling wines that are "creamy," in that they have about half of the bubbles of traditional Champagne (3-4 atmospheres instead of 6). Rare outside of France. It is important to notice that it is not the same as the town of Cramant in the Champagne region. It is also a term for sparkling wines of high quality made outside of Champagne. The 3 notable types are:

Crémant d'Alsace - Sparkling wine of the Alsace region made in the méthode champeniose. Usually made from Pinot Blanc and Sylvaner. Must be aged in the bottle a minimum of 9 months.

Crémant de Bourgogne - Sparkling wine of the Burgundy region made in the méthode champeniose. The best are made from Pinot Noir and Chardonnay, just like Champagne, but Pinot Blanc and/or Pinot Gris may also be used. My favorite is the red variety, made from Pinot Noir. Unlike rosé style Champagne, which only has a slight Pinot character, the Crémant de Bourgogne Rouge is a true sparkling red wine. Must be aged in the bottle a minimum of 9 months.

Crémant de Loire - One of the best known sparkling wines of France, outside of Champagne. Chenin Blanc is the most common grape variety. Must be aged in the bottle a minimum of 12 months. This wine can be a relative bargain compared to some Champagne, and is often found at weddings or other events where a great quantity may be consumed.

Crianza *(cree-ahn-zah)* The Spanish term for oak aging. The terms "con crianza" or "vino de crianza" on the label require that the wine has been aged for at least one year in oak. Similarly "sin crianza" means that the wine was never aged in oak before bottling.

Criots-Bâtard-Montrachet *(cree-oh bah-tar mon-rah-shay)* One of the Grand Cru vineyards that surround the famed white wine vineyard of Montrachet in Burgundy.

Crisp A wine tasting term used to imply that a white wine has a refreshing acid balance. It is used much the same way one may say the taste (not texture) of a fresh green apple is "crisp."

Crozes-Hermitage *(craw'z air-mee-tahj)* A northern Rhône appellation. The wine may be red or white, and is produced from any of the 11 villages that surround the better Hermitage appellation. Reds are 100% Syrah and whites are Marsanne with some Roussane.

Cru *(crew)* The French term for growth, in wine it has many more conno-tations. It refers to a specific vineyard, but is also used to indicate quality (e.g. grand cru in Burgundy, or cru classés in Bordeaux). In Beaujolais it means one of the top 10 communes, and in Champagne individual villages are considered grand cru or premier cru (as opposed to individual vineyards in other parts of France).

Cru Bourgeois *(crew boor-j'wah)* The so called lesser wines of Bordeaux, France. Those that do not rank in the five classified growths (1st growth - 5th growth). Wines of this class were once considered a bargain. Increasingly, Bourgeois wines of note are fetching prices that rival the classified growths.

Cru Classe *(crew- clah-say)* French for classified growth. Those wines of Bordeaux that have been ranked, from 1st to 5th growth. The first classifi-cation took place in 1855 and a few modifications have been made over the years. Saint-Emilion does not use the 1st - 5th rating system, instead it uses a more confusing premier grand cru classe, and grands cru classe.

Crush The English language term (especially in California) for the harvest.

Cultivar A cultivated grape variety. Some use this as a more precise term than "grape variety."

Cuvaison *(coo-veh-zohn)* The French term for maceration. The practice of leaving the skins in contact with the juice during fermentation to extract color, tannin, and aroma. The period of time the wine is left macerating is referred to as the "cuvage." There is also a winery by this name in Napa Val-ley in California.

Cuvée *(coo-vay)* From the French term cuve meaning a vat or tank. It now usually refers to a specific lot or batch of wine. The term is sometimes used on a wine label to signify that the wine comes from a special batch of wine. It also refers to a blend of wines.

D

Dao *(dah'-oh)* One of the principal wine regions of Portugal. It is known for its well aged red wines.

Decant To transfer wine from a bottle into a crystal or glass container (a Decanter). This is primarily done with older red wines and Port which have developed sediment. The careful transfer of the wine into a fresh container allows the sediment to be left in the original bottle resulting in clearer wine.

Decanter The glass or crystal container that one decants into. In practice it could be a clean bottle; however, tradition dictates that it be an impressive vessel for the wine.

Degree Days Also known as the "heat summation method." A scale created by the University of California at Davis in the 1930s to determine the suitability for vineyards in any given climate. Modern instrumentation has largely supplanted this scale. The total accumulative number of degrees above 50F during the growing season. If the temperature for any given day rises to 70F that day would add 20 points to the summation. Over the 200 days of the California growing season the total would range from less than 2,500 degrees days for the coolest areas, classified as Region I, to region V with more than 4,000 degree days.

Demi-Sec *(deh-mee seck)* Literally this French term means half-dry. In practice it refers to the sweetest style of Champagne a house will make.

Demijohn Any very large bottle, usually around 10 gallons. Often used by amateur wine makers as a vat or storage container. May be covered in straw or rest in a wooden frame. From the French dame jeanne which has the same meaning.

Denominación de Origen *(deh-noh-mee-nah-th'yon' deh oh-ree-hen')* The Spanish term for their appellation laws. Established first for the wine growing region of Rioja in 1926. Often abbreviated DO.

Denominazione do Origine Controllata *(deh-noh-mee-nah-t'zee-oh'-neh dee oh-ree-jeen-eh con-troh-lah'-tah)*   The Italian term for their appellation laws, established in 1963. Abbreviated DOC.

Denominazione do Origine Controllata e Garantita *(eh gah-rahn-tee-tah)* The highest level of the Italian DOC laws. The wines must not only be typical of their region, but must pass a blind tasting. The first wines that began using this designation went on sale in the mid 1980s. Abbreviated DOCG.

Dessert Wine   Legally, in the US, this refers to fortified wines such as Port or Sherry, but also to the very inexpensive "more bang for your buck" sweet wines that are the favorite of college students and the stereotypical "bowery bum." In fine wine terms it refers to those wines that are destined to be enjoyed after a meal. All of the wines of this class are sweet but well balanced. They include the Sauternes of France, the Beerenauslese and Trokenneerenauslese of Germany as well as similar wines from most growing regions of the world. Port and a few other fortified wines are often considered Dessert Wines, while Sherry and other drier fortified wines are more properly Aperitifs.

Dézaley *(deh-zah-lay)*   One of the most celebrated white wines of Switzerland. Created on the shores of Lake Geneva from the Chesselas grape.

Disgorging   The process of removing the sediment from sparkling wine as the final step of the "methode champenoise." All of the sediment that has been building up in the bottle over the years has ended up in the neck of the bottle. The bottle is plunged into a freezing brine solution and ice forms in the bottle. The top is removed and the "plug" of ice is forced out by the pressure in the bottle. A small amount of wine is lost, and is replaced by other wine that has been mixed with sugar. This "dose" of sugar (or in French "dosage") determines how sweet the final sparkling wine will be. The French term is "dégorgement."

Doctor   One of the most famous vineyards in Germany. Located in the village of Berkastel on the Mosel river. Bernkastler Doctor, as it is usually referred to, is planted entirely with Riesling.

Dolcetto *(dohl-chet'-oh)* One of the principal grapes of Northwestern Italy. The best known wines made from this variety bear its name.

Dôle *(dohl)* The most highly regarded red wine of Switzerland. Made from the Pinot Noir and Gamay grapes, it is a light refreshing wine.

Domaine *(doe-mehn)* The French term for estate. A term that can cause a great deal of confusion, especially in Burgundy, France. There are several similar sounding phrases that seem to suggest the wine is estate bottled. Look for these phrases: Mise du domaine, Mis en boutille a la domaine, Mis en boutille a la propriété.

Domäne *(doe-may'-nuh)* A rarely used German term for estate. Mostly reserved for state-owned vineyards.

Dosage *(doh-saj)* The addition of sugar and wine to sparkling wine after disgorging. The amount of sugar added determines the style of the sparkling wine.

Double Magnum A large wine bottle, which holds the same as four normal bottles (3 liters). This is one of the more common large format sizes, and is also referred to by its capacity as a Three Liter bottle.

Dry The opposite of sweet in wine parlance. This term is used to denote a wine that has no residual sugar. Often this word is misused to refer to a wine with a minimal amount of "fruit." Most wines are dry with sweeter varieties being primarily white.

Dry Extract A technical wine tasting term. If you place wine in a centrifuge and remove all of the water, the powder that is left will be the dry extract. The amount of flavor that a wine has can be directly attributed to the dry extract. The body of the wine is also a function of dry extract.

Dulce *(dool'th-eh)* Literally sweet in Spanish, the term usually refers to the sweetening agent added to some Sherry.

Dumb A wine tasting term to mean a wine that is not showing up to its potential. Dumb, in this context, refers not to intelligence but to the inability to speak. While trying to avoid words that are anthropomorphic, this one seems particularly well suited.

E

Earthy A wine tasting term. It means just what it sounds like, a slight taste or aroma of soil. The French use a term "goût de terroir" that is often used to mean the same thing; although it can also mean that the wine has typical tastes for the region.

Echézeaux *(eh-sheh-zoh)* One of the best known Burgundy Grand Cru vineyards. Situated in the town of Flagey-Echézeaux, but it is grouped by convention with the other Grand Crus of the bordering commune of Vosne-Romanée. Do not confuse with the more expensive and intense vineyard, Grands Echézeaux, which is next door.

Edelfäule *(eh-dell-foy-luh)* Literally noble rot in German. This term refers to the mold Botrytis Cinerea. The French also call it noble rot (pourriture noble). This mold is responsible for reducing the water ratio in grapes, making them very sweet and useful as dessert wines.

Edna Valley An American Viticultural Area south of San Luis Obispo in California (an area broadly referred to as the Central Coast). One of the few transverse valleys in the US (meaning it points to the sea). This makes the region much cooler than surrounding growing regions and is ideal for Chardonnay and Pinot Noir.

Egri Bikavér *(eh'-gree bee'-kah-vair)* The famous "Bull's Blood of Egri", a red wine from Hungary. Once famous the world over, the versions that you find in most stores now is a thin and uninspiring red wine. Often it is primarily made from Merlot (the local name is Kekfrankos) with the addition of Cabernet Sauvignon. I look forward to trying a better representative of this wine than that which is found on most US wine store shelves.

Einzellage *(ay'n-t sel-lah-guh)* The German term for a single vineyard worthy of being mentioned on a label. Any German wine that carries a vineyard name may be considered a wine of quality. The name of the town usually comes first on the label as in the case of Piesporter Goldtröpfchen.

Eiswein *(ice-vine)* The German word for ice wine. This is an intense dessert wine that has been made from very ripe grapes (without Botrytis) that were frozen on the vine. The frozen water is removed during pressing, leaving a very sweet must.

Elegant A dubious wine tasting term. It refers to a well balanced wine that has subtle complexity. I say it is a dubious term because it is anthropomorphic (giving human traits to inanimate objects) and should be avoided. That said, I am guilty of using the word myself.

Emilia-Romagna *(eh-meel'-yah ro-mah'-n yah)* The Italian region north of Tuscany that is situated around the city of Bologna. Many visitors to Italy ignore this region because of the great deal of industry that is evident. What they do not realize is that this is the center of gastronomy for Italy. Parmesan cheese and Proscuitto Crudo both hale from nearby Parma, and Bologna is the cross roads for food from all over Italy. The most famous wine of the region is Lambrusco, a light, sometimes sparkling wine. Lambrusco is often overlooked as well, because the overly commercial Riunite is technically a Lambrusco.

Enology - also **Oenology** The science of wine production.

Enophile - also **Oenophile** A wine lover.

Enoteca *(eh-no-teh'-kah)* An Italian wine bar, often run by the regional wine authority, where you may sample many local wines.

Entre-Deux-Mers *(ahn-truh duh mair)* French for between two seas and a reference to the Bordeaux wine district situated between the Dordogne and Garonne rivers. A huge amount of rather indifferent white wine is made here.

Erzeugerabfüllung *(air'-t zoo-gher-ahb'-foo-lung)* This rather imposing German word is found on labels of wines that have been Estate Bottled.

Est! Est! Est!!! Other than the name, this is a rather forgetable Italian white wine. The name is an example of marketing that has withstood the ages. The story goes that a German Bishop in the 1100s sent a servant ahead to Rome with instructions to chalk Est (it is in Latin) on the side of every tavern with decent wine between the Bishop's home and Rome. That way the Bishop would not have to suffer through poor wine on his trip to visit the Pope. In the town of Montefiacone the servant was so enamoured of the wine that he scrawled the now famous epitaph. The Bishop, upon arriving in the town, was said to have agreed with his servant's taste to such an extent, that the Bishop never ventured on, living out his life drinking the wine he loved. Perhaps it was a different wine than what is sold today.

Estate Bottled - Estate Bottling Wine that was bottled by the vineyard owner. Many wines are still bottled and produced from grapes that are purchased on the open market, often for the lowest price. This designation assures that the winery had control over the grapes from beginning to end so that they could produce a high quality wine. In the US the vineyard need not belong to the winery, if there is a long term exclusive contract for the grapes of the vineyard (which also must be in the same geographic location as the winery). See also Domaine for the French equivalent of this designation.

Esters A scientific term. It relates to components in wine formed by the combination of acids and alcohol. They contribute the fruity, perfume-like smell to wine. In wine the most important esther is ethyl acetate.

Extra Dry A sparkling wine (or even authentic Champagne) that is slightly sweet. This term often leads to confusion since Dry means without sweetness, but Extra Dry for some reason means slightly sweet. While this is an English language term, it is still found on some French and other imported wines.

Extract - Dry Extract A scientific term often used in wine tasting. It liter-ally refers to what would be left in a centerfuge once you have removed the liquid. In wine, the term is used to indicate that a wine has a lot of flavor, especially when the wine would indeed be shown in a laboratory to have a greater amount of dry extract. The terms "heavy", "intense", and "big" are related to the amount of extract in the wine.

F

Faded A wine tasting term for a wine that has lost all or much of its flavor and aromas over time.

Fat In the US this term often infers that the wine is lacking in acidity. In other parts of the world the term fat is used to indicate a full, well balanced wine, and is a compliment.

Fatigue When a wine is subjected to shaking and jostling, either through the winemaking process, or shipping, it becomes fatigued. The further the wine has travelled, or the more severe the trip, the longer it will take to re-cover. Also called Bottle Shock or Bottle Fatigue. Usually a temporary condi-tion which a month or more of rest will cure.

Fendant *(fahn-dahn)* A popular white wine and grape in Switzerland. As is the case for so many wines that are light and fresh, it is often best enjoyed locally. Elsewhere in Switzerland the grape is known as Dorin, and in France is is called Chasselas.

Fermentation The process that turns grapes into wine. Specifically the metabolization of the sugars by the yeast, into alcohol, carbon dioxide and heat.

Feuillette *(fuh-yet)* A small oak barrel. At 36 gallons (136L) it is slightly more than half the size of a regular barrel, which averages about 60 gallons (225L).

Fiasco *(fee-ask'-coh)* The straw covered bottle of Chianti fame. Like most regional bottles, this one has become rarer as bottles have become increasingly standardized.

Figeac, Château *(fee-jahk)* One of the better known estates in St. Emilion (a region in Bordeaux, France).

Filtering A wine making technique used to ensure clarity and sterility in wine. Careful use of precise filtering pads and agents allow the winemaker to target specific foreign substances to remove, based on their size. Some winemakers feel that filtering reduces the quality of wine. Emile Peynaud, the preeminent University of Bordeaux enologist (enology being the science of wine) had this to say about the filtering debate: "Resistance to the practice of filtering arose from the reproach made that it tended to thin down and emaciate the wines. Nevertheless, if every precaution is taken... it may be stated that the mechanical action of filtering has never had a negative influence on quality. To suggest the contrary would mean conceding that the foreign substances... which filtration is precisely designed to remove, have a favorable taste function." From "Knowing and Making Wine."

Finesse One of the wine tasting terms I most recommend avoiding because it is vague and anthropomorphic. When not applied to wine the term suggests "subtlety in performance, skill" (Random House Dictionary). Wine is inanimate, it has no skills, and does not perform. Subtlety is further defined as "elusively thin or tenuous" (Random House Dictionary) and these terms are not a compliment for wine. I suspect the term is most used to express admiration for the balance of a very fine wine, one where the balance between the fruit, acidity and tannins are harmonious enough to keep any one from standing out.

Finger Lakes The main wine producing area in New York state. The region, which is about 300 miles northwest of New York City is dotted with lakes. These help to keep the ground from freezing in winter, and so help improve the conditions for vines. While wine has been made here since the early 19th century, the results had always been spotty. Once planted almost exclusively to French Hybrids (crosses between native American grapes and the European wine grapes) the Finger Lakes are now as likely to produce the better known white wines, Chardonnay and Riesling.

Fining The method for clarifying wine. Depending on the cause of the cloudiness, different agents can be used. Most, like gelatin, and egg whites, are proteins, while another is Bentonite, a form of clay. The general concept is to add a substance to the wine that the cloudy particles will stick to, and fall to the bottom. The winemaker then draws the clear wine off the top.

Finish The final flavors you taste in the wine. Often confused with "aftertaste." I distinguish the finish as being the taste you notice just as you swallow or spit a wine, as opposed to the aftertaste which are those flavors you notice after you swallow the wine, and which linger in your mouth for some time. Tannin is one of the common components that are noticeable in the finish of a wine.

Fino *(fee-noh)* A dry type of Sherry (a fortified wine from Spain). It is one of the styles of Sherry which is created by the presence of flor (A type of yeast found on some wine).

Fixin *(fee-san)* The northernmost wine village of the Cote de Nuits in Burgundy, France. Not well known, and without a Grand Cru to bring it recognition, Fixin continues to make some stellar red wines from the Pinot Noir grape. Any time you run across a wine from this commune, it is likely to be worth trying. This is doubly true as Fixin may be the remaining relative bargain in Burgundy.

Flor *(flore)* A special type of yeast found on the surface of wine. In the Sherry district of Spain, the flor yeast help to make the finest Sherries. On other wines it is a pest and must be controlled. It is also the Spanish word for flower.

Fortified Wine A class of wines that have been made sweet by interrupting the fermentation process with the addition of a neutral distilled spirit. The spirit kills the yeast before they have finished converting all of the sugar. Port and Sherry are both fortified wines.

Foxy A wine making term for the smell of native American grape varieties. The best example is the Concord grape that most Welch's grape juice is made from. The term originated with the early settlers who called the native grapes Fox grapes.

Franken *(frahn'-ken)* A large German wine region that specializes in dry white wines made from the grape Silvaner. While many German wine regions produce flowery and somewhat sweet wines, the wines of Franken tend to be clean and crisp. This has earned them a following, especially among those who are looking for dry German wines to drink with food. The region is sometimes known as Franconia in English language texts.

Free Run In wine making, it is the juice that appears after crushing, but before pressing. It is the highest quality juice for wine making.

Fresh Most wine is intended to be enjoyed young. When this young wine has ample acidity in the balance, it is often referred to as fresh.

Friuli-Venezia Giulia *(free-oo'-lee veh-net'-zee-ah joo'-lee-ah)* The wine region in the northeastern corner of Italy. The wines tend to be high quality, and the labels are usually marked with the name of the grape. This makes the wines friendly and easy to buy for most Americans. Merlot and Pinot Grigio (Pinot Gris) are among the best known red and white grapes grown here.

Frizzante *(free-zahn'-teh)* The Italian term for a wine that is slightly sparkling. Some wines may exhibit this spritz or sparkle by accident, but more often it is intentional. The French use the term "pétillant" although I prefer this Italian term.

Fruit Wine basically has three components. Fruit, acidity and tannin. All three must be in balance to make a decent wine. The fruit encompasses all the tastes and smells that that are not sour (acid) or bitter (tannin). Every grape variety and style of wine exhibits different fruit. In some wines such as Zinfandel the fruit can be very noticeable (Zin has so much fruit it is often described as jammy). Other wines such as Cabernet Sauvignon have less obvious fruit.

Fruity Some young wines have an aroma that can only be described as fruity. Beaujolais is one of the best known examples.

G

Gamay *(gam-may)* The grape of the Beaujolais region of France. It produces a light styled red wine. While this grape variety is found on the labels of some California wines, it is probable that the grape is not actually Gamay, but a light Pinot Noir clone or even the easily forgotten Valdiguie of southern France.

Garnacha *(gahr-nah'-shah)* The Spanish name for the grape referred to in France as Grenache. Very popular in Spain, it is the grape responsible for Spain's best known red wine, Rioja.

Gavi *(gah'-vee)* One of Italy's best known white wines. Made from the Cortese grape around the town of Gavi, in the northwestern part of the country, the Piedmont.

Gevery-Chambertin *(jev-ray shahm-bair-tan)* One of the highest quality, and highest quantity villages of the Côte de Nuits, in Burgundy, France. Not only are there a number of Premier Cru vineyards that can be outstanding, but more than a third of all the red Grand Cru vineyards in Burgundy can be found around this single town. The most famous vineyard is Chambertin, which lent its name to the town. Clos de Béze is a close second, and as such often appears as Chambertin-Clos de Béze. The other seven vineyards each have Chambertin appended to their own names, to show that they are considered slightly less regarded than Chambertin and Clos de Béze. The 9 Grand Crus are: Chambertin, Chambertin-Clos de Béze, Chapelle-Chambertin, Charmes-Chambertin, Griotte-Chambertin, Latriciéres-Chambertin, Mazis-Chambertin, Mazoyères-Chambertin (usually bottled as Charmes-Chambertin), and Ruchottes-Chambertin.

Gewürztraminer *(geh-vairtz'-tra-mee'-ner)* One of the great white wine grapes of the world, often overlooked in the US. The name means spicy traminer (traminer being a related type of grape). The pungent aroma of the grape can be delightful, and because of the name of the grape, the nose is referred to as spice. The use of the word spice without qualification, there are many types of spice, is reserved for discussions of Gewürztraminer. Often made in a sweet style, except in Alsace, France, where they make wines rich and full, rather than sweet.

Gigondas *(jee-gohn-dahs)* A wine from the Southern Rhône region of France. As with most Southern Rhône red wines, Gigondas is based on Grenache. The total amount of Grenache may only be 65%, so varying amounts of Cinsault, Syrah and Mourvèdre are also used in the blend. The wines tend to be tannic with a great deal of extract (that is they are heavy and dark) and require at least 5 years before drinking.

Gisborne A wine region on the north island of New Zealand. Situated on the east coast, this region is one of the largest by volume. Many of the grapes are used by the large producers, and as such there are not many wineries here. Chardonnay is the main grape of the region.

Givry *(jee-vree)* One of the higher quality wine towns in the Côte Chalonnaise section of Burgundy, France. Most of the wine is red, from the Pinot Noir grape.

Glycerol One of the alcohols found in wine as a result of fermentation. Sometimes referred to as glycerin, this can be misleading. Glycerin is marketed as a sweet, and syrupy liquid, used for soap making and adding viscosity to some liquors. The amount of glycerol found in wine is too small to make the wine thick (in fact, dry wines are slightly less viscous than water). It can contribute to the sweetening effect of the alcohol, since glycerol is much sweeter than most sugars, but again, it is only found in very small amounts (less than 1/10 of the alcohol found in wine). It has nothing to do with the formation or quantity of tears or legs found on a glass of swirled wine.

Goulburn Once a prominent wine region in Australia, it would have faded into obscurity if not for the single winery Tahbilk (they used to have Château in front of their name, but recently dropped it). Tahbilk can trace its roots back to 1860 when it was the original wine producer in the region. History has gone full circle and Tahbilk has stood the test of time.

Goût de Terrior *(goo-de-tare-wah)* A much used, little defined French term. Literally it means taste of the soil. Often used to describe the earthy flavors found in some wines. Just as often used to credit the conditions of soil and climate, for the particular taste of a wine or region.

Gran Reserva *(grahn reh-zehr-vah)* A Spanish term for a red wine that has been aged for a minimum of five years (with at least two in wood) before being released. For whites and rosé, it is four years before release and six months in wood.

Grand Cru *(grahn crew)* The French term for great growth. In the Burgundy and Alsace region this signifies the highest designation for a vineyard. In the Champagne region the term refers to the villages which may sell their wines for 100% of the asking price.

Grand Cru Classe *(grahn crew clah-say)* French for great classed growth. Found on the wines of St.-Emilion, Graves, Médoc and Sauternes regions of Bordeaux.

Grand Vin *(grahn van)* French for great wine this term has no legal meaning and is often used on wines that are not particularly great.

Graves *(grahv)* One of the wine producing regions of Bordeaux, France. The city of Bordeaux itself has largely encroached on the area, making for an almost urban vineyard setting. The word literally means gravel and so important is gravel for drainage in vineyards, that the region is named for this notable feature. Red and white wines are produced here, with the best known producer being Ch. Haut Brion. Cabernet Sauvignon, Merlot and Cabernet Franc are the chief red grapes, and Sauvignon Blanc and Sémillon for white wines.

Green A wine tasting term for wines made from under ripe grapes. The wine will have the smell of vegetation and be highly acidic.

Grenache *(greh-nah'sh)* A red wine grape of the Rhône Valley of France, and elsewhere (especially Spain). In the southern Rhône Grenache replaces Syrah as the most important grape (Syrah being more important in the north). It is also the grape of Lirac and Tavel, two of the arguably best rosé wines (also from the Rhône). Grenache is also responsible for the exceptional, and rare, fortified wine, Banyuls.

Grosslage *(gross'-lah-guh)* German for large vineyard. In German wine law, it is a collection of individual vineyards (Einzellagen) that share common traits. This allows the wines to be marketed under either their vineyard name, or the often better known Grosslage name.

Grüner Veltliner *(groo'-ner felt-lee'-ner)* A wine grape grown almost exclusively in Austria where it produces a light and simple wine. Recent marketing and production advances have lead to a worldwide surge in popularity of these wines.

H

Halbtrocken *(hahlb-trock-en)* German for half-dry. Wines with this designation may contain no more than 1.8% residual sugar.

Half Bottle A small bottle that holds .375L.

Haraszthy, Agoston A possible or at least a self proclaimed, Hungarian Count, and an unquestionably flamboyant figure. Haraszthy made his mark on the American state of Wisconsin (where he founded what is now known as Sauk City) before moving west to California. There he founded the Buena Vista winery in Sonoma, which is still in operation today. In 1861 he contrived to be sent to Europe by the Spanish governor of California in order to obtain cuttings of various wine grapes. For this he is often heralded as the "Father of California viticulture." Count Haraszthy's final claim to fame would come several years later, in Nicaragua, where he once again relocated, still hoping to make a fortune. It was here that the good Count was eaten by alligators.

Hard In wine tasting terms this relates to a wine that is tannic, particularly one that is so tannic that it is out of balance. This is a function of youth for some wines, and these wines will "soften" with age.

Harsh A hard wine with excessive acidity will be "harsh." The acid accentuates the tannins and increases the drying sensation known as astringency.

Haut-Brion, Château *(oh bree-ohn)* The highest rated, and best known vineyard in the Graves district, in Bordeaux, France. So highly prized is this vineyard, that it was included with the famous vineyards of Margaux, Latour and Lafite in the 1855 classification of the Haut-Médoc, even though it is many miles away from the other vineyards. Like the wines of the Haut-Médoc, Haut-Brion is primarily made from the grape Cabernet Sauvignon. Unlike the afore mentioned wines, Haut-Brion has a higher ratio of Cabernet Franc than Merlot, which often allows the wine to be softer and rounder than the others. They also produce one of the finest white wines of the region. Haut-Brion Blanc is a blend of the white wine grapes Semilion and Sauvignon Blanc. Haut Brion was purchased by the American financier and politician Clarence Dougless Dillion in 1935. His granddaughter still owns and operates Haut-Brion to this day.

Haut-Médoc *(oh meh-doc)* The Médoc is a wide peninsula of land formed by the Gironde River and the Atlantic Ocean, just northwest of the city of Bordeaux, France. It is subdivided into the lower (Bas-Médoc) and upper (Haut-Médoc) regions. To be confusing, the Haut-Médoc is further south, and closer to the city; but, it is also the more important region from a wine point of view. The Haut-Médoc is home to the renown vineyards of Margaux, Latour, Mouton and Lafite. It is the land of many Châteaux, and when most people speak of Bordeaux, this is the wine they have in mind. From north to south, the wine producing communes are St. Estèphe, Pauilliac, St.-Julien, and Margaux. The order is important as the wines tend to become lighter the further south you travel.

Hawkes Bay Sometimes referred to in the press as the "Bordeaux of New Zealand." The inference is not only due to the Cabernet and Merlot based wines from the region, but as well to the variability of vintages that plagues Hawkes Bay. Chardonnay and rich, oak aged Sauvignon Blanc are the whites of the region.

Heavy Used in wine tasting to imply that the wine is out of balance towards the tannins. This type of wine is more than just "hard" it is tannic to a fault, and may not soften enough with age to be enjoyable.

Hectare The metric unit for measuring land area. It is 10,000 square meters. One hectare = 2.471 acres.

Hectoliter The metric unit for measuring volume. It is 100 liters. One hectoliter = 26.42 gallons (US) = 133 bottles of wine (11 cases).

Herbaceous A green, vegetable smell in wine. For example, Sauvignon Blanc is grassy when subtle, herbaceous when overpowering. It is considered a negative attribute when it is more than slightly noticable.

Hermitage *(air-mee-tahj)* One of the most important wine making regions of the Rhône Valley, France. Heralded for its rich, earthy wines, both red and white. The red wines are made from the Syrah grape. The whites are more rare, and are made from Marsanne and Roussanne. The name is derived from a thirteenth century knight, Gaspard de Sterimberg, who laid down his weapons here, in favor of the religious life. He built a chapel on the hill, and became a hermit.

Hessische Bergstrasse *(heh-see-shuh bairg-strah-suh)* A tiny German region that primarily produces white wines from the Riesling grape. Most of the wine is consumed locally.

Hochheim *(hawk-heim)* An important German wine making town. It overlooks the Main river, but it is considered part of the Rheingau.

Hock A British term for the German wines of the Rhine. Derived from the wine town Hochheim.

Hospices de Beaune *(oh-speece duh bone)* A charitable institution in the Burgundy region of France. It is the beneficiary of a famous wine auction, held every year on the third Sunday in November. A local 15th century hospital has long been the recipient of the charity. Over the centuries a great deal of vineyard land has been bequeathed to the Hospice. It is the sale of these wines that draws the crowds to the picturesque city of Beaune, every year. Approximately 15,000 wines from various Burgundy vineyards, are produced and sold at the auction. The wine is sold in a barrel and it is up to the buyer to bottle and age the wine before reselling. The words Hospice de Beaune are often printed on the label, but the final quality of the wine is dependent on the bottler.

Hot The burning sensation of excessive or out of balance alcohol in wine. Usually found in the nose, rather than the taste.

Hunter Valley The oldest vineyard region in Australia. About 100 miles northwest of Sydney. Traditionally Shiraz (the Syrah grape of the Rhône Valley, in France) is king here, with Sémillon being the white grape of choice. Bowing to international tastes, Cabernet Sauvignon and Chardonnay are now almost 50% of the total vines planted.

I

Ice Wine This is an intense dessert wine that has been made from very ripe grapes (without Botrytis) that were frozen on the vine. The frozen water is removed during pressing, leaving a very sweet must. In German it is known as eiswein. A modern technique called cryroextraction utilizes a freezer in place of mother nature.

Imbottigliato *(im-boh-tee-l'yah'-toe)* Italian for bottled. "Imbottigliato all'origine" is the term for estate bottled.

Imperial A large bottle (6 liters), equivalent to eight regular sized bottles.

Indicazione Geographica Tipica *(in-dee-katz-ee-oe-nee jee-oe-graf-ee-ca tee-pee-cah)* A relatively new quality designation for Italian wines. It is used for wines that are typical of what is being made in the region, but may not be made with the official grapes or in a traditional style. Many of these wines are simple, but some are the most expensive wines in Italy. Usually abbreviated to IGT.

J

Jerez de la Frontera *(heh-reth' duh lah fron-teh'-rah)* The city in southern Spain that is the home of Sherry. The word Sherry comes from a rather poor attempt to pronounce the name of the town. The full name harkens back to the days when this was a frontier town on the border between the Christians and the Moors.

Jeroboam A large bottle (4.5 liters), equivalent to to six regular sized bottles (four in Champagne - 3 liters).

Johannisberg *(yo-hahn'iss-bairg)* One of the most famous German wine towns. It is situated in the middle of the Rheingau region. Because of the fame of this village, the word Johannisberg is sometimes (in the US only) added to the Riesling grape, Riesling being the principal grape of this region in Germany. "Johannisberg Riesling" was adopted in the US to distinguish it from the now rare Franken Riesling (which is actually the grape Sylvaner).

Jug Wine A term used for low quality wines that are sold in large bottles, or jugs. While this type of wine is rarely written about, it is important to remember that most of the wine made in the world is in fact, of jug wine quality.

Jura *(joo-rah)* The name used for the département (like a state), mountain range, and wine growing region in eastern France, near the Swiss border. Not well known, for the wines do not travel well, it is a pleasant area, with nice, much varied, but ultimately simple wines.

Jurançon *(joo-rahn-sohn)* A white wine region in the Pyrenees, in the southwest of France. Most of the wines are made dry today, but the area was once famous for its dessert wines. Visitors may still be able to find examples of this increasingly rare sweet wine. The wines are made from local grape varieties, and are rarely found outside of the area.

K

Kabinett *(kah-bee-net')* The entry level designation for quality German wines (QmP). Drier than other wines of the class, a Kabinett must be made from grapes with at least 16 percent sugar at harvest. The result is a drier (although not necessarily dry), lighter styled wine that is low in alcohol. The term comes from the practice of the wine producers reserving some wine for their own use, by locking it away in a cabinet.

Keller *(kel-ler)* The German word for cellar.

Kir *(keer)* A cocktail made by adding creme de cassis (a black-currant liquor) to white wine. A "Kir Royale" is made with Champagne instead of white wine. Named after a former mayor of Dijon, France, Canon Felix Kir.

Klevner *(klev-ner)* In the Alsace region of France this name is sometimes used for the white wine grape Pinot Blanc. It can also be used for a wine that is a blend of Pinot Blanc and Auxerrois. Near Zurich, Switzerland, the name is used for a red wine made from the grape Pinot Noir.

L

La Tâche *(lah tah'sh)* One of the Grand Cru vineyards of Burgundy, France. The red wine made from this vineyard is one of the most sought after Pinot Noirs in the world. Situated in the commune of Vosne-Romanée, the entire vineyard (just less than 15 acres) is owned by the Domaine de la Romanée-Conti (D.R.C.). Less than 2,000 cases of this wine are made a year.

Labrusca One of the species of grape native to North America. The Concord grape is the best known example. Most wine grapes come from the species Vinifera.

Lafite-Rothschild, Château *(la-feet rot-sheeld)* One of the Bordeaux, France properties designated a First Growth in 1855. Situated in the commune of

Pauillac, this is one of the most famous, and expensive wines in the world. The wine is made from Cabernet Sauvignon with a small amount of Merlot, Cabernet Franc, and Petit Verdot. Designed for long term aging, this wine is the benchmark for many Cabernet producers. Aproximately 25,000 cases produced annually.

Lafleur, Château *(lah-fluh'r)* A tiny, but exceptional property located in the Pomerol commune in Bordeaux, France. Since Pomerol was overlooked in the 1855 Classification, Lafleur has no official ranking. Only about 1,000 cases are made each year.

Lage *(lah'-guh)* The German term for vineyard. Hence "einzellage " and "grosslage ."

Lake County North of Napa and east of Sonoma in California, Lake County does not have proximity to the ocean or altitude to cool the vineyards. The warmer growing climate has been a boon for Zinfandel, and has led to some very popular, although slightly sweet, Chardonnay. While it has a long history, it is only recently that the quality of Lake County's wines have become recognized.

Lambrusco *(lam-broos'-coh)* A lightly sparkling wine, made from the grape of the same name. It is from the Emilia-Romagna region of Italy. Produced both in a dry or slightly sweet style, it is best know in the US as the brand Riunite (which is one of the sweetest examples made). In Italy, it is easier to find the drier styles, and they are a great match for the rich foods of the region. Lambrusco is made just west of Bologna, which is considered to be the capital of Italian gastronomy.

Languedoc *(lahn-guh-doc)* A region in the south of France that stretches along the Mediterranean from the Rhône river to the beautiful medieval walled city of Carcassone in the west. Most of the wine made here is what we in the US would call "jug wine." What wine of quality that does originate here comes primarily from the western sub regions of Corbières and Minervois and tends to be rather coarse reds.

Languedoc-Roussillon *(lahn-guh-doc roo-see-yawn)* This combined region produces almost 40% of all the wine in France. Most of it is generic, but the Corbières and Minervois sections of Languedoc and much of Roussillon produce high quality wines. In many ways it is a shame that these better sections should share in the stigma of the larger region. The best dry wines of the region are Red and can be made from any number of grapes including Syrah and Mourvèdre although economics dictate that most of the wines are based on Carignan, Cinsault or Grenache. Fortified wines based on Muscat and even Grenache are also found in the region, and can be among the best examples in the world.

Late Bottled Vintage Port A style of Port created originally for restaurants. Since Vintage Port throws a great deal of sediment, it can be difficult for a restaurant to deal with. The solution was to age the Vintage Port in barrels for four to six years, before bottling. This allows the wine to be ready to drink when released as opposed to Vintage Port which may require decades of aging before it is at its best. With an LBV there is little to no sediment so decanting is not necessary. This style of wine is delightful, but is no substitute for actual Vintage Port. Often abbreviated as LBV.

Late Harvest By harvesting later, the grapes are riper, and sweeter. This is appropriate for making sweet, dessert style wines. Some Late Harvest wines are almost dry, opting for increased alcohol and intensity rather than sweetness, as in the Alsatian "vendange tardive" (French for late harvest). In the US the term usually refers to a lightly sweet wine. Select Late Harvest refers to a sweeter wine, and Special Select Late Harvest to a very sweet wine. This is consistent with the German terms Aulese, Beerenauslese, and Trokenbeerenauslese.

Latium *(lah'-tyum)* The wine region in Italy around Rome. Most of the wine made here is white from the ubiquitous Trebbiano grape.

Latour, Château *(la-toor)* A First Growth wine of Bordeaux, France. This property, situated in Pauillac is one of the best known and respected in the world. This wine is primarily composed of Cabernet Sauvignon. Latour is made to age, it has been said that Latour is the longest lived of all Bordeaux wines. Around 23,000 cases are made each year.

Latricières-Chambertin *(lah-tree-s'yair shahm-bair-tan)* A Grand Cru red wine vineyard in Burgundy, France. Situated adjacent to the Chambertin vineyard (also a Grand Cru) it is allowed to append the name of its more famous neighbor to its own.

Lees The sediment from young wines while still in the barrel, tank or vat. Racking is the process of removing the wine and leaving the lees behind. Some white wines, such as Chardonnay, are often aged in contact with the lees in order to give the wine more flavor (see sur lie).

Legs A much over used and meaningless wine tasting term. It refers to the streams that are seen on the side of the glass after swirling (also called tears). While too many so called experts explain this as being related to the body, or the amount of glycerin in the wine, it is actually a function of the alcohol, and has no relation to the quality of the wine at all.

Léoville… *(leh-oh-vell)*
Léoville Barton *(bar-tohn)*
Léoville Las Case *(lahss cahz)*
Léoville Poyferré *(p'wah-feh-ray)* Three, Second Growth Bordeaux, France vineyards from the commune of Saint-Julien. Often considered to be better than other wines of their class (especially the first two). Cabernet Sauvignon based, these wines are made for aging. As one may suspect, the three were once one, they were broken up around 1826.

Liebfraumilch *(leeb-frao-milsh)* One of the best known German wines. The name means blessed mother's milk. Prior to the enactment of the German wine laws in 1971 the term was used to mean almost any German wine from the Rhine region. Since the laws have gone into force, along with an update in 1983, the term now is used to designate wine made from a strictly delimited area of one of four regions. The region's name must also appear on the label. While the great grape of Germany, Riesling, can be used, it is rarely found in Liebfraumilch. In order to keep the costs down, and production up, most Liebfraumilch is made from Müller-Thurga, Sylvaner and Kerner. Liebfraumilch tends to be lightly sweet, simple, and very inexpensive.

Light The opposite of heavy. A wine without much tannin in the balance. The wine may still be complex, and full of flavor. Such wines are often enjoyable young, but rarely age. Uncharacteristically, there is a legal meaning for Light Wines in the US. They must be less than 14% alcohol. This is the same alcohol limit for all table wines in the US, making the legal definition of Light Wine redundant.

Liguria *(lee-goo'-ree-ah)* A wine producing region of Italy that stretches along the Mediterranean from the French border down to Tuscany. The region is also unofficially known as the Italian Riviera and is dotted with famous resort towns.

Limousin *(lee-moo-zan)* A forest in central France that is a major source of oak for wooden barrels. The barrels made from this oak impart a stronger taste than oak from other French sources, and so Limousin oak has somewhat fallen out of favor around the world.

Limpid Literally this word means transparent, as in pure water. Used in wine tasting to imply a wine that is clear and bright. Occasionally misused by those who associate the homonym "limp" with the word, and assume it must mean something negative. It may be best to avoid this term, using "clear" instead.

Liqueur A sweet, flavored, alcohol based drink. Used in the world of wine to mean something completely different. In the champagne method of making sparking wines "liqueur de tirage" is the mix of sugar solution and yeast added to the wine, to create the secondary fermentation, which will in turn produce bubbles. Again in sparkling wine production, the term is also used as "liqueur d'expédition" which is the sweeting agent added to the finished sparkling wine, which will determine the final style (from Extra-Dry, which is sweet to Brut, which is dry). Liqueur is also used in Sauternes, the dessert wine making region of Bordeaux, France, to refer to the sweetness of the wine. Finally, also from France, there is the occasionally used term "vin de liqueur," which refers to a wine made sweet by adding spirits to stop the fermentation process. This type of wine is more often called "vin doux naturel."

Liquoreaux *(lee-co-ruh)* A French term for a sweet white wine, such as Sauternes or Coteaux du Layon, that has retained residual sugar without the addition of spirits, as opposed to "vin doux naturel."

Liquoroso *(lee-kwoh-roh'-soh)* An Italian term for a dessert wine that is made sweet by adding spirits to stop the fermentation process while there is still sugar left unfermented. The English term is "fortified wine."

Lirac *(lee-rack)* A dry rosé wine from the Rhône region of France. Produced primarily from the Grenache grape, many consider this, along with its neighbor Tavel to be some of the most successful rosé wines made.

Lodge A warehouse in Vila Nova de Gaia, Portugal, used for storing and aging Port. In Bordeaux, France the equivalent word would be "chai" and in the Sherry producing town of Jerez, Spain, the term is "bodega."

Loire *(l'wahr)* The Loire Valley is one of the major wine producing regions of France. Most of the wines tend to be light and enjoyed young. A notable exception is my favorite sweet wine, Coteaux du Layon which ages for decades. The principal white grape is Chenin Blanc, and further to the east, Sauvignon Blanc. Less red is produced, and it is often made from Cabernet Franc (also used for rosé wines in the region). Because of the beauty of the country side, many castles (Châteaux) have been built along the Loire river and its tributaries, making this a popular, and delightful, tourist destination. This is a huge area with many different types of wine.

Lombardy A principal wine producing region of Northern Italy.

M

Macebeo *(mah-cah-beh'-oh)* The principal white wine grape of the Spanish Rioja region where it is known locally as Viura. Simple and crisp with a floral quality, this grape helped revolutionize the white wines of the Rijoa region by replacing the easily oxidized Malvasia grape.

Mâcon *(mah-cawn)* A major town in southern Burgundy, France, that has lent its name to a wide region, the Mâconnais. Most of the wine produced is white, fresh, simple and made from Chardonnay.

Mâconnais *(mah-cawn-nay)* A large wine region in southern Burgundy, France. Most of the wine produced is white, fresh, simple and made from Chardonnay.

Madeira *(muh-deh'-rah)* A Portugese island in the Atlantic Ocean, off the coast of Morocco. The fortified wines from this region are unique in that they are purposefully baked and oxidized, prior to bottling. In times gone by this was accomplished by shipping the wines on a sailing vessel, the longer the journey the better, although today modern techniques favor specially designed heating tanks. Since the wine is in contact with oxygen from inception, it turns a dark brown color, the process of which is known for all wines as "maderization" or one would say the wine has "maderized." The wines are made in several styles, and are usually labeled with the name of the grape variety used. Sercial is the driest style, and is usually served before a meal. Verdelho is a bit sweeter, and a great accompaniment with cream soups. Boal, or Bual is noticeably sweet, and Malmsey is the sweetest and is usually served after a meal. Madeira was once a very popular wine. In the 19th century it was the most popular wine in the US. Towards the end of the 19th century, the twin plagues that devastated Europe, oidium and phylloxera, did not skip the island of Madeira. In the process of replanting, and re-inventing themselves, Madeira producers started to use a single grape variety, Tinta Negra Mole, for all the wines, while still labeling them with the original grape names to indicate style. This not only led to confusion, but a noticeable decline in quality. Since entering the European Common Market in 1986, Madeira has had to conform to the European labeling laws, which require at least 85% of the grape mentioned on the label. This has led to a resurgence in planting of the original grape varieties. Madeira is almost certainly the longest lived of all wines. I have had many examples from the early 19th century that were in fine shape. The cost of these ancient wines are surprisingly reasonable, and you should never pass up the opportunity to try one. Beware of the word "solera" on the label, as this means that only a drop or two of wine from the date listed are actually in the blended wine itself.

Maderized A wine tasting term for a wine that has been affected by oxidation. In extreme examples the wine (usually white wine) has begun to turn brown. This process is identical to the browning that occurs in an apple that has had a bite taken out of it. The term comes from the wines of Madeira, which are very brown, due to a great deal of oxidation, and being baked.

Magnum A large wine bottle, which holds the same as two normal bottles (1.5 liters). The larger the bottle, the slower the wine ages. A magnum is the perfect size for aging great red wines, as it ages the wine slowly, but not too slowly.

Malbec *(mahl-bec)* One of the red wine grapes of Bordeaux, France (where it is called cot or pressac). While it is rarely used for more than adding a bit of color, it is one of the five grapes allowed, along with Cabernet Sauvignon, Cabernet Franc, Merlot and Petite Verdot. South of Bordeaux is the region of Cahors where Malbec is the chief grape used in what historically has been called their "black wine." Argentina is the new champion of Malbec, where it is one of the most important grapes planted.

Malolactic Fermentation A secondary fermentation that changes the tart malic acid (found in green apples) into the softer lactic acid (found in milk). Common in red wine, but used almost exclusively in Chardonnay for white. One of the byproducts of this process is a chemical called diacetyl which is responsible for the buttery taste of some wines. Often abbreviated ML.

Malvasia Since ancient times this has been an important grape throughout the Mediterranean. In recent years it has become less popular and is increasingly being replaced by fruitier, lighter white wine grapes. The distinct amber color of wines made from this grape are a reminder of how easily it becomes maderized. In fact this is the grape known in Madeira, Portugal as Malmsey. Italy is the final bastion for this grape, where it is used to make sweet wines, or when blended with Trebbiano, to make dry whites such as Orvieto and Frascati.

Manzanilla *(mahn-thah-nee'-yah)* One of the styles of Sherry. Very dry, and some say, almost salty.

Marc *(mar)* The French word for pomace (the solids left after making wine). Also a brandy distilled from pomace (eau-de-vie de marc). In Italy the brandy is known as Grappa.

Marche *(mahr'-kay)* The Marches, as it is known in English, is an south eastern Italian region along the Adriatic Sea. This is the home of the well known white wine Verdicchio (which is both the wine and the grape name).

Margaux *(mar-goh)* The southernmost of the quality wine producing regions of the Haut-Médoc, in Bordeaux, France.

Margaux, Château *(mar-goh)* A First Growth Bordeaux, France, producer, from the town of the same name. Sometimes used as an example of why not to rely on the 1855 classification to rate wines. While the wines from this property are now as good as a First Growth should be, this could not be said during the 60s and early 70s. The winery had run into disrepair, but since it was listed as a First Growth in 1855, there was no way for consumers to know that it was a poor example of what should have been a great wine. Turned around in the late 70s and early 80s by its current owners, Margaux is once again a First Growth in more than name. Cabernet based, like the other First Growth wines of the region, Margaux tends to be softer than some of its northern counterparts.

Margret River An up and coming wine region in Western Australia. The cool climate has proved to be one of the most successful in Australia, and there is every reason to believe the production of quality wines from the region has just begun.

Marlborough Possibly New Zealands finest wine region. Located on the northern end of the southern island, Marlborough is a cool growing region with long dry autumns. This is important since the grapes would not have a chance to ripen fully if the region had rain around the time of the harvest. Sauvignon Blanc made the region well known, but it is Pinot Noir that may ultimately make its mark on Marlborough.

Marsala *(mar-sah'-lah)* Often relegated to the kitchen, this is the best known fortified wine of Sicily, Italy. While still popular as a cooking ingredient, it is not usually a favorite among lovers of fortified wines. The wine itself is vinified dry, and a sweeting agent "mosto cotto" (cooked must) is added to give it the distinctive brown color and flavor.

Marsannay *(mahr-sah-nay)* This tiny commune in the northernmost section of the Cote d'Or of Burgundy, France, has almost been taken over by furniture stores and auto dealers. Red, white and rosé wines are all made here, making it unique in Burgundy. The wines are simple and light and rarely found outside of the region.

Marsanne A white wine grape of the Rhône Valley, France. It is noticeably earthy and richer than most other white wine grapes.

Mataro Another name for the grape Mourvèdre. One of the red wine grapes of southern France and the Rhône Valley. It is the grape of the very tannic, and darkly colored Bandol (from the south of France). It is these very characteristics that makes the grape important for blending. It is one of the 13 grapes found in Châteauneuf-du-Pape. The grape has a following in California where it is used for blending with Syrah or Zinfandel, or even bottled on its own.

May Wine A relatively rare German white wine that has had the herb woodruff added to it, and then sweetened.

Mazis-Chambertin *(mah-zee sham-bair-tan)* A Grand Cru red wine vineyard in Burgundy, France. Allowed to add the name of its famous neighbor, Chambertin, to its own because of its proximity and high quality.

Mazoyères-Chambertin *(mah-z'oy-air sham-bair-tan)* Another of the Gevery-Chambertin Grand Cru Burgundies that is allowed to append the Chambertin name to its own. Usually sold as Charmes-Chambertin.

McLaren Vale A quality wine growing region in the Southern Vales region of Australia.

Médoc *(meh-doc)* A wine growing region in Bordeaux, France. The Médoc is split in two, with the Haut-Médoc (upper Médoc) being the southern portion, and the higher quality of the two (in fact most of the highest quality Bordeaux red wines come from the Haut-Médoc). The remaining portion, the Bas-Médoc (lower Médoc) is rarely seen on wine labels, the term Médoc itself being more common.

Mendocino County The northernmost wine region in California's North Coast. The quality of the wines from the region have improved greatly in the last few decades, and some exceptional sparkling wine has started to be produced.

Mercurey *(mair-coo-ray)* A wine producing commune in the southern Burgundy region of France. Specifically located in the Côte Chalonnaise, it is the best known red producer in the region. The red wines are made from Pinot Noir, and the tiny amount of white made, is from the Chardonnay grape.

Merlot *(mair-low)* One of the best known red wine grapes. Often blended with Cabernet Sauvignon. In the Haut-Médoc region of Bordeaux, France, it is second to Cabernet Sauvignon; but, across the river in Saint-Emilion and Pomerol it is the primary grape. It ages somewhat more quickly than Cabernet Sauvignon, because it is lighter in tannins.

Méthode Champenoise *(meh-toh'd shahm-peh-n'wahz)* First a dry, still wine is made. It is then bottled. A small amount of sugar and yeast is added to the bottle, which is then sealed. The yeast turns the sugar into carbon dioxide, heat and alcohol. The carbon dioxide dissolves in the wine, making the wine bubbly. Once the process has finished, the bottle of wine still contains the sediment from the yeast. Through a process known as riddling, the bottles are slowly turned upside down (over a period of weeks or months) until the sediment is in the neck of the bottle. The neck is then plunged into a very cold salt water solution, which freezes a bit of the wine around the sediment. The bottle is opened and the chunk of ice, complete with all of the sediment, is removed. The bottle then needs to be refilled to replace the lost wine. At this point, some Champagne is added, along with a solution of sugar, which will determine the final sweetness and style of the wine.

Methuselah / Methuselem An oversized bottle (6 liters) used for Champagne. It holds eight normal bottles.

Meursault *(muhr-soh)* A popular wine producing village of Burgundy, France. Located in the Côte de Beaune, it produces primarily white wine from the Chardonnay grape. A small amount of red wine is produced from Pinot Noir.

Microclimate In meteorological terms this is the effect of geography on weather on a very small scale. In wine tasting, this term, like the French term Terrioir (see goût de terrior) has been expanded to include the geology as well as geography of any given area. In total, it refers to the different conditions any individual vineyard may face. The vineyards of Burgundy, France are a living example of this effect. While many of the vineyards are tiny, they each have a taste characteristic that is noticeably different from their neighbor.

Mildew The same fungus that plagues home owners can be found in the vineyard, with the same undesirable results. There are two types in the vineyard, "downy" and "powdery." It is the powdery type that is known as Oidium and devistated the vineyards of Europe in the late 19th century. It is now controlled by the careful use of powdered sulfur or copper sulfate in the vineyard.

Millésime *(mee-leh-zeem)* The French term for vintage, the year of harvest that appears on a bottle.

Minervois *(mee-nair-v'wah)* One of the best known red wines from the Languedoc-Roussillon region of southern France.

Mission The grape carried by the Franciscan monks to the New World. It is probably the same as the Pais grape of Chile and the Criolla grape of Argentina. Never a quality grape, it has largely been forgotten about and removed from vineyards throughout the New World. A small amount can still be found in California, and the best wines made from it are sweet and fortified.

Mittelrhein *(mit' l-rine)* A tiny and very picturesque wine region in Germany along the Rhine River. Most of the wine is white and made from the Riesling grape. It is rarely exported.

Moelleux *(m'wah-luh)* A French term for a wine that is ever so slightly sweet. There is no real English equivalent. The term "threshold" is applied in the US to wines that have measurable residual sugar, but do not taste sweet to most people.

Moldy Just what it sounds like. Grapes (usually red) that were affected by mold and used to make wine anyway will have this off taste and odor.

Monopole *(mawn-o-pole)* The French term for a vineyard that has a single owner, hence a monopoly on that wine. Primarily used in Burgundy, where it is rare for a vineyard to have only one owner.

Monterey County Until recently this county in California was better known as the setting for Steinbeck novels than for wine. In the early 1960s large concerns began to make wine of varying quality from the region. The wine improved, and so the number of wineries increased. Today Monterey County is still home to some of the best values in California wines, as well as a few well known, but pricier producers.

Monthelie *(mohn-teh-lee)* An almost unknown red wine producing commune in the Cote de Beaune section of Burgundy, France. The wines tend to be rich and well priced.

Montrachet *(mon-rah-shay)* A Grand Cru white wine vineyard of Burgundy, France, planted entirely to Chardonnay. The vineyard was much larger in times gone by, but has been broken up into smaller portions over time. Half the vineyard lies in the commune of Chassagne-Motrachet, as do the adjacent Grand Cru of Bâtard-Montrachet (in part). The other half of the vineyard is in Puligny-Montrachet along with the Grand Crus Bâtard-Montrachet (in part), Bienvenues Bâtard-Montrachet and Chevalier Montrachet. Montrachet is the source of confusion and error for some wine drinkers. The two towns each appending the name of the vineyard (common in Burgundy) means that some people refer to the wines from the towns collectively as Montrachet. This can be a costly mistake should you order Montrachet in a restaurant, as the Grand Cru vineyard produces some of the most expensive white wine in the world.

Montrose, Château *(mohn't-rose)* A Second Growth Bordeaux, France property. It is (along with Ch. Cos-d'Estournel) the highest rated vineyard in the village of Saint-Estèphe. Keeping with the generalization that the harder wines are in the north of the Haut-Médoc, Ch. Montrose is indeed a harder styled wine. Based on Cabernet Sauvignon, as are all Haut-Médoc wines, this wine will age well.

Morey-Saint-Denis *(moh-ray san deh-nee)* A village in the northern end of the Côte de Nuits in Burgundy, France. A producer of very high quality red wines, it is unusual to see the village name on a label. Much of the vineyard land is Grand Cru, and would be sold with the name of the vineyard only. Besides the namesake Grand Cru vineyard, Clos Daint-Denis, Clos de la Roche, Clos de Tart, Clos des Lambray and a part of Bonnes Mares are all found in this tiny village, situated directly south of Gevery-Chambertin. The grape for the reds are Pinot Noir, and a tiny amount of white is made from Chardonnay.

Morgon *(mor-gawn)* A wine producing village in the Beaujolais region of France. The wines here are less fruity and more complex than its neighbors. Those who would support the claim that Beaujolais can improve with age, usually point to the wines of Morgon as an example. As with all Beaujolais, the grape for this red wine is Gamay.

Moscato *(moss-cah'-toh)* The Italian name for the Muscat grape. This is the grape of Asti Spumante, Italian's famous sparkling wine (the drier versions in Italy are far superior to the exported versions). The Italians make a wide range of Moscato wines, some fortified, some sparkling.

Moscato d'Asti *(moss-cah'-to dah'ss-tee)* One of my favorite wines, it is often overlooked in the US. Lightly sparkling, lightly sweet, and light in alcohol, this wine is light in everything, except flavor. Made from the Muscat (known locally as the Moscato) grape in the town of Asti, in the Piedmont region of northern Italy. Only the finest grapes go into the production of Moscato d'Asti, with the bulk of them being utilized to make the better known, and fully sparkling, Asti Spumante.

Mosel / Moselle *(mo'-zl / mo-zell')* The river that runs through part of the Mosel-Saar-Ruwer wine region in Germany. Moselle is the English spelling. Many of the very best vineyards in Germany can be found along the banks of this river as it winds it way through the region.

Mosel-Saar-Ruwer *(mo'z'l sahr roo'-ver)* One of the highest quality wine regions in Germany. It includes two of the tributaries to the Moselle River, the Saar and the Ruwer. The finest vineyards are found on steeply terraced hills, overlooking the rivers. The best wines are made from Riesling, but increasing amounts of Müller-Thurgau, Elbling and Kerner are being planted. Some of the best known wine growing regions in Germany can be found here: Zeller Schwarze Katz, Piesporter and the Bernkastler vineyards. The Bernkastler Doctor vineyard in particular is heralded by many as the source of their favorite German wine.

Mou *(moo)* A French term for a wine that is soft or thin to a fault. Not well known in the US, but a good term to know as there is not really an English equivalent.

Moulis *(moo-lee)* One of the smaller wine growing villages in the Médoc district of Bordeaux, France. It is notable as the home of Chasse-Spleen, one of the best known Cru Bourgeois (lesser Bordeaux wines).

Mourvèdre *(moor-ved'r)* One of the red wine grapes of southern France and the Rhône Valley. It is the grape of the very tannic, and darkly colored Bandol (from the south of France). It is these very characteristics that makes the grape important for blending. It is one of the 13 grapes found in Châteauneuf-du-Pape. The grape has a following in California where it is used for blending with Syrah or Zinfandel, or even bottled on its own. Sometimes called Mataro.

Mousse *(moose)* The French term for the foam found on sparkling wines or beer. Often called "head" in English.

Mousseux (moo-suh) The French generic term for sparkling wine. Champagne, from the Champagne region is always referred to by name.

Mousy A wine tasting term for the smell and taste of a particular bacterial spoilage in some faulty wines.

Mouton-Rothschild, Château *(moo-tohn rot-sheeld)* A First Growth Bordeaux, France property. Rated as a second growth in the 1855 classification, it was elevated by decree in 1973. For many wine enthusiasts, Mouton is best known as the wine with the incredible art labels. With only three exceptions, since 1946 an original work of art has been commissioned for the label. Marc Chagall, Salvador Dali and Andy Warhol are among the artists who's works have graced the Mouton labels. In 1953 there was the 100th anniversary label. In 1973 the painting was from the Chateau's collection rather than commissioned for the label. It was an homage to Picasso, mourning the passing of the artist, while celebrating Mouton's elevation to First Growth. The 1977 was the third exception, when the label was a commemoration of the visit of the Queen Mother (of Great Britain). The wine is rightfully as famous as the labels, and like all of the wines of the region, it is based on Cabernet Sauvignon.

Müller-Thurgau *(mew'-lair toor'-gau)* The most planted grape in Germany. A cross of Riesling and Sylvaner. The wines it makes tend to be low in acid, and somewhat dull, compared to Riesling. Widely planted in New Zealand as well.

Musar, Château *(moo-sahr)* A Cabernet Sauvignon based wine from Lebanon. This wine has received much press and critical acclaim over the years. I do not share this opinion, finding the wine to be very expensive, overly hard, lacking in fruit, and having a distinct baked flavor. All or most of these may be blamed on the US distributors and importer, so perhaps the wine shows better in the correct circumstances. It may also be that this is the best wine made in the Middle East, and so allowances have been made by the critics.

Muscadet *(mus-cah-day)* A light, dry white wine made around the town of Nantes, France, where the Loire river flows into the Atlantic ocean. Because of the style of the wine, and the geography of the area it is produced in, it is often acclaimed as the perfect accompaniment to seafood. The Sèvre-et-Maine appellation is added to the name of the wine made from this smaller delimited area. Once this was a small percentage of the wine made, now most Muscadet exported comes from Sèvre-et-Maine. In addition, the wine is sometimes aged on the lees (sediment) to add flavor, and this too is noted on the bottle, giving the wine the resulting tongue twister name: Muscadet Sèvre-et-Maine Sur Lie. Muscadet is the local name for the grape used, which is known elsewhere as Melon de Bourgogne.

Muscat *(moos-cat or muss-cat)* Considered the original wine making grape, and the progenitor of all wine making grapes (of the species Vinifera). The grape comes in many sub-varieties and even colors. Nearly every wine making region of the world has some sort of Muscat based wine. The aroma of the grape is distinct, and has lent its name to the word "musk." A list of the Muscat based wines would take pages, the good news is that the word Muscat or Moscatto appears on many of the labels. Almost without exception, Muscat based wines are somewhat, to very sweet. Muscat raisins and table grapes can also be found on occasion.

Musigny *(moo-see-n'yee)* A Grand Cru Burgundy, France vineyard. While the red wine is made from Pinot Noir and constitutes by far the largest proportion of the 3,000 cases a year of wine produced from this vineyard, a tiny amount of white wine from Chardonnay is made and labeled Musigny Blanc. This is the only Grand Cru white wine made in the Côte de Nuits. Like all of the Grand Cru reds of Burgundy, this wine is unforgettable in a decent vintage.

Must The crushed grapes and juice that will be fermented into wine.

Musty The off smell of a wine that has been in contact with old or poorly cleaned wooden casks. It is similar to a moldy smell, or even the "corked" smell of an off wine. If you experience this smell, and think it may be a corked bottle, try opening another bottle of the same wine, if it still exists, it is likely musty, and not corked.

N

Nahe *(nah'-huh)* One of the major wine growing areas of Germany, and for many, as high a quality as the Mosel, and the Rheingau. A visit to Bad Kreuznach, the wine capital of the region, will not only yield exceptional Rieslings, but you may soak in the therapeutic baths and gamble your nights away in the casino.

Napa Valley Easily the best known wine region in the US, this area of California has been making wine for generations. Some of the best known names in California wines can be found here, and certainly some of the most expensive. Cabernet Sauvignon based wines have proven to be the most successful, although Chardonnay and many other grapes continue to be planted. The valley floor can be very hot. Too hot for some varieties, and so the hills that overlook the Napa River valley are dotted with vineyards. The legal term Napa Valley also includes several neighboring valleys and mountain sides.

Navarra *(na-var)* A wine making region in northern Spain, once only known for its rosé wines. Increasingly, red wines of note have been coming out of this region.

Nebbiolo *(neh-b'yoh'-loh)* The principal grape of the Piedmont region of northern Italy. The wines Barolo, Barberesco, and Gattinara are all made from Nebbiolo. Barolo in particular tends to be hard in youth, and to reward extended aging.

Nebuchadnezzar The largest of the Champagne bottles. It holds 20 ordinary bottles (15 liters). They are very impressive, until you try to pour from one.

Négoçiant *(neh-go-see-ahn)* The French word for a trader or merchant. In wine terms it is the merchant who buys the wine in cask, and then bottles, labels and sells it. There is also a growing trend among negociants to buy the grapes and make the wine themselves.

Neuchatel *(nuh-shah-tel)* A popular Swiss white wine, made from the Chasselas grape along the shores of Lake Neuchatel.

New York Third after California and Washington State in wine production, New York has been producing wines since the earliest days of the US. Few US wine lovers think of New York in the same regard as they would California. This is changing as small wineries have begun planting Vinifera (European grape varieties such as Cabernet and Chardonnay) in place of the more traditional Hybrids and native American grapes. You are now more likely to be offered a New York Riesling than the once ubiquitous White Concord. The Concord, a native American grape, is now relegated to making juice, which it does best. Sparkling wines continue to be produced in New York, in response to the cool climate (crisp tart grapes are required for sparkling wine). New York has a ways to go before it can lose the stigma it gained from centuries of indifferent wines, but it is moving in the right direction.

Nierstein *(neer'-sh'tine)* The leading wine village in the Rheinhessen region of Germany.

Noble Rot A term for Botrytis Cinerea. The special mold that is responsible for many of the world's greatest dessert wines. It creates micro lesions in the skin of the grape, and then removes the water from inside the grape. The result is fruit with a much higher ratio of sugar, suitable for creating sweet wines. The mold can also be harmful when it attacks dry wine vineyards (it is usually called Gray Rot when it is a pest). The French call Botrytis "pourriture noble" - noble rot.

Nouveau *(noo-voh)* The French word for new. It has taken on a new meaning and a life of its own when paired with Beaujolais. Beaujolais Nouveau is shipped in mid-Novemeber, just a few days after the harvest. Using the Carbonic Maceration method, the wine is made much more quickly than by traditional methods, but looses complexity in the process. The new wine becomes a center piece of marketing as cases of it are flown around the world to celebrate its release.

Nuits-Saint-Georges *(n'wee san johr'j)* The wine town in Burgundy, France, that lent its name to the Côte de Nuits which starts here and runs north. The town is home to some very good reds wines, and many First Growths (1er Cru), but no Grands Crus.

Nutty A wine tasting term for a wine that exhibits flavors reminiscent of nuts, especially hazelnut. In some cases this can be a sign that the wine is oxidized. Sherry and Tawny Ports are both very nutty, and very oxidized (hence the brown color).

O

Oak Used to make containers for storing and aging wine, specific types of oak are used for small barrels to impart flavor and tannins to the wine. The newer the barrel, the more flavor it imparts. Oak is critical for making long-lived red wines, and some whites. It can sometimes be over used to hide flavors or to make up for lackluster crops. Oak in wine should always be subtle, and in balance. Beware of any wine where the oak is the defining character. In larger containers, and older barrels, the oak does not impart much if any flavor, and so less expensive oak is used. There is a certain amount of air exchanged through the pores of a small oak barrel that can help to develop the aromas of the young wine (secondary aromas). Again, this process is diminished in larger oak barrels because of the volume of wine they hold. On the average, oak barrels hold around 60 gallons (225 liters).

Oechsle *(uh'k-sleh)* The German scale of measuring the sugar content of must (in the US we use the Brix Scale). The aim of such scales is to determine the potential alcohol content of the finished wine. This is a critical measure of when to harvest.

Oeil de Perdrix *(uh'y duh pair-dree)* Literally eye of the partridge in French. The term is used to connote a color of wine. It is a browning pink color. The term is old, and rarely used much anymore, but seems to have referred to rosé wines that were slightly oxidized. You may run across the term in reading old notes, or from overly poetic wine writers.

Off A very general word for any wine that is not quite as it should be. Usually used by a taster familiar with the wine, who is pronouncing that this bottle or sample is somehow damaged. Especially used to describe an odor that may be due to a problem with the wine.

Oidium *(oh-ee'-d'yum)* The powdery mildew fungus that devastated the vineyards of Europe in the mid-nineteenth century. Like the phylloxera plague that would follow, Oidium was brought from America. It is now controlled in the vineyard by spraying.

Oloroso *(o-lo-ro'-soh)* A Sherry that has not been aged in the presence of flor. Dry, as is all Sherry when aging in a barrel, this is the Sherry that is often sweetened and sold as Cream Sherry.

Oporto *(o-port-oh)* The city on the Douro river in Portugal that gave Port its name. The Port trade is actually conducted across the river in Vila Nova de Gaia because of the fire danger the aging Port presents.

Oregon This Pacific Northwestern state is well known for its Pinot Noir wines. The climate has proven that it can produce remarkable wines; however, as is the case with so many of the finest cool regions, the vintages can be variable. Riesling, Chardonnay and Pinot Gris are white varieties that have been successfully planted in Oregon.

Organoleptic *(or-gan-o-lep'-tic)* Examination with the senses as opposed to a chemical or physical exam. This is the highest form of wine tasting. An expert must be able to taste the wine and have a good idea of what it is, and more importantly, what it should be. A laboratory analysis can aid the winemaker in determining if the wine has finished a particularly stage, or needs to be adjusted, but only a taster can determine quality and marketability.

Originalabfüllung *(o-reeg'-ee-nahl-ahh'-foo-lung)* The older German term for estate bottled. It was largely replaced in 1971 by the term "erzeugurabfüllung."

Orvieto *(ohr-v'yay'-toh)* A well known Italian white wine made from the Trebbianno grape in the Umbria region.

Otago The southernmost wine region in New Zealand. In fact, the southernmost wine region in the World. Nestled in the mountains, the climate is different than almost anywhere else in New Zealand. Vineyards, reminiscent of those in Germany's Mosel (one of the northernmost growing regions) are perched on hillsides with an exposure designed to eke out every bit of solar radiation possible. Pinot Noir is being planted here, as is Riesling. These grapes too are found in the cool climates of Germany, and the comparison is inevitable. Time will tell how this region does, as most of the plantings are fairly recent, but there are high hopes.

Oxidized A wine tasting term for a wine that has absorbed oxygen. In extreme examples the wine (usually white wine) has begun to turn brown. This process is identical to the browning that occurs in an apple that has had a bite taken out of it. Also known as "maderized."

P

Palomino *(pal-o-mee-noh)* The main grape used for Sherry production. Also used sparingly in the New World where it never seems to perform as well.

Paso Robles A wine growing region in California, south of the bay, and south of Monterey as well. Look for Cabernet Sauvignon and Zinfandel from this region.

Passe-tout-grains *(pahss too gran)* Usually called "Bourgogne Passe-tout-grains." A blend of Gamay and Pinot Noir (at least 33%) from southern Burgundy, France. A rarity that is worth trying when you find it.

Passito *(pah-see'-toe)* An Italian wine making technique. The grapes are dried on mats until they turn to raisins. The result is a much higher sugar ratio in the grapes. Mostly used for dessert wines, but also used to make the dry red wine Reccioto della Valpolicella Amarone.

Pasteurization The process of sterilizing liquids by heating. Rarely used for fine wines, but occasionally used for simpler wines, especially if they contain residual sugar.

Pauillac *(paw-yack)* One of the principal wine growing towns in the Haut-Médoc, in Bordeaux, France. This is the home of Mouton, Lafite and Latour.

Pedro Ximenez *(peh'-dro hee-meh'-nez)* A wine grape grown primarily in Spain, with some plantings in Argentina and Australia as well. Throughout Spain it is used to make rather simple white wines. It is also used to make Sherry-like wines around the world. In the actual Sherry producing region of Spain it is becoming increasingly rare, in favor of the Palomino grape, and is usually used for blending. It is often called PX.

Penedès *(peh-neh-dess')* A wine producing region in Spain, just west of Barcelona. Most of Spain's sparkling wine, Cava, is produced here. There has been an explosion of red wines produced in the area, many from the Cabernet Sauvignon grape. The well known producer Torres is one of the leaders in the region, as well as Jean Leon who helped to made Spanish Cabernet popular in the US.

Perfume Used by some wine tasters to describe the abundant floral quality of some white wines. It should be used exclusively for those aromas that derive from the grape itself (primary aromas).

Perlant *(pehr-lahn)* A French term for a wine that has some, but very little sparkle. It is for wines that are less sparkling than what the French call "pétillant," and the Italians call "frizzante."

Perth Hills A tiny wine growing region in Western Australia that is east of the city of Perth. This is one of the newest wine regions in the country. By planting at altitude, the grape growers here are able to escape the heat that plagues the neighboring Swan Valley.

Pétillant *(peh-tee-yahn)* The French term for a wine that is slightly sparkling. Equivalent to the Italian term "frizzante."

Petit Verdot *(peh-tee vair-doe)* One of the blending grapes used in Bordeaux, France. Added to Cabernet Sauvignon, or Merlot based wines for its tannins.

Petite Sirah A wine grape found primarily in California. Once thought to be related to the Syrah grape of the Rhône Valley in France, it is now known to be the grape Durif. It has been said that this grape is "neither petite, nor Syrah." It yields wines with a deep color that tend to be rather simple and tannic, but enjoyable young.

Pétrus, Château *(peh-troos)* A wine of the Pomerol region of Bordeaux, France. In 1855 when the region was being classified, Pomerol was on the wrong side of a river, without a bridge. As a result, the Pomerol region has never been classified. If it had, Pétrus would certainly be the highest rated wine in the region. With only 4,000 cases produced a year, Pétrus is consistently one of the most expensive and sought after wines in the world. Usually made from 100% Merlot (a small amount of Cabernet Franc is planted, and is used only when needed). One can not write of Ch. Pétrus without mentioning Jean-Pierre Moueix *(mo-ex)*, whose guidance over the past four decades has turned this nearly obscure vineyard into the powerhouse it is today.

pH Wine makers, and wine writers often talk about the total acidity (TA) in a wine. It is only half the story. pH is the measure of how strong the acid is in wine. The lower the number, the stronger the acid. A wine with a low TA may still taste tart if the pH is low enough. To be confusing pH is essentially backwards when talking about acidity. The higher the number, the more alkaline (the opposite of acidity) a solution is. The technical answer is that pH is a measurement of the number of hydrogen ions a solution contains. In dry table wine the range, very generally, is around 3.1 - 3.6.

Phalz *(fahl'tz)* One of the Anbaugebiete (specified wine regions) of Germany, and the most up and coming. Also referred to as the Rheinpfalz, and sometimes known in English speaking circles as the "Palatinate." Stretching for 50 miles, just north of Alsace from the French-German border, the Phalz produces red and white wines of distinction. Pinot Noir, known as Spatburgunder in German, is the red wine grape of the region, where it produces a very light styled wine. Riesling is king here, but Müller-Thurgau is a close second, with a variety of other grapes constituting 60% of the vineyards. While the second largest German region by size, it may be the largest by volume of wine produced. The words Phalz and Palatinate both derive from the Latin palatium, meaning palace. The Roman emperors constructed their imperial residences on a hill in the region 2000 years ago, and the name still sticks.

Phylloxera *(fil-lox'-er-ra)* A small insect that was responsible for the most devastating plague in wine history. A native of North America, the phylloxera louse is happy to live off the leaves of the native North American grapes. It was accidently exported to Europe where it found a new type of grape to live off of (Vinifera). Instead of the leaves, it found that the roots of this new type of grape was a delicacy. It so liked the roots of Vinifera that it changed its life cycle to exclude males and the winged form of the insect, learning to specialize as a female only, root eating monster. This made phylloxera much harder to detect, and to destroy. The late 19th century saw this insect spread throughout Europe, and even to the wine making regions of the New World, where it nearly wiped out the wine making industry. Many solutions were tried, but it was the grafting of native North American root stock (which is resistant to the bug) to the Vinifera grape vines that was finally found to be effective. This technique is used world over to this day. Phylloxera is mostly controlled except in areas where through greed, ignorance or accident, root stock that is not resistant is used. Such was the case in California in the 80s and 90s where phylloxera was found to be rampant in the famous vineyards of Napa Valley and elsewhere, primarily due to the wrong choice of root stock.

Pichon Longueville Comtesse de Lalande, Château *(pee-shoh'n long-veel coh'n-tess duh lah-lahnd)* A Second Growth vineyard in the village of Pauillac, in Bordeaux, France. It is often considered to be better than its peers and is given the unofficial designation "Super Second." Adjacent to its brother vineyard (see below) this wine is often called Pichon-Lalande to reduce confusion. A greater proportion of Merlot, and the more southernly vineyard, make this wine softer than Pichon-Baron, or even other wines in the region.

Pichon-Longueville, Château *(pee-shoh'n long-veel)* A Second Growth vineyard in the village of Pauillac, in Bordeaux, France. Until the mid-nineteenth century this was a huge vineyard, but it was divided, with part going to the sisters (see above) and this part going to the son. Because of the potential of confusion with its sister vineyard, this property is often called Pichon-Baron. A Cabernet Sauvignon based wine, it is usually of a style somewhat more tannic than its sister vineyard or its adjacent neighbor, the First Growth, Ch. Latour.

Piedmont / Piemonte *(peed-mont / p'yay-mon'-the)* One of the most important wine producing regions in Italy, it is situated in the northwestern corner of the country, up against the Alps. This is the home of the intense red wines Barolo and Barberesco, as well as the refreshingly light sparkling wine Moscato d'Asti and the well known sparkler Asti Spumante. Piemonte is the Italian name for the region

Piesport *(peez-port)* A tiny, but very famous German wine making town. With steep, rocky vineyards that overlook the Moselle River, the Rieslings produced here are among the world's best. The renown Groldtropfchen vineyard is located in this village.

Pineau des Charentes *(pee-no day shah-rahn't)* A somewhat obscure sweet, fortified wine made in the Cognac region of France. It is made by adding Cognac to unfermented grape juice (instead of partially fermented wine).

Pinot Blanc *(pee-no blahn)* A relative of the Pinot Noir, this white grape is planted in abundance in Alsace, France; California and Oregon. At one time this grape was found in the vineyards of Burgundy, alongside Chardonnay. While Burgundy plantings are now rare, it would seem that much of the Pinot Blanc taken from Burgundy to be planted elsewhere, is actually Chardonnay. This is especially true in Italy, where producers of Pinot Blanco are pleasantly surprised to find they have the better selling Chardonnay planted instead, and have rushed to change the name of their wines. The wines made from Pinot Blanc tend to be very crisp due to high acidity.

Pinot Grigio *(pee'-no gree-d'joh)* The Italian name for the grape and wine produced from the Pinot Gris grape. Most of this popular wine is rather bland and uninspiring.

Pinot Gris *(pee-no gree)* A relative of the Pinot Noir grape. This "grey" member of the family is important in Alsace, France, where it is known as Tokay d'Alsace and in Germany where it is called Ruländer, and best known for many as the Italian Pinot Grigio. The Alsatian examples are some of the richest and most flavorful.

Pinot Meunier *(pee-no muh-n'yay)* A cousin of the Pinot Noir grape, and like Pinot Noir, one of the red wine grapes used in Champagne. Curiously it is rarely mentioned in Champagne where nearly half the vineyards are planted to Pinot Meunier.

Pinot Noir *(pee-no n'wahr)* One of the most important red wine grapes in the World. At home in Burgundy, France, it is also found throughout the New World. In California many of the best examples are found in Santa Barbara county. Oregon too boasts exceptional Pinots, and New Zealand is proud of their up and coming contributions. It is also used to make high quality sparkling wines in Champagne and elsewhere. By pressing very gently, the red color which comes from the skins of the grape, does not leech into the juice, allowing sparkling wines made with Pinot Noir to remain relatively clear. Rosé Champagne is usually (but not always) made by adding red wine at the end of the process. Pinot Noir tends to be high in acid, and low in tannin, which makes it easier to enjoy in its youth, and one of the best wines to enjoy with food. Pinot Noir is a very hard grape to grow, and a very hard wine to make. This makes vintage fluctuations common, as well as less than stellar results from some producers, even in good years.

Pinotage *(pee-no-tahj)* An important grape in South Africa. The result of crossing Pinot Noir and Cinsault (which is known as Hermitage in South Africa). While the South Africans are very proud of the wines made from this grape, I have not had the pleasure of tasting one of note. Like many wines that travel so far, it may be a combination of factors that lead to a degradation of quality.

Pipe A large oak barrel that is tapered at the ends. At 522.5 liters or 138 gallons it is about twice the size of the average barrel. Used primarily for Port.

Piqué *(pee-kay)* A French term, it means a wine that has begun to sour.

Plastering A confusing term. It means either the addition of substances such as calcium sulfate before fermentation in order to increase acidity, or calcium carbonate to reduce acidity. Since both of these are a white powder that is added to a liquid, as is plaster, it may explain the term, but not why it can mean two potentially opposite results.

Plonk A common slang term for bulk or jug wines.

Pomace All of the seeds, skins, pulp and stems left over after fermenting and pressing the red wine. The French call this "marc" and distill it into a brandy by the same name. The Italians call this brandy "grappa."

Pomerol *(paw-meh-rawl)* A wine producing village in Bordeaux, France. Unique among French wine producing regions, this one has no classification system. In 1855 when most of Bordeaux was being classified, Pomerol was less accessible than it is now, and was largely ignored. The wine makers of the region have resisted classification ever since. The home of the very expensive and renown Ch. Pétrus, Pomerol may be one of the highest average quality regions in Bordeaux. The wines here are produced primarily from Merlot, with varying amounts of Cabernet Franc added when the vintage calls for it.

Pommard *(po-mar)* A well known wine producing village in Burgundy, France. Situated at the northern end of the Côte de Beaune, it produces primarily red wines from the Pinot Noir grape.

Porron *(poh-rone)* An odd looking glass or ceramic wine drinking vessel from Spain. It is shaped like a bag with two horns. One end is wider, to allow pouring in the wine. The other end is a spout. The drinker raises the Porron high over their head and allows the stream to run down into their mouth. More for celebration than everyday use, it is now seen mostly at festivals for the delight of the tourists.

Port   A Portuguese, sweet red wine that is made by adding neutral grape spirit (brandy) to the unfinished wine. This is the process known as "fortification." Port is made in several styles. Vintage Port is made in years that are exceptional. It is bottled young, and ages in the bottle for decades. An aged Vintage Port throws a good deal of sediment and must be decanted before serving. Late Bottled Vintage Port is aged for several years in a barrel before it is bottled. It is a short cut method that allows the wine to be served with a minimum of fuss. It never will have the complexity of a fine Vintage Port, nor the price. Character Port is a house style that is not vintage dated. It is a simple, inexpensive style that will not improve with age. The label will not say "Character Port," it will have a brand name instead. Tawny Port has been aged in a barrel for a number of years (usually listed on the label). As the Port throws sediment, it is racked into a new barrel, leaving the sediment behind, as well as the coloring agent. The result is a lightly brown (tawny) colored wine that is nutty and complex. 10, 20 and 40 year old Tawnies are common. There is also a White Port made from white wine grapes. It is a drier, aperitif style. It is rarely seen in the US. Outside of the European Economic Community, which controls the legal use of the term Port, there are several Port style wines made in a similar fashion. Australia and the US are both producers of these Port styled wines.

Porto   The legal name for Port exported to the US, in order to reduce confusion with US made port style wines. It must appear somewhere on the label. The exception is for Port that is bottled in England prior to export to the US.

Pouilly-Fuissé   *(poo-yee fwee-say)*   A Chardonnay based white wine from southern Burgundy in France. Very popular in the US.

Pouilly-Fumé   *(poo-yee foo-may)*   A dry white wine made from Sauvignon Blanc in the Loire region of France.

Pourriture Noble   *(poor-rit-ch'yer no-bluh)*   French for noble rot a term for Botrytis Cinerea, the special mold that is responsible for many of the world's greatest dessert wines. Botrytis creates micro lesions in the skin of the grape, and then removes the water from inside the grape. The result is fruit with a much higher ratio of sugar, suitable for creating sweet wines. The mold can also be harmful when it attacks dry wine vineyards (it is usually called gray rot when it is a pest).

Pourtgieser A red wine grape popular in Austria. It has no connection to Portugal at all.

Premier Cru *(preh-m'yay crew)* French for first growth. In Bordeaux it refers to the very top estates. In Burgundy it refers to those vineyards that are distinctive enough to be listed on the label, but not great enough to stand on their own (as are the Grand Cru vineyards).

Press A piece of wine making equipment used to press the juice out of the grapes. In the case of red wine this is done after fermentation.

Press Wine When making wine, the juice that is extracted without pressing is of the highest quality, and is called "free run." In order to extract the rest of the juice, the grapes must be pressed. This is often done multiple times. Each succeeding press yields juice of a lower quality. The term "press wine" is mostly used to connote this lower quality juice. In order to make an inexpensive wine from expensive grapes, such as Cabernet Sauvignon, or Chardonnay, the grapes must be pressed many times in order to increase the quantity produced. In some cases, only this press wine is used, the free run juice being used for higher quality wine. Since this press wine is often bitter, it becomes necessary to leave a small amount of sugar in the wine to hide the bitterness.

Primeur *(pree-muh'r)* A French term for wines that are consumed shortly after harvest. The best known example is Beaujolais Nouveau.

Primitivo *(pree-mee-tee'-voh)* A red wine grape found in Italy. It was thought for some time that this was the origin of the Zinfandel grape of California. Current DNA methods suggest that the Primitivo may actually have come from the Zinfandel, rather than the other way around.

Prohibition A period in US history that outlawed the sale of alcoholic beverages, by the 18th amendment to the US Constitution. It lasted from 1920 until 1933 when it was repealed by the 21st amendment to the US Constitution. During this period the consumption of alcoholic beverages doubled. Because of the great profits to be made, bootlegging and smuggling became common, and a great deal of violence was introduced into American society.

Proof A method of expressing the alcohol content of spirits. Wine has the actual percentage listed. In the US proof is double the percentage of alcohol. So a 100 proof spirit, contains 50% alcohol. In Great Britian it would be 57.06% by volume. This is an important distiction, because Scotch Whiskey imported into the US will say 80 proof when it has 40% alcohol, but the same whiskey in Great Britain will only say 70 proof.

Prosecco *(pro-seh-coh)* A white wine grape of Italy. In the US it is best known as a sparkling wine made from the same grape. In Italy the wine may be sparkling, lightly sparkling, or even still.

Provence *(pro-vahn'ss)* A huge wine making area in the south of France. The emphasis tends to be on quantity more than quality, with over 40 million cases produced each year.

Pruning One of the most important steps in vineyard management. Conducted during the dormant period in the vineyard. The goal is to shape the vine for the coming growing season, with a specific goal in mind. The goal may be to increase or decrease the amount of grapes to be produced, or to make the grapes easier to harvest by machine, or a host of other considerations.

Puget Sound A small wine region in western Washington that is centered around the city of Seattle. While most of the wine boom in the state has been in the eastern regions, this area is one of the oldest in the state, and is home to some of the better known wineries.

Puglia *(poo'-lyah)* A southeastern Italian wine producing region. Every country has a region that excels in making bulk wines, and this is Italy's.

Puligny-Montrachet *(poo-lee-n'yee mohn-rah-shay)* A white wine making village in the Côte de Beaune in Burgundy, France. The famed vineyard Montrachet straddles this town, and Chassagne-Montrachet, both of which have appended the famous vineyard names to their own.

Pulp The center of the grape which contains the juice. It is surrounded by the skin of the grape, where tannin, and in the case of red wines, the coloring agents are found. The pulp in turn surrounds the seed, or pip, which is also a source of tannin.

Punt The indentation in the bottom of a Champagne bottle. Originally designed to strengthen the bottle, so that it could withstand the internal pressure of the sparkling wine, it is now found on many wine bottles. It not only increases the strength, but it makes it easier for the bottle makers to stack the bottles on end.

Puttonyos *(poo'-tun-yosh)* In the production of Tokaji Aszu wine of Hungary, baskets of very ripe grapes, effected with botrytis, are added to the base wine to sweeten it. The baskets are themselves known as puttonyos, and the label of the wine will indicate how many puttonyos have been added. Three is common for the drier styles, with five being used in the sweetest. Six puttonyos wines exist, but are nearly legendary. There also exists an even more legendary wine, Essencia which is made entirely from the puttonyos grapes.

Q

QbA The complete phrase is "Qualitätswein bestimmter Anbaugebiete" which is almost always abbreviated to QbA in the US and on the wine label. It means quality wine from a specified region. It is a legal designation under the 1971 German wine laws. A QbA wine must have a minimum sugar level at harvest, but may be chaptalized (have sugar added). It must come from one of the 11 specific growing regions of Germany, and the name of the region must be on the label.

QmP "Qualitätswein mit Prädikat" which translates from German to quality wine with distinction. Almost always abbreviated in the US, and on the wine label. A legal designation under the German wine laws of 1971. As well as this phrase the label must identify the wine as belonging to one of these six classés from driest to sweetest: Kabinett, Spätlese, Auslese, Beerenauslese, Eiswein or Trokenbeeranauslese (see each listed individually). The rules for QmP are similar to those of QbA, except that the wine may not be chaptalized (have sugar added). These are the highest quality wines made in Germany.

Quarts de Chaume *(cahr duh show'm)* A Grand Cru vineyard in the Coteaux du Layon district of the Loire, France. This is a sweet Chenin Blanc white wine that ages very well. It is very rare, and it is one of my favorite wines.

Quinta *(keen'-tah)* The Portugese term for a vineyard estate. Similar to "château" in Bordeaux, France.

R

Racking An important step in wine making. The transfer of the young wine from one barrel, where it has thrown some sediment, to a new barrel, leaving behind the sediment. Not only does this help to clarify the wine, it is an opportunity for the wine to come into contact with air. A certain amount of oxygen is required at this stage of a wine's development, in order to produce necessary aromas (secondary aromas). Racking must be conducted carefully, as too much oxygen will be more harmful than beneficial for the wine. Heavy red wines may be racked three or four times. Lighter reds and whites may only be racked once or twice.

Rainwater Once a trademark for a particular Madeira, it is now a generic term for a lighter, not too sweet, style.

Rancio In an odd twist of wine jargon, this term, which literally means "rancid" in Spanish is used to describe the browning effect, and nutty taste that wines take on when purposefully exposed to air during aging. It is not considered a negative trait in these wines. Madeira is one such wine, and it has lent its name to the term "maderized' which has a similar meaning, but is used with a negative connotation for wines that were not meant to be oxidized. Common sense would dictate that these two terms are reversed, and yet, this is how they are used. Tawny Port, Marsala and Banyuls are all wines that could be described as rancio.

Ratafia *(rah-tah-fee'-ah)* Any of several aperitifs made by adding brandy to unfermented grape juice. The best known example may be the Pineau de Charentes of the Cognac region, although Ratafias are found in the Champagne and Burgundy regions of France as well. The name is said to come from the tradition of toasting the ratification of a new treaty with such a concoction.

Rebe *(reh'-buh)* The German word for vine. Hence the name of the grape Sheurebe which was created by a man named Sheu.

Récolte *(reh-colt)* The French word for "harvest," or "harvesting." A similar word seen on some French wine labels is "récoltant" which refers to the fact that the wine maker has harvested their own grapes, and as such the wine is estate bottled.

Rehoboam *(ree-o-boa-em)* An oversized bottle (4 1/2 liters) that holds six regular bottles of wine.

Rémuage *(rem-you-ah'j)* The French term for "riddling." The practice of turning and inverting bottles of sparkling wine, made in the champagne method, over a period of a week or more, until the sediment has all collected in the neck of the bottle, for easy removal.

Reserva *(reh-zehr'-vah)* A Spanish term that is regulated by law to mean a red wine that has been aged for at least three years before release, at least one of which must have been in a barrel. For rosé and white wines it is two years before release and six months in wood.

Reserve In the US, the term reserve has no legal meaning. It implies that the wine is from the better part of the production; however, it is often used on the label of very cheap wines that have not been reserved from anything. Since this term has meaning in Spain and Italy, it is confusing for the consumer.

Retsina *(ret-see'-nah)* For millennia the Greeks have added pitch (pine resin) to their wine to help preserve it from bacterial spoilage. While this seems odd in a time of high technology, it was the technology of the time. Retsina is the direct decedent of these wines, and is still flavored with pitch to this day. The white or rosé wines are an acquired taste, but are quite popular among those who grow up with the flavor. For the rest of us, well, it is an acquired taste.

Rhein *(rine)* The German spelling for the Rhine River.

Rheingau *(rine'-gaoh)* Historically one of the highest quality German wine producing regions. The Rhine River flows primarily northwest through Germany, except for here, where it takes a southwest course for about 20 miles. It is the direction of the river that allows the vineyards to have a south facing view, critical for ripening the grapes in this cold growing region. Here you will find Johannsberg, a region that for the US is literally synonymous with Riesling. The influx of faster maturing and easier to grow grapes has not reached this part of Germany, as it has in so much of the country. Instead, Riesling continues to be the primary grape of the region, which in no small way helps to define the quality of the wines. Critics charge that the wines of the region have been declining in quality as producers rush to meet the demand for their wines. In 2000 the German government made a stab at correcting the problem by assigning a new vineyard classification system, not unlike that used in the Burgundy region of France. Critics now point out that the system is less than effective as it gave 33% of the vineyards the superior rating (as compared to Burgundy where 3% of the vineyards are Grand Cru and 11% Premiers Cru).

Rheinhessen *(rine-hess'-en)* The largest of Germany's wine regions. You will find very little Riesling here, with the wines being made primarily of Müller-Thurgau and/or Sylvaner. As with so many large growing regions around the world, the emphasis here is on quantity over quality.

Rheinpfalz *(rine'-fal'tz)* One of the Anbaugebiete (specified wine regions) of Germany, and the most up and coming. Also referred to simply as the Pfalz, and sometimes known in English speaking circles as the "Palatinate." Stretching for 50 miles, just north of Alsace from the French-German border, the Phalz produces red and white wines of distinction. Pinot Noir, known as Spatburgunder in German, is the red wine grape of the region, where it produces a very light styled wine. Riesling is king here, but Müller-Thurgau is a close second, with a variety of other grapes constituting 60% of the vine-yards. While the second largest German region by size, it may be the largest by volume of wine produced. The words Phalz and Palatinate both derive from the Latin palatium, meaning palace. The Roman emperors constructed their imperial residences on a hill in the region 2000 years ago, and the name still sticks.

Rhine Wine It would seem obvious that this phrase relates to those wines made in the Rhine Valley of Germany; however, in a never ending attempt to confuse consumers and to belittle the place names of Europe, under US law a Rhine Wine can be any white wine with less than 14% alcohol.

Rhône *(rone)* One of the largest rivers in western Europe, its valley is the home to one of the most important wine regions of France. In the northern end of the French Rhône Valley we find Côte-Rôtie and its intense Syrah based wines. Just a stones throw south, the white grape Viognier is at home in the town of Condrieu. Hermitage is further south, and further south still is Châteauneuf-de-Pape with its 13 allowable grape varieties. France is not the only country that the Rhône flows through, or the only one to make wines in its valleys. The Swiss too count the Rhône as their own, and produce wines all along its banks.

Ribera del Duero *(ree-bair'ah del doo-eh-roh)* While this wine region in Spain is not well known among many wine lovers, it is the home of two of Spain's greatest producers, Vega Sicilia and the Alejandro Fernandex, maker of Pasquera. The region is in the north of Spain at 2600 feet, along the Duero River, the same river that will become the Douro in Portugal on who's banks the grapes for Port are grown. The red wine grape here is the Tempranillo, which is also responsible for the high quality of Spain's most famous red wine, Rioja. Tempranillo is known locally as Tinta del Pais.

The incredible quality of Vega Sicilia has in the last few decades prompted more producers and consumers to pay attention to this high altitude treasure.

Rice Wine Made throughout Asia, and best known as the Japanese Saké, this is not a wine at all. The first criteria for wine, both legally and from the point of view of quality, is to be made from grapes. This is not to say that a wonderful beverage cannot be made from rice, it simply should not be called wine.

Richebourg *(reesh-boor)* A Grand Cru red wine vineyard in the commune of Vosne-Romanée, in Burgundy, France. Even among its peers of Grand Cru vineyards, this is one of the best known.

Riddling One of the steps to making sparkling wine in the champagne method. The practice of turning and inverting bottles over a period of a week or more, until the sediment has all collected in the neck of the bottle, this allows the sediment to be easily removed. Known in French as "rémuage." Once done exclusively by hand, it is now largely done by machine.

Riesling *(rees-ling)* One of the greatest white wine grapes. Found originally in Germany, and still the most important quality grape there, it has now made its way around the world. Riesling makes wines that are fruity, but well balanced with acidity. This makes for long lived white wines, and some of the best sweet wines in the world.

Rioja *(ree-oh-ha)* One of the best known wine production regions in Spain. Red wines are made from Tempranillo and Grenacha (the Grenache of France). Whites are primarily made from Viura. The region is proud of its heritage, which dates back to the 19th century when groups of wine makers from the Bordeaux region of France settled here, trying to escape phylloxera. The insect finally made its way south of the border to Spain, but not before the Bordelais had made their mark. Because of the hot weather the wines can suffer from being baked before and during vinification. This led to inconsistent quality, and damaged the reputation of the region. Enter modern wine making techniques, along with temperature controlled vats, and Rioja is undergoing a renaissance of sorts. This is doubly true for the white wines which were once brown and maderized, but are now fresh and fruity.

Riperia The most common species of native North American grape vine. Because it is highly resistant to phylloxera, it is often used to create new crosses of root stock.

Riserva *(ree-zair-vah)* In Italian wine laws this term can only be used for wines that have been aged for a period before release. The length of time varies by region. It is three years for Chianti Riserva, but five for Barolo or Brunello Riserva. Unlike the similar Spanish term, Italian wines do not necessarily have to be aged in barrel to qualify for Riserva.

Rivesaltes *(reev-sahlt)* A town just north of the French-Spanish border that has lent its name to a variety of fortified dessert wines from the region. Some are sold as "Muscat de Rivesaltes" and are made from that grape. Others are simply sold as "Rivesaltes" and may be made from the grape Grenache, in a semi successful imitation of Banyuls.

Rkatsiteli *(ruh-kat'-see-tel'-ee)* Practically unknown to wine lovers in the US, this may be the second most widely planted white wine grape in the world (after the equally unknown Airen of Spain). Almost exclusvely found in Russia and Bulgaria.

Robe *(roab)* A French wine tasting term. Usually translated to mean color, it seems to also refer to the overall appearance of a wine.

Robust A commonly used wine tasting term which belongs to the group of terms I would suggest you avoid. Anthropomorphic and vague, it seems to be used for a wine that is not showing any signs of fault, and is high in dry extract (rich and mouth filling). It is not clear if this term applies to or alludes to the amount of tannins in the wine. It is also not clear if it indicates quality or just the "weight" of the body of the wine.

Romanée, La *(roh-mah-nay)* A Grand Cru red wine vineyard from Vosne-Romanée in Burgundy, France. Incredibly small, even by Burgundy standards, this celebrated vineyard only produces enough grapes to make about 300 cases of wine a year. This is the true "smallest appellation in France" a accolade often mistakenly given to Château-Grillet in the Rhône.

Romanée-Conti *(roh-mah-nay cohn-tee)* A Grand Cru red wine vineyard from Vosne-Romanée in Burgundy, France. Considered by some to be the finest of the elite group of Grand Crus. With only 600 cases made in a good year it is one of the most collectable and expensive French wines. Completely owned (a monopole) by the Domain de Romanée-Conti (DRC).

Romanée-Saint-Vivant *(roh-mah-nay san vee-vahn)* A Grand Cru red wine vineyard from Vosne-Romanée in Burgundy, France. Adjacent to Romanée-Conti and Richbourg this vineyard is nearly as large as both of them combined. Perhaps it is its size, or the neighborhood it is in, but this vineyard is rarely accorded the attention of the other vineyards of Vosne-Romanée. A total of approximately 2,500 cases are produced each year.

Rosé *(ro-zay)* The French word for pink and the wines that are close to that color. Rosé wines suffer from an image problem. It may be that white wine and red wine drinkers feel that rosé does not fit either niche, rather than being a bridge between them. It may also be that the sweet and simple rosé wines from the 60s and 70s made people think that all rosé wines are uninspiring. Certainly the "white zinfandel" and blush wines made in the US haven't helped the reputation any (even if they are rarely called rosé wines). In fact there are dry rosés such as the famed Tavel and Lirac of the Rhône Valley in France that deserve more recognition. Served well chilled, these wines are great for hot summer days or picnics where a heavier red or white wine would simply be too much. Many regions of the world produce rosé wines, and many of them are best enjoyed locally. Certainly there are many rosé wines that are easy to dismiss, but it is a shame to dismiss the entire class out of hand. Technically these wines are also known as Blanc de Noirs (white from black) or Vin Gris (grey wines).

Roses Many a traveler has photos of roses planted at the end of a row of vines. The usual explanation is that these flowers are decorative and traditional. The truth is that roses are the canary of the wine world. Roses are very susceptible to oidium (powdery mildew) and when they exhibit signs of this fungus, the grapes are sprayed to stave off infestation.

Rosso *(ross'-oh)* Italian for red and used as part of the name for some red Italian wines.

Rosso di Montalcino *(ross-oh dee mon-tahl-t'chee'-noh)* The lighter version of the Italian wine Brunello di Montalcino, made from the same grapes, in the same vineyards, but without oak (or in fact any) aging.

Rotten Egg The odor of hydrogen sulfide (the additive to household gas that allows you to smell it escaping). Rare in wine, and most unfortunate when it occurs. Almost always attributed to poor handling of grapes and the wine during production.

Rotwein *(rot-vine)* The German term for red wine.

Rouge *(rooj)* French for red. Red wine would be vin rouge.

Rouge Valley The southernmost wine growing region in the State of Oregon.

Rough A wine tasting term for a wine that is astringent, and tannic out of balance. Mostly a term for young wines. Rough wines rarely soften enough with age to be really enjoyable. By the time the roughness has gone, so has all of the fruit.

Round A wine tasting term applied to a wine that is well balanced. Often used as in "a well rounded wine."

Roussanne *(roo-sahn)* A white wine grape from the Rhône Valley in France. It has been amost completely replaced by Marsanne in the region. It is still occasionally used in a blend with the richer Marsanne, where it adds a subtle complexity to the wine.

Roussillon *(roo-see-yawn)* The wine region just north of the Spanish border around the city of Perpignan. Even though the region is lumped together to form Languedoc-Roussillon, it has a very distinct character of its own. The people of the region consider themselves to be Catalans, an ethnic identity that extends south of the border as far as Barcelona in Spain. This is the home of the fortified wines Rivesaltes and the rare and incredible Banyuls. A great deal of simple table wine is also made here, most of it using Cinsault as the base, along with Grenache and even Syrah and Mouvedre in the blend.

Ruby Cabernet An American cross between the Cabernet Sauvignon and Cinsault grapes. It was supposed to be a commercial alternative to the slow ripening Cabernet when it was created at UC Davis back in 1948, but it turned out to be rather disappointing. Very little of this grape is still planted in California, and what remains has been relegated to making bulk wines in the Central Valley.

Ruby Port A wood port, meaning it has aged in a barrel for some time, usually three years. The term Ruby Port is rarely used anymore, and when it is, it may mean a blend of red and white ports served as an aperitif in the cafés of Europe.

Ruchottes-Chambertin *(roo-shot sham-bair-tan)* A Grand Cru red wine vineyard from Gevery-Chambertin in the Burgundy region of France. At eight acres, it is not the smallest Grand Cru vineyards, but it may be one of the least known. About 1,000 cases of wine produced a year.

Rüdesheim *(roo-dess-heim)* A small wine producing town in the Rheingau region of Germany. The Rieslings from the area are popular with tourists who flock to the picturesque town, which in turn goes out of its way to accommodate the throngs.

Ruländer *(roo-lahn-der)* The German name for the Pinot Gris grape.

Rully *(ro-lee)* A small red and white wine producing town in Burgundy, France.

Ruwer (roo-ver´) A tributary of the Moselle River, and part of the Mosel-Saar-Ruwer region. Little wine is produced here, although it can be of very high quality, and the river is not much more than a stream.

S

Saale-Unstrut *(zahl' oon-shtrut)* A tiny, and northerly German wine region. In what was once considered East Germany, this region produces dry white wines near the city of Leipzig.

Saar *(sahr)* A tributary of the Moselle River, and part of the Mosel-Saar-Ruwer region. The region is so cold that the Riesling grape only gets ripe enough to make fine wines a few years out of a decade. The rest of the time the wines go to make Sekt, the German sparkling wine, which like all sparkling wines starts with an acidic base. As with all cold growing regions, the emphasis here is on ripening and finding a southern exposure for the grapes. Since the Saar runs north through the wine producing area, its banks are not lined with vineyards, as are so many other German rivers. Instead it is the side valleys, with their south facing slopes that are home to the vines. The wines in a great year are unsurpassed, and unforgettable. It is this potential alone that keeps this region under vine.

Saar-Ruwer *(sahr-roover)* A Bereich (group of villages and vineyards) in the Mosel-Saar-Ruwer region.

Saccharomyces *(sac'eh-ro-mi'sez)* The genus of yeast responsible for the primary (sugar) fermentation in wine. They turn the grape sugars into alcohol, carbon dioxide, and heat.

Sachsen *(zahkh'-zuhn)* The smallest of the German wine regions. It is centered around the city of Dresden in what was once East Germany. The region produces dry white wines.

Saint-Aubin *(san't-oh'ban)* A tiny wine producing village in the Côte de Beaune region of Burgundy, France. Just northwest of Chassagne-Montrachet and Puligny-Montrachet, Saint-Aubin produces primarily red wine that tends to be of a lighter style.

Saint-Emilion *(san't eh-mee-l'yon)* One of the principal wine producing towns and regions in Bordeaux, France. The wines here tend to be based on Merlot with Cabernet Franc as Cabernet Sauvignon does not ripen well in the cool clay soil. The town itself is charming, and a favorite tourist destination. Ancient cellars (the French term being cave) carved out of the limestone honeycomb the area. Saint-Emilion has been classified several times, in 1955, 1969, 1985 and as recently as 1996. This allows properties to be elevated, or even demoted, in sharp contrast to the neighboring Haut-Médoc which still relies on its 1855 classification. Wines may be Premiers Grands Crus Classés (first great growth class), or Grands Crus Classés or simply Grand Cru. The top designation is further devided into A and B to allow the exemplarily producers, Ch. Ausone and Ch. Cheval-Blanc to be recognized as being better than even the best. Various outlying villages, the "satellite towns" append their name to Saint-Emilion on their labels. These wines tend to have a higher concentration of Cabernet Franc and be lighter that the Grand Cru Saint-Emilion wines. There is a growing trend of modernization and individuality in the region, especially among the unclassified producers. This has drawn attention and critical acclaim to wines that heretofore have been largely ignored.

Saint-Estèphe *(san't ess-teff)* A wine producing village in the Haut-Médoc region of Bordeaux, France. As it is situated at the northern extreme of the Haut-Médoc, the wines from here tend to be more tannic, longer lived and less subtle than others in the region. Cabernet Sauvignon is the chief grape in the wines, followed by Merlot and Cabernet Franc.

Saint-Joseph *(san jo-sef)* An appellation in the northern Rhône Valley in France. It produces red wines from Syrah and a small amount of whites from Marsanne.

Saint-Julien *(san joo-l'yan)* A wine producing commune in the middle of the Haut-Médoc region of Bordeaux, France. Some consider this the sweet spot of the Haut-Médoc. It produces wines that are not as hard as Saint-Estèphe, nor as soft as Margaux. While no First Growth properties were classified here in 1855, it has a wealth of producers considered better than their class.

Saint-Péray *(san peh-ray)* A white wine producing village in the northern Rhône Valley of France. This is also the home of a well respected sparkling wine made in the champagne method. The wines, whether still or sparkling, are made from the Marsanne and Roussanne grapes.

Saké *(sah-kee')* A Japanese rice based alcoholic beverage often erroneously called rice wine.

Salmanazar *(sahl-man'-a-zar)* An oversized wine bottle (9 liters) that holds 12 regular bottles.

Sampigny-les-Maranges *(sahm-pee-n'yee leh mah-rahnj)* A red wine producing village at the southern end of the Côte de Beaune in Burgundy, France. The wines are sold under the name Côte de Beaune-Villages.

San Luis Obispo A California wine region that is south of Paso Robles (although technically part of Paso Robles is in San Luis Obispo County) and continues south to Santa Barbara County. This is a wide and general area that has many types of wine, and producers of varying quality. Since the cost of land in Napa and Sonoma Counties has surpassed the budget of many would be grape growers, San Luis Obispo has been growing at an amazing rate.

Sancerre *(sahn-sair)* A wine producing village in the Loire valley of France. The crisp Sauvignon Blancs produced here and in the neighboring Pouilly-Fumé are the bench marks for this white wine grape.

Sangiovese *(san-joh-vay'z eh)* One of the most important red wine grapes of Italy. Found primarily in the Tuscany region of central Italy. There are several distinct clones of this grape, each of varying quality. The Brunello clone is responsible for the wine of the same name, and is of the highest quality. Other clones are responsible for the wines of Chianti, Vino Nobile di Montepulciano and Carmignano. Critics point to the ideal vineyard conditions of some Chianti producers, whose wines do not live up to the potential of the vineyard, as an example of how important clonal selection can be.

Sangria *(sahn-gree'-ah)* An iced red wine and fruit mixture from Spain. The concept of adding fruit and/or sweetening agents to wine is of ancient origin. Originally used to hide the fact that the wine has gone bad, today it is a delightfully cool drink for a hot day. Similar products (e.g. wine coolers) make the rounds every generation in the US, but it can not compare to the carefully crafted Sangria of Spain. One of the secret ingredients in my personal recipe is the addition of Spanish brandy, which is slightly sweet.

Santa Barbara Directly south of San Luis Obispo in California, the city and county of Santa Barbara is a hidden jewel. Two of the main growing regions in Santa Barbara County are the Santa Maria and Santa Ynez valleys. Both of these valleys directly face the ocean, capturing the breezes that make these some of the coolest growing regions in California. For this reason Pinot Noir, and Chardonnay have done very well here. Syrah from the region has also been impressive and Viognier and Riesling, more lovers of cool climates, thrive here as well.

Santa Cruz Mountains Just South of the Bay and overlooking the famed Silicon Valley of San Jose, the Santa Cruz Mountains are home to a few hearty wine makers who's names are near and dear to all California wine lovers. One of California's longest lived and most respected Cabernet Sauvignon comes from here. The intensity of this cab is due in no small measure to the infertile soils of the region.

Santa Maria Valley One of the coolest growing regions in California, this valley is located in Santa Barbara County, far to the south of the better known Napa and Sonoma Valleys. California is warm, and it can be too warm for quality grape growing in many regions. Generally, the further south in California you go, the warmer it gets. Santa Maria Valley is efficiently cooled by the ocean breezes making it ideal for the cool loving Pinot Noir and Chardonnay grapes.

Santa Ynez Valley The charming Danish town of Solvang used to be the main attraction to this valley. Located in Santa Barbara County, California. Tourist now are just as likely to come for wine tasting. The cool ocean breezes keep this valley temperate enough to grow world class Pinot Noir, Chardonnay and Syrah. The wineries here are not as numerous as those way to the north in Napa, and the tourist are not anywhere near as common. For those who intrepidly explore, either in person or by popping a cork, this is a region not to miss.

Santenay *(sahn-t'nay)* One of the better red wine producing villages of the Côte de Beaune in Burgundy, France. Located at the southern tip of the Côte d'Or the wines tend to be softer than those from the Côte de Nuits in the north, but well balanced and well priced.

Sardinia *(sar-din'-ia)* A large island off the coast of Italy. For generations the wines here were coarse reds, or almost "sherry-like" whites. Modern wine making has allowed the producers of this area to discover an entirely new direction, with lighter, fresher tastes.

Sassicaia *(sah-see-cah'-yah)* A Cabernet Sauvignon based red wine from the coast of the Tuscany region in Italy. The wine is very consciously based on the wines of the Haut-Médoc in Bordeaux, France, and indeed even the grape cuttings originate from there. This wine forever changed the landscape of Italian wines. Even though it had no official classification, it was one of the most expensive and critically acclaimed wines of Italy. It was at the forefront of a class of wines that have been called "Super Tuscans" each based on Cabernet Sauvignon, even though, at the time, Cab was not an allowed grape anywhere in the Tuscany region. Because of the great popularity of these wines a new DOC designation was created in the region of Bolgheri for these wines, and a DOC Bolgheri Sassicaia was created for this wine alone. This wine has become so popular, that counterfeiting has recently become a problem.

Saumur *(saw-muhr)* A wine producing area in the Loire Valley of France. Most of the wine here is sparkling, and based on the Chenin Blanc grape and the red wine grape Cabernet Franc (in Champagne they also use a white wine and red wine grape, Chardonnay and Pinot Noir). Still versions of the red, rosé and white wines are also produced.

Sauternes *(saw-tairn)* The dessert wine from the district of the same name in Bordeaux, France. Made from the Sémillon grape, with varying amounts of Sauvignon Blanc, and occasionally Muscadelle, the wine is the product of the botrytis mold, which concentrates the sugars in the already over-ripe grapes. The intensely sweet grapes have too much sugar to be completely converted to alcohol, and the result is a wine with 14% alcohol and about 5% residual sugar. This gives Sauternes a sweet tart flavor that is ideal not only after a meal, but with rich foods such as foie gras (one of the greatest food and wine pairings). While it is now rare except as cooking wine, American producers have been known to use the name of the region for their own dry wines, usually without the final "s", as in Sauterne.

Sauvignon Blanc *(so-vee-n'yohn blahn)* A white wine grape planted around the world. In France it is found in Bordeaux, where it is usually blended with Sémillon to make a rich styled wine, but with very little varietal character. The Loire Valley of France is home to the villages of Sancerre and Pouilly-Fumé which may produce the truest expression of this grape. California versions are sometimes called Fumé Blanc, a relic of a marketing ploy that popularized the grape, but confused the consumer since there is no clear cut difference between wines labeled Sauvignon Blanc and Fumé Blanc. New Zealand is another bastion of Sauvignon Blanc. The distinct "freshly cut grass" aroma of Sauvignon Blanc can range from barely noticeable to overwhelming.

Savennières *(sah-ven-yair)* A village located in the Anjou region of the Loire Valley in France. Like most of the region the wines here are white and made from Chenin Blanc. Unlike the rest of the region these wines are always dry.

Savigny-les-Beaune *(sah-vee-n'yee leh bone)* A small but prolific red wine producing village in the northern end of the Côte de Beaune in Burgundy, France. The wines are light, well priced and of good quality

Savoie *(sah-v'wah)* A wine producing district on the easternmost edge of France. Most of the wines are dry, crisp white wines, that do not travel well.

Scheurebe *(shoy'-reh-buh)* A German white wine grape made by crossing Sylvaner and Riesling in 1916 by George Scheu (rebe means vine in German). The grape is lower in acid than the traditional German wine grape Riesling, but it is more susceptible to botrytis (the special mold that concentrates the sugar in the grape). This allows for dessert style wines that are easier and more profitable to make, but without the longevity of a wine made from Riesling.

Schloss *(sh'loss)* The German word for castle. Often used in the same way the French use chateau, to mean the vineyard, the wine and the property.

Schloss Johannisberg *(sh'loss yo-hah'-niss bairg)* The most famous vineyard in Germany, and one of the few that does not need to have its village name appear on the label along with the name of the vineyard. Situated in the Rheingau region this may be the oldest Riesling vineyard in the area.

Schloss Vollrads *(sh'loss vuhl-rahd'z)* The largest vineyard in the Rheingau region of Germany. This is one of the few vineyards that does not need to list the name of the adjoining village on the label. Famous for its drier styled wines, critics charge that this vineyard has not been living up to its potential of late.

Sec *(sek)* The French term for dry (meaning a wine without any residual sugar). The exception is Champagne. No one wanted to admit to drinking sweet wines, so sec is a term that was adopted for the sweetest style of Champagne. This is why "extra dry" is use for the slightly sweet style, and brut (meaning "raw, rough or unrefined") had to be used for the driest style.

Secco *(seck'-oh)* The Italian term for dry (meaning a wine without any residual sugar).

Sediment In a young wine still being made, the sediment is the remnants of the wine making process itself. These tiny particles drop to the bottom of the barrel or tank, and the wine is then racked - moved to a fresh tank or barrel - and the sediment left behind. If the wine is not perfectly clear when bottled, rare in modern winemaking, the particles are called haze or clouds rather than sediment. In a wine that has been bottled, sediment is the collective solids that form at the bottom of the bottle over time. This is made up of the tannins and coloring agents (phenolic compounds) that have precipitated out of solution. This is why a wine becomes lighter in color, and less tannic as it ages. Wine is decanted when it has sediment so that the clear wine can be enjoyed, and the sediment thrown away. Sparkling wine made in the champagne method has its own form of sediment. This forms after the yeast have created the bubbles in the wine during a secondary fermentation. The process of riddling and degorging is used to remove the sediment. On the bottom of a cork or in white wines there can be another form of sediment. This comes from the harmless crystals of potassium bitartrate (cream of tartar in the spice section of the grocery store) which precipitate out of the wine when the temperature is dropped. Because these crystals are sometimes mistaken for sugar, or even glass, most white wines are cold stabilized to allow this crystal to be removed before bottling. A commonly used expression is to say that a wine has "thrown sediment", meaning that sediment has accumulated.

Sekt *(zekt)* The German term for sparkling wine. About 25 million cases of Sekt are produced in Germany each year.

Sélection de Grains Nobles *(selek-shawn duh grahn no-b'l)* The sweet wines of Alsace, France. Most have been affected with botrytis (a special mold that concentrates the sugars in the grape). Alsatian wines are usually dry, and these are the notable, and rare, exceptions.

Sémillon A white wine grape, found primarily in the Bordeaux region of France. Often has Sauvignon Blanc blended with it to add acidity. This duo is responsible for the dry wines of the area as well as the dessert wines of Sauternes. Sémillon is also found in the New World, especially parts of Australia where it is still a popular white wine grape.

Sercial *(sair-s'yahl)* The driest style of Madeira.

Setúbal *(shtoo'-bahl)* A fortified Muscat wine from Portugal. It is made in the rancio style, meaning that it is brown like a Sherry or Tawny Port. This type of wine is made in many parts of the world, but Setubal is one of the very finest, and worth looking for.

Sèvre-et-Main *(sev'r eh meh'n)* A wine region in the far western corner of the Loire Valley, where the river meets the Atlantic Ocean. A dry white wine is made here from the Muscadet grape, and goes by the original name Muscadet Sèvre-et-Main.

Seyval Blanc *(say-val blahn)* One of the most successful of the French Hybrids (crossings of North American native grapes and classic European grapes). Interestingly enough this is a popular grape in England where the conditions for growing wine grapes are poor, even if the desire is high. The Canadians have made amazing ice wines from this variety, and it continues to have a following in New York and elsewhere.

Sharp A wine tasting term used when the acid in a wine is out of balance or strong. It would fall between "tart" and "sour" on a scale of perceived acidity.

Sherry *(share-ee)* A fortified wine made in the Sherry district in southern Spain around the city of Jerez de la Frontera. The wine is made primarily from the grape Palomino. The grapes are brought into the winery and pressed. The first pressed juice (that of the highest quality) is reserved to make the "Fino" styles. The remaining "press wine" will be used for the "Olorosos" style. The wine is vinified in the traditional manner, until dry. That wine which is to become Fino is placed into a partially filled barrel, so that the special yeast called "flor" can develop. The Olorosos wine is placed in completely filled barrels and fortified to 18% alcohol to prevent spoilage or the accidental introduction of flor. Once the Fino wine has developed flor, it is first fortified (to 17%) to prevent the further growth of flor and then allowed to continue to age, and oxidize, developing a rich dark brown color and nutty flavor. If the bodega (warehouse) is near the ocean town of Sanlucar de Barrameda, the fino will be allowed to develop into the very dry Manzanilla style. Some claim to be able to taste the salt of the ocean breezes in this wine. This is where the Solera system comes into play. Six or more barrels are stacked up. Each of the barrels contains wine of different ages, in different proportions. Wine is drawn from the oldest barrel, and replaced with the next oldest, and so on. The theory is that in this way you "train" the younger wines. The final solera barrel may contain a fraction of wine that is fifty years old or even more. The Sherry that is brought to market is a blend of the wine from these barrels. Sherry, like Champagne, is sweetened just before bottling to determine its final style. The sweetening agent is often concentrated grape juice from the Pedro Ximenez grape (PX is also increasingly being used on its own to make very sweet styled Sherrys). A final fortification is also performed before bottling to bring the final product up to 19% alcohol. The Olorosso style Sherry that did not benefit from the introduction of the flor yeast is usually sweetened heavily and ends up as Cream Sherry.

Shiraz *(shee-raz)* The Australian name for the grape Syrah. Most of the vines planted in Australia (where Shiraz is one of the most planted red wine grapes) can trace their ancestry back to France, via South Africa. This circuitous route means that the vines left France before the twin plagues of oidium and phylloxera of the last half of the 19th century. As France recovered from the devastation, new clones of old favorite grape varieties were often chosen to be replanted in the vineyards. That means the Syrah that ended up in Australia is from an older clone than is found in most of the Rhône Valley today. In this way Shiraz may be a distinct clone of the Syrah grape, and entitled to its own name.

Short One of the most important measures of quality in fine wine is how long the flavors stay in your mouth after swallowing or spitting. A short wine is one of poor quality, that does not linger.

Sicily *(sis-ill-ee)* This island is not only the largest in the Mediterranean, it is also one of Italy's largest producers of wine. Marsala has long been the best known wine of Sicily. The oxidized white wine, that so many know for cooking, typified the wines made here until only a few years ago. New plantings on cooler hillsides and modern techniques have allowed the new generation of Sicilian wine maker to produce lighter, fruitier wines.

Sick An old fashioned wine tasting term for a wine that is very faulty, such as being cloudy with an odd smell. This term is anthropomorphic, and implies that the wine can somehow become well again. It is best avoided.

Sierra Foothills Far to the east of the Pacific Ocean, further even than the great farming expanse of the Central Valley of California, the foothills of the Sierra Mountains begin to rise. Here, where gold was once found and miners clamored for refreshment, a wine industry sprang up in the 19th century. More than a century later, a growing number of wineries have made these foothills their home. Here the venerable Zinfandel vine was planted many generations ago, and now has matured to offer some of the most intense juice anyone has made wine from. Zinfandel reigns here, but new grape varieties are slowly being planted as the region expands.

Silky A wine tasting term for a specific mouth feel that is evident in the very finest of red wines. It is related to balance and is usually used when the wine is old enough for the tannins to have softened.

Simple A wine tasting term for a wine that has very little complexity. That is, it doesn't have a lot of different flavors. Most wines are simple to some degree, with only the greatest wines being complex.

Skin The outer layer of the grape, usually called hulls or husks in scientific circles. This is where most of the color comes from in red wines, and a great deal of the tannin. Many grapes have light colored pulp, and if were not left in contact with the skins would have very little color; this is how rosé wines are made. Different grape varieties have different skin characteristics. Some are thick with a fair amount of tannin, such as Cabernet Sauvignon, which yields dark, tannic wines. Others, such as Nebbiolo, have thin skins and even more tannin, yielding lighter colored wines that are heavy in their youth. Others still, such as Pinot Noir, have thin skins and low tannins, making for crisp, fruity wines that are more approachable when young.

Smooth A wine tasting term that refers to a tactile sensation in the mouth (mouth feel) associated with the acids, rather than the tannins in the wine (see soft). Technically a wine is smooth due to the presence of lactic acid, which in turn is present in the wine due to malo-lactic fermentation. This secondary fermentation turns the tart, "sharp" malic acid, found in green apples, into the "smooth" lactic acid found in milk. The opposite of smooth is sharp.

Soapy An off odor in some faulty wines. Technically, it may be due to fatty acids produced by the yeast that end up as salts in the wine, notably caprylic acid salts. The term soapy is also used for a wine that has very little acid in the balance. There is some debate on the use of the term, as flat seems to cover the meaning.

Soave *(s'wah'-veh)* The best known Italian white wine, it comes from the Verona region in the northeastern portion of the country. Made from the Garganega grape, with the ubiquitous Trebbiano sometimes used in the blend. Most Soave is uninspiring, made to fill the world wide demand for the name, with little regard to quality. There are exceptions among the smaller producers who struggle to provide a wine of interest for the discriminating consumer. Soave Classico comes from the smaller, more defined, and original, Soave region.

Soft A wine tasting term that refers to the lack of apparent tannins in a wine. If the wine is well aged, or in a style that is enjoyed young, soft is a plus. If the wine is meant to age, and is soft in its youth, it is a minus, as one would expect to find tannins to help the wine age.

Solera *(soh-leh'-rah)* A system of blending wines used primarily for Sherry and Madeira. Basically it is a way to add older wines to the new wine, in order to maintain a consistent style. As a small portion of the old wine is removed from the cask, it is replaced with an equal portion of new wine. The old wine is then added to the new wine. In this way the high quality of the older wine is thought to improve the quality of the younger wine, while the younger wine replenishes the cask of older wine. Some Sherry, and especially Madeira will be labeled with the word "solera" and a date. This is a marketing ploy. It simply means the year that the Solera was started, and the bottle may at best, contain trace amounts from that year.

Solid A rather vague, but commonly used wine tasting term. Usually used when the wine is showing no obvious flaws and is in balance. It is not clear if this is to be considered a compliment, or just a way of saying there is nothing wrong with the wine.

Sommelier *(so-mel-yay)* A rather formal name for a wine steward or wine waiter. There is a Master Sommelier designation for those that have passed a rigorous exam, although very few people selling wine in a restaurant have such training. It has been said that the term itself goes back to the days when wine was driven to market in cask on a mule train. The mule driver was the "sommelier" and since he also sold the wine, the name stuck. Beware of anyone who brandishes this title unless they are indeed a Master Sommelier.

Sonoma Valley / County The Russian River has carved a wide and fertile valley for this Northern California wine region. West of Napa, and closer to the ocean, Sonoma is a collection of micro-climates that range from hot and dry, to foggy and cool. Almost every type of wine grape known can be found somewhere in this sprawling region. Some of this may be due to the long tradition of grape growing in the region. In Sonoma, a near legendary figure named Haraszthy planted some of the earliest European grape varieties in California. Generations of immigrants and wine makers followed, giving the region a tradition of wine making that still permeates every nook and cranny of the valley.

Sophisticated A wine term that should almost certainly be avoided. Originally it was a euphemism that meant that the wine had not been tampered with to make it seem better. This meaning is largely forgotten, and was never well known outside of professional circles. It is more likely to be used now to mean a wine that is complex. When used in this way the term is anthropomorphic and vague. When used in the original context it is more specific, although few people will understand that it means unadulterated.

Sound A wine tasting term that means the wine is free of defects. It is the minimum expected of a wine, and therefore can not be construed as a compliment.

Sour A wine tasting term for a wine that has too much acidity in the balance. This is beyond tart, and usually means the wine has a serious defect, such as it is turning into vinegar (technically it has too much volatile acidity). This should be considered rare, and marks a wine that is not drinkable.

Spanna *(spah'-nah)* The local name for the Nebbiolo grape in the Piedmont region of Italy. Some wines from the region are also labeled and sold under this name.

Sparkling Wine That class of wines which has been carbonated. The highest quality versions are carbonated through the action of yeast in a sealed bottle. This is the champagne method, and all Champagne is made this way. Another method is to start in the bottle, but then transfer all the wine to a tank and filter out the sediment. This is known as the transfer method. Less expensive sparkling wines are made in a tank, with the yeast again adding the carbon dioxide. These wines are then bottled. The final method is to add carbon dioxide to the finished wine, much as you would for a soda pop, no quality sparkling wine is made in this method. Champagne is a method and a region in France. Sparkling wines should only be called Champagne when they come from that region in France. This is the law in Europe, but the US and Australia still allow domestic sparkling wines to be labeled with the Champagne name.

Spatburgunder *(sh'pat'-boor-gun-der)* The German name for the Pinot Noir grape. While Germany produces mostly white wine, the red it does make comes mostly from the Pinot Noir grape.

Spätlese *(sh'pay't-lay-zuh)* The German term for late picked" It is a QmP (quality wine without sugar added) designation. Most wines of this level are only slightly sweet.

Spice / Spicy A wine tasting term. Use carefully. Gewürztraminer (which means spicy traminer) is the only grape that you should use the unqualified term spice for (in reference to its aroma). For every other type of wine, it is important to specify what kind of spice you mean (after all there are many spices). Black pepper spice is common in red wines, and woody spices (such as clove and cinnamon (from aging in oak barrels) are found in some white wines.

Split The name for a quarter bottle of wine (.187 liters), especially Champagne.

Spritz The English language term for slightly sparkling. The French call it "pétillant," the Germans "spritzig" and the Italians use my favorite term "frizzante." Some wines, such as Moscato d'Asti are made to have very light carbonation. Other wines may have a small amount of dissolved carbon dioxide by accident. This term applies to both conditions.

Spritzer Usually white wine and soda water mixed together. The white wine spritzer is a common request in bars in the US. Wine purists often consider the combination to be contemptible, and yet it is a tradition many centuries old. In warmer regions it is still not uncommon to add some sparkling water to wine (even red wine) to make it more refreshing.

Spumante / Spumanti *(spoo-mahn'-teh / spoo-mahn'-tee)* Italian for sparkling. Most Italian sparkling wines are made with the transfer method, although a growing number of quality wines are being made in the champagne method (called metodo classico in Italian). Asti Spumante is one of the best known Italian sparklers, with Prosecco being another. Spumanti is the plural version of the word.

Stabilizing Any number of wine making procedures that make the wine more stable. The most common example is "cold stabilization" which is used to ensure that tartaric precipitants do not appear in white wine if it has been chilled and then warmed again. Filtering and fining are common examples of stabilization that are used to improve and maintain the clarity of wine. Pasteurization is sometimes (but not often) used to reduce the chance of bacterial spoilage, and/or to reduce the effect of shipping.

Steely A wine tasting term used primarily for very crisp, dry, white wines. The high acid balance of these wines can leave a metallic impression on the palate. Chablis, the great Chardonnay of the Burgundy region of France, is often said to be "steely." Flinty is another term that seems to have the same or similar meaning.

Steen The name for Chenin Blanc in South Africa, where it is a very commonly planted grape.

Stemmer A piece of wine making equipment used to remove the stems from the grape bunches before the grapes are pressed and fermented. The stems can leave a bitter flavor, and are rarely used in white wine. Some red wines benefit from the tannins that the stems impart, and so are added back in. Stemmer machines are often combined with a crusher and are known as "stemmer crushers."

Stemmy A wine tasting term for the flavor of stems in some wines. The taste is bitter and full of chlorophyll and so is sometimes also called "green." This should be considered a fault in wine, as it rarely improves the flavors.

Still Any wine that is not sparkling.

Stuck A wine making term. "Stuck fermentation" and "stuck wine" are the same thing. A wine sticks during fermentation when the yeast can no longer metabolize the sugar, or there are not enough viable yeast left to do the job. Heat and/or the lack of oxygen are the two most common reasons for a stuck fermentation. This is a very bad situation as it can be difficult, or even impossible, to get the fermentation restarted.

Sturdy A rather vague wine tasting term. It seems to be used for wines that are tannic, but not to a fault, and are otherwise well balanced.

Sugaring The practice of adding sugar (grape sugar ideally) to the unfermented grapes (must). This is done when the grapes are not ripe enough on their own to produce enough alcohol. Common for lesser quality wines in cool growing regions such as Germany, it is illegal in many other parts of the world. Another term is Chaptalization.

Sulfites / Sulfur A much maligned element of wine making. While it can be overused and ruin the flavor of the wine if not used carefully, it is an integral part of most wine making. Sulfur Dioxide, the gas form of sulfur, is sprayed on the vines to control fungus. Barrels are treated with sulfites (sulfur combined with another element, usually metallic) to kill unwanted bacteria. Sulfites are also added to the juice prior to fermentation to prevent browning and to control the yeast that come in from the fields with the grapes. It is also used to stop fermentation on some sweet wines, so that residual sugar can be left in the wine. Sulfur adds control to the wine making process, and those few wines that are made without it tend to be very poor. The amount of sulfur that can be in wine is controlled by law. Because the smell and taste of sulfur in wine can be ruinous, the sulfur is almost always very carefully applied and is used in amounts well below the legal limits and in amounts too small to cause health considerations for most people.

Sultana Another name used for Thompson Seedless grapes. Since making wine from this common grocery store variety of grapes has a deserved attached stigma, the name Sultana is much more common for wine. Common in Australia where it makes a great deal of sweet fortified wines (which is what it is best for). Thompson Seedless is the most planted grape in California, and while it is mostly used for raisins and table grapes, a huge amount is still used to make jug wines.

Supple A very common wine tasting term. As with many wine tasting terms, it is rather vague. It literally means "compliant or yielding." When applied to a wine it seems to mean a wine that is easy to drink without being too simple. The lack of tannins in the balance seems to be one of the primary requirements for a wine to be supple.

Sur Lie *(soo'r lee)* The French term for on the lees. Wines that have been aged in contact with these dead yeast cells gain some measure of complexity.

Swan District This is the original wine district in Western Australia. Just north of the city of Perth, this is a very warm region that seems best suited for the fortified dessert wines that are found here. As interest in producing wine in the Perth region grows, it is the cooler hillsides that are being cultivated, while the Swan District continues to fall out of favor.

Sweet There are four basic tastes: sweet, sour, bitter and salty (all other flavors are actually related to smell). Of these, only sweet is pleasant. In dry wine the alcohol adds a slight sweet taste to help balance the tannins and acids. Sweet being the opposite of dry in wine, sweet wines contain some amount of sugar. This can vary from a barely noticeable 1% up to an intense 10% or more. Since too sweet is the definition of "cloying" all decent sweet wines have a good deal of acidity (which is sour) to balance out the sugar. The best sweet wines are actually more "sweet-tart."

Sylvaner / Silvaner Historically one of the major white wine grape varieties of Germany. Not as long lived or as intense as the Riesling grape, Sylvaner is still popular in parts of Germany. The Müller-Thurgau grape has taken Sylvaner's place in much of the rest of Germany. Silvaner is the German spelling.

Syrah One of the great red wine grapes. At home in the Rhône valley of France, it has made its way to Australia where it is known as Shiraz as well as California where it is still known as Syrah.

T

T-Budding A vineyard management term. The root of a vine takes decades to grow and can be very extensive. If a vine is in place, but no longer a desirable varietal, for whatever reason, just the top can be replaced, and the roots left intact by a grafting process known as T-Budding. The old vine is removed just above the soil line. The new graft is inserted into a T shaped incision made into the remains of the old vine. The process is quick and successful.

Table Wine A US legal term that encompasses all wines that are between 7% and 14% alcohol. The term is used in Europe to mean a wine that was not made under the rules of any specific controlled area. Winemakers who are interested in pushing the boundaries of wine production in their area often can only bottle their wines as the local equivalent of table wine. Since some of these wines are of very high quality, and can command higher prices than the usual wines from the region. As such, it can be a very confusing term. Table Wine can be either: most wines (as in the US), a wine of lower quality or distinction, or a wine of distinction that does not conform to a standard.

Tafelwein *(tah'-fel-vine)* German for table wine.

Tank A large container for making or storing wine. Wood was a traditional material for centuries, but that was replaced by cement tanks which in turn have largely been replaced by stainless steel, with modern temperature controls. Some wine, such as Pinot Noir, can still benefit from the proper use of classic wooden, open topped tanks. Also called a vat.

Tannin Those compounds responsible for the bitter and astringent tastes in wine. They are found primarily in the skin and seeds of the grape, as well as stems (which are not always included in the wine making process). Because white wines have little to no contact with these parts of the grape, white wines have little tannin. Aging in oak barrels can also add (oak) tannin to wines. Tannin is required for aging red wine. Not all tannic red wines will age well, but few red wines without strong tannins will age well either. Technically the tannins are known collectively as "phenolic compounds."

Tar / Tarry Some wines have a dark flavor that wine tasters call tar. It is not the overwhelming stench of a tarred road, rather it is a flavor so dark, that only tar seems to fit. Rhône wines can have this, as well as the Barolos of Italy. If it is too pronounced it is not a positive thing.

Tart A wine tasting term for a wine that is noticeably acidic. As long as the acid is not overwhelming, it is only tart. A stronger acid flavor would be harsh and a very strong acid flavor would be sour. Dessert wines are often sweet/tart as the acid and residual sugars balance each other.

Tartar Tartaric acid is the main acid in wine. Some of it can crystalize in a chilled wine. Since the crystals are unsightly, and can cause concern for the consumer, some white wines in particular are cold stabilized to remove the crystals before the wine is released. The crystals are flavorless and harmless.

Tastevin *(tahst-van)* A flat, usually silver, cup that was once used to taste and evaluate wine. Since it is flat like a saucer, it is almost useless for smelling the wine. The bottom of the shiny container has a series of bumps, designed to shine light through the wine at various angles at once. In the dimly lit cellars, it was difficult to determine the clarity of the wines without this tool. Clarity is less of an issue than it used to be in wine, and glasses are much more effective, so the tastevin has mostly been relegated to novelty.

The exception is Burgundy, France where it is still traditional. Beware of a wine steward wearing one of these on a chain around their neck. Chances are this person is attempting to hide their lack of knowledge behind a façade of snobbery.

Tastevinage *(tahst-vee-nahj)* There is an organization in Burgundy, France, composed of wine lovers and professionals, called the Chevaliers du Tastevin. This group blind tastes a series of wines, and those considered worthy are given their seal of approval, the "Tastevinage." The label is elaborate and easy to spot, but the wines may or may not be of distinction.

Tavel *(tah-vel)* A dry rosé wine from the Rhône region of France. Produced primarily from the Grenache grape, many consider, along with its neighbor Lirac to be some of the most successful rosé wines made.

Tawny Port A Port that has been aged in a barrel instead of a bottle. The process allows the wine to take on a nutty aroma, and to lose its red color over time (turning a tawny brown). The best examples are usually labeled in decades, such as a 10-year-old, 20-year-old or 40-year-old. Inexpensive tawny ports may be a blend of red and white port, and do not resemble the real thing in any way. The US and Australia make fortified wines that they continue to label "port" and the tawny versions of some of these are a relative bargain.

Tears Another name for "legs." A much over used and meaningless wine tasting term. It refers to the streams that are seen on the side of the glass after swirling. While too many so called experts explain this as being related to the body, or the amount of glycerin in the wine, it is actually a function of the alcohol, and has no relation to the quality of the wine at all.

Terroir *(tair-wah'r)* While this literally means soil in French, it has many more implications. It may also be used to mean the surrounding weather patterns such as the English language term "microclimate." For some, the term may mean how typical the wine is of the region the "expression of terroir." Like many French wine tasting terms this one has been adopted by English speaking wine professionals, although it is no more easily defined when used in English. It is often used in conjunction with the French word for "taste" as in "goût de terroir."

Tête de Cuvée *(tet duh coo-vay)* Literally, French for head blend. The term is unofficial, but is often used to mean the top of the line from any Champagne house. For example Dom Pérignon is the tête du cuvée from Moët.

Thief A glass or metal tube used to extract wine from a barrel. The French call it a "pipette."

Thin A wine tasting term for any wine that has little flavor. Technically it is used for a wine that has little dry extract (what is left after you remove all the liquid).

Thompson Seedless The green grape found in the grocery store. It is often called a 3-way grape because it is used for table grapes, raisins and wine. The wine that is made from it tends to be without distinction. It is the base of many wines in the US that are called "chablis" (Chablis actually being a region in France). In Australia, where it is called Sultana, it is responsible for simple, but delicious fortified wines. Because it is a 3-way grape, Thompson Seedless is the most planted grape in California. French Colombard is the most planted wine grape, but some years more wine has been made from Thompson Seedless.

Tignanello *(tee-n'ya-nell'-oh)* An Italian wine made in the Chianti region by the well known Antinori firm. Since its inception in 1971, this wine has broken tradition with the Chianti region and produced a wine of character that does not follow the rules. The wine tends to be mostly Sangiovese, as is Chianti, but without the white wine in the blend that softens Chianti. The addition of Cabernet Sauvignon takes this wine even further from its Chianti roots.

Tokay d'Alsace *(toe-kay d'al-zass)* The local name for Pinot Gris in Alsace, France. Some Alsatian wines are bottled with the name Tokay. Do not confuse this with the Hungarian wine of the same name. There is no relation either to the grape or the wine. The EEC now stipulates that the name Pinot Gris must also appear on the bottle to help reduce confusion.

Tokay / Tokaji *(toe-kay)* The great white wine of Hungry, made from the Furmint grape. Tokaji Furmint is dry, and rare outside the region. Tokaji Szamorodni is a bit sweeter, but no less rare. Tokaji Aszu is the sweet version, and the one most likely to be found in the US. It is made slightly different than other dessert wines. Baskets of very ripe grapes, effected with botrytis (which reduces the amount of water in the grape, making it sweeter), are added to the base wine to sweeten it. The baskets are themselves known as puttonyos, and the label of the wine will indicate how many puttonyos have been added. Three is common for the drier styles, with five being used in the swetest. Six puttonyos wines exist, but are nearly legendary. There also exists an even more legendary wine, Essencia which is made entirely from the puttonyos grapes.

Tonneau *(tuh-noh)* A measure of wine in Bordeaux, France equivalent to 100 cases (1200 bottles). The term is not used much any more, as most wine makers simply talk about cases or bottles.

Topping The winery practice of replacing evaporated wine in the barrel. This "head space" is also called "ullage." This is an important step to reduce the oxidation of the wine, and to ensure quality.

Touraine *(too-rehn)* A wine producing region in the Loire Valley of France. The well known Vouvray is made in this region. More red and rosé is made here than elsewhere in the Loire, and it is primarily made from Gamay and Cabernet Franc. The white wines are based on Chenin Blanc and Sauvignon Blanc.

Transfer Method One of the more economical (and common) ways to make a sparkling wine. The wine is placed in a closed bottle, to allow yeast to make the bubbles, as in the champagne method, but then the bottles are opened, and all "transferred" into a tank to be blended. This blend is then filtered (as opposed to riddling in the champagne method) and rebottled. A key phrase on the bottle may be "fermented in the bottle" as opposed to "fermented in this bottle" which can only be said of wine made in the higher quality champagne method. Champagne from the Champagne region can not be made via the transfer method.

Treading This is the classic image of a group of people stomping on grapes. The technique (almost extinct now) was used to crush the grapes, to improve the color of the wine and to speed the start of fermentation, rather than to press the juice out of the grapes, as many people may think. It was particularly important for making Port, which is deeply colored, and benefited greatly from the technique. Some Port producers still hold to the tradition, but most opt for modern wine making techniques which yield similar results, with greater control.

Trebbiano *(treh-bee-ah'-noh)* The white wine grape responsible for more wine than any other (there are other varieties that have more plantings, but the yields are so high Trebbiano makes the most wine). Throughout Italy Trebbiano, seems to pop up in a vast majority of white wines. Often blended with grapes that have more character, Trebiano's main claim to fame is that it is easy to grow, and it yields more wine per vine than almost any other grape. The wines it makes tend to be thin, and boring. It is for exactly this reason that in France (where it is called Ugni-Blanc or Saint-Emilion) the grape is used as the base for Cognac, and Armagnac and other brandies. Trebbiano has spread to most major wine making regions of the world to the dismay of critics everywhere. Because of the huge number of names for this grape, some wine makers may not even know that they are using Trebbiano.

Trentino-Alto Adige *(tren-tee'-no ahl'-to ah'-dee-jay)* The northernmost of Italy's wine producing regions. A large amount of red wine is made here as well as whites, and even sparkling wines. This is a huge region with a great many wines and a great many grape varieties.

Troken *(traw'-ken)* The German word for dry. Legally it means a wine that has less than 1% residual sugar. The Germans have been experimenting more with drier wines, to give them more universal appeal, and to match more cuisines. Halbtroken, meaning half-dry has also become popular.

Trokenbeeranauslese *(traw'-ken-bear'-en-ouse'-lay-zuh)* The top German wine. Sweeter and more expensive than any other of the QmP class. The English language term would be "individual berry special select late harvest." The grapes must not only be late harvested, but they must be dried (troken) to an almost raisin state before picking. This intense dessert wine, which is usually abbreviated to TBA, is only made in very special vintages, often less than once a decade. It ages unbelievably well. I have tasted 40 year old examples that still seemed to be quite young.

Trotanoy, Château *(troh-tahn-wah)* One of the top producers in the Pomerol region of Bordeaux, France. Considered, unofficially since there is no official classification in Pomerol, to be second only to Ch. Pétrus. The 2,000 or so cases of this wine produced each year is made primarily from Merlot.

Tuscany *(tuss-can-ee)* A wine region in central Italy that extends from the city of Florence to the south. Some of the best known Italian wines come from this region. Notable are the Chianti wines, and Brunello di Montepulciano. The rising trend to create Cabernet Sauvignon based, or blended wines, has led to the unofficial designation "Super Tuscans" for these expensive and much sought after wines. Sangiovese (or Brunello as one of the clones is called) is the important red wine grape of the region. Malvasia is the important white for quality, and Trebbiano for quantity.

U

Ugni Blanc *(oo-n'yee blahn)* The French name (or at least one of the many French names) for the Trebbiano grape. In France this rather undistinguished grape (that is responsible for more wine than any other grape) is often used to make the base wine that will be distilled into brandy. Cognac and Armagnac are two well known brandy regions that use the grape.

Ullage *(oo-lehj)* The amount of air that results in a barrel or bottle due to evaporation. In the barrel the missing wine is replaced to keep the wine from becoming oxidized (topping). In theory the same could be done with old bottles of wine (this is called recorking). It is rare to see recorked bottles of wine, and if it is done, there needs to be a complete explanation of the process and a certificate from the company that performed the task. The amount of ullage in a bottle greatly influences the value of the wine at auction.

Umbria *(oom'-bree-ah)* The central Italian region that is home to the well known white wine Orvieto.

Umpqua Valley A wine region in western Oregon, just south of the Willamette Valley.

United States The history of wine making in the US starts as far back as the 16th century when missionaries planted grapes and made wine in what is now New Mexico. By the early 19th century commercial wine making ventures had begun in the eastern states, propelled by the interest of Thomas Jefferson and others. The eastern states proved to be too cool for quality wine making, and growers started to look further west for ideal climates. As the population moved west, so did the wine. The discovery of gold in California brought thousands of settlers. Some hoped to strike it rich by pulling wealth out of the ground, and others hoped that the way to riches lay in planting in the ground. Spain controlled California then, and it was the Spanish governor that commissioned Agoston Haraszthy to travel to Europe with the express intent of bringing back vine cuttings to jump start the wine industry. Spain and the gold are gone, but the vines remain. Throughout the state, anywhere the climate is cool enough to accommodate grapes, you will find vines planted. California is not the only place that wine is made in the US. The Pacific Northwest states of Oregon and Washington, as well as the eastern state of New York all have thriving wine industries. In fact, it may surprise many people to learn that most states have wineries, and vineyards. The US is far behind Europe in both production and consumption of wine, but thanks to research and modern techniques, many of which originated in the US, the quality of American wines rival that of the rest of the world.

Usé *(oo-zay)* A wine tasting term from the French for "worn out." A more common English language term is "over the hill."

V

Vacqueyras *(vah-kay-rahss)* A red wine producing town in the southern Rhône Valley in France.

Valais *(val-ay)* One of the most important wine producing regions of Switzerland. The red Dôle and the white Fendant wines are both from this region.

Valdepeñas *(val-deh-pay'-n'yahss)* A wine producing district in central Spain, known for its light reds.

Valençay *(vah-lahn-say)* A wine region in the Loire valley of France. Known for its simple wines.

Valle d'Aosta *(vah'-leh dah-aw'ss-tah)* The smallest wine producing region in Italy. Skiers know the area for the famed Courmayeur ski resort, which is just on the other side of Mount Blanc from France's famed ski town, Chamonix. The crisp, dry white wines of the region are enjoyed by skiers, but rarely seen elsewhere.

Valmur *(vahl-moor)* One of the Grand Cru vineyards of Chablis, in the Burgundy region of France. The wine is made from the Chardonnay grape, and is often cleaner and more crisp than other Chardonnay or even other white Burgundy.

Valpolicella *(vahl-poh-lee-t'chell-ah)* One of the best known red wines of Italy. The name which means valley of many cellars, is a testament to the region, north of Verona where it is made. When the vintage permits, a portion of the grapes are brought from the vineyard to be dried on straw mats. The sweet version of the wine, which is hard to find in the US is called Recioto della Valpolicella and the better known dry version is Recioto della Valpolicella Amarone, or simply Amarone.

Varietal Wine Any wine that takes its name from the predominant grape variety. This is very common in the US and the rest of the New World, but in Europe, wines are usually labeled with the place name. In the US there must be 75% of the named grape. Elsewhere the percentage varies, but is rarely, if ever, lower.

Vat Another name for a tank. A container for fermenting, storing and blending wine. Wood was a traditional material for centuries, but that was replaced by cement vats which in turn have largely been replaced by stainless steel, with modern temperature controls. Some wine, such as Pinot Noir, can still benefit from the proper use of classic wooden, open topped vats.

Vaucluse *(voh-clooze)* A French département (equivalent to a state) that encompasses the southern Rhône Valley.

Vaud *(voh'd)* The other major wine producing region of Switzerland (after the Valais). The white wine Aigle is one of the best known from the area.

Vaudésir *(voh-deh-zeer)* One of the Grand Cru vineyards of Chablis, in the Burgundy region of France. The wine is made from the Chardonnay grape, and this vineyard is often considered the finest among the Grand Crus of Chablis.

VDQS / Vins Délimités de Qualité Supérieure *(van deh-lee-mee-tay' duh cah-lee-tay' soo-pehr-yur')* the French designation for wines of superior quality, that do not quite make it to the top echelon status of Appellation Contrôlée. As with AC wines, those labeled VDQS must adhere to regional rules of production.

Vega Sicilia *(vay'-gah see-see'-l'yah)* A Spanish wine that is very famous, among a select few. The producer's top label, Vega Sicilia Unico, is often aged for decades before bottling, and sells for prices that rival the finest Bordeaux or Burgundies.

Vendage *(vahn-danj)* The French term for harvest or vintage. As with the Italian term "vendemmia" and the Spanish "vendima" vendage refers to the actual harvest, rather than the year (which is how vintage is commonly used in English). The French term for the year that appears on the label is "millésime."

Vendage Tardive *(vahn-danj tahr-deev)* French for late harvested. The term is used in the Alsace region where a tiny amount (sometimes less than 1%) of the grapes are picked late. While this practice results in a sweeter style wine elsewhere, the Alsatians ferment the wine until it is dry, producing instead a very rich, and intensely flavored wine.

Vendima *(ven-dee'-mee-ah)* The Spanish term for harvest or vintage. It refers to the actual harvest, rather than the year (which is how vintage is commonly used in English).

Veneto *(veh'-neh-toe)* A large Italian wine region that includes the cities of Venice and Verona. Nearly a fifth of all the DOC wines of Italy come from this region. Soave and Valpolicella are two of the best known wines that are produced here.

Veraison *(veh-ray-zohn)* A viticultural term originally from the French. Young grapes are tiny, hard and green. As they swell and ripen they take on the color they will be when they are harvested. Veraison is the point where the grapes just start to turn color.

Verdelho *(vair-day'-l-yoh)* Originally a white wine grape used to make a medium dry style of Madeira. Now the term is common, even if the grape is not often used.

Verdicchio *(vair-deek'-ee-oh)* An Italian white wine made from the grape of the same in the Marche region. There are several versions made, but the best known in the US comes in a curved bottle, reminiscent of the clay amphora that stored wine in ancient times.

Verduzzo *(vair-doot-soh)* An Italian white wine and grape. Many of the best examples are somewhat sweet.

Vermouth Some may be surprised to find out that this classic addition to a martini starts out as wine. In a technical sense a vermouth is any wine that has been infused with herbs or fruits. The Vermouth that.is well known today comes in either a white (dry) or red (sweet) version. The name vermouth comes from the German word wermut which means wormwood a common ingredient in Vermouth. Wormwood is incredibly bitter and has been used for medicinal purposes since the dawn of time.

Vernaccia di San Gimignano *(vair-nah'-t'chah dee san-d'jee-mee-n'yah'-noh)* A well known Italian dry white wine and grape. San Gimignano itself is a quaint tourist town, not far from Florence. It is famous for its towers, and visitors often come home with a taste for the local wine.

Vert *(vair)* French for green. A wine that is green will have the smell of vegetation and be highly acidic.

Vielle Vigne *(v'yay veen-yuh)* The French term for old vines. The concept is important because older vines yield more intense juice.

Vieux *(v'yuh)* The French word for old. Sometimes found in the name of the producer or vineyard. The feminine form of the word is "vielle."

Vigne *(veen-yuh)* The French word for vine. Related words are "cep de vigne" which refers to the actual grape vine and cépage which means grape variety.

Vigneron *(vee-n'yeh-rohn)* The French term for someone that works in a vineyard. It is also sometimes used in a more general sense for anyone who works anywhere in a winery. See also Viticulteur.

Vignoble *(vee-n'yohb'l)* The French term for a wine producing region. Can also be used for a single vineyard or estate.

Vila Nova de Gaia *(vee-lah no-vah deh gah'-yah)* The town in Portugal where all the Port "lodges" (warehouses) are located. It is across the Douro river from the city of Oporto, because of the danger of fire.

Vin *(van)* French for wine.

Vin Blanc *(van blahn)* French for white wine.

Vin Bourro *(van boo-rew)* The French term for a wine that has just been pressed. It is not uncommon for vineyard workers and others to consume this incredibly young wine. It is often still sweet, and full of carbon dioxide, since the wine is not altogether finished fermenting.

Vin de Paille *(van duh pah'y)* A wine made in the Jura region of France by first drying the grapes on straw mats. This is the French term, but the Italian Vin Santo is one of the best known examples of wines made in this style. This process increases the ratio of sugar to water in the grape. The result is a wine that either has more alcohol, or that is somewhat sweet, or both.

Vin de Pays *(van duh peh-yee')* The third category of French wines after AOC and VDQS. This category was created in 1973, almost 50 years after the others. It includes the simple wines found throughout the country. As with the other categories these wines must conform to local standards for grape variety and yield.

Vin de Table *(van duh tabl)* The lowest category of French wine. Most of these wines simply have the name of the producer on them, and may contain any wine from anywhere.

Vin Doux Naturel *(van doo nah-too-rel')* Literally this means naturally sweet wine in French. To be confusing it refers to wines that are not naturally sweet at all, but have had neutral grape spirits added to them to stop the fermentation process while there was still some unfermented sugars left. The process is called "fortification." Quite a few Muscat based wines are made this way in France, as well as the rare and incredible Banyuls. Often abbreviated to VDN.

Vin Gris *(van gree)* French for grey wine. It refers to wines that are made from red wine grapes (which are called black grapes) but are almost without color. A Rosé is a pink wine, made the same way, but with more color.

Vin Jaune *(van jawn)* This French "yellow wine" is made in the Jura district. By all accounts it most resembles a light Sherry.

Vin Santo *(veen sahn'-toe)* An Italian white wine from the Tuscany region. Made from Trebbiano and Malvasia grapes that have been dried before making the wine. The very sweet grapes are then fermented in small barrels that have some air in them, allowing the wine to maderize (oxidize). The result is a slightly brown wine that is either sweet, or very dry and alcoholic.

Vineyard A group of grape vines. The boundaries of a vineyard may be determined by ownership or by geological / geographical considerations.

Vinho Verde *(veen'-yoh vair'-day)* This Portuguese "green wine" may be red or white, and is often slightly sparkling. Green in this case refers to the youth of the wine, rather than its color. The wine is produced far up the Douro river, almost to the border of Spain.

Viniculture This term is used for the entire scope of wine. For the business and science of growing grapes, making the wine, and then selling it.

Vinifera *(vin-if'-er-ah)* There are over 40 species of grape, each belonging to the genus Vitis. Vinifera is the species responsible for almost all wine. The original Vinifera is often thought to be the Muscat grape, but the use of these grapes goes back long before written history. Cabernet Sauvignon, Chardonnay, and indeed almost any grape variety you can name, are all Vitis Vinifera.

Vinification The process of yeast turning grape juice into wine.

Vino *(veen-noh)* Italian for wine.

Vino da Tavola *(vee-no dah tah'-voh-lah)* The Italian term for table wine." As with other European countries, this is the lowest designation for wines. Since some of Italy's greatest wines are made in a style or grape variety inconsistent with their regions, this lowly designation has appeared on the label of some of the most popular and expensive Italian wines.

Vino Nobile di Montepulciano *(veen-no noh'-bee-leh dee mon-teh-pool-t'cha'-noh)* An Italian red wine from the Tuscany region. Made from the Sangiovese grape in and around the town of Montepulciano. The region neighbors the southern Chianti area, and many examples are similar in style to Chianti.

Vinous *(vin-us)* A wine tasting term used for wines that have no real flaws, but the best thing you can say about them is that they taste like wine.

Vintage This term refers both to the actual grape harvest as well as the year of the harvest. The term is also applied to wines that bear this year of harvest on their labels. Wines that are a blend of years are considered non-vintage wines (or N.V.). Until modern winemaking allowed fine wine to age consistently, dates were not associated with wines, and the "freshest" wine was the wine that was most in demand.

Vintage Port The most expensive, and longest lived style of Port. These wines are only made in years of exceptional quality, usually only a few times a decade. They are bottled when they are young, but are intended to age for 20 years or more before they are consumed. As they age, Vintage Ports will throw sediment and will need to be decanted before serving. This is the best wine to buy to celebrate the life of a child, as the wine will age in much the same way as a person. First the parent, and then the offspring can celebrate 12 milestones in their life with a case of Vintage Port. In its youth the Vintage Port is but a hint of what it will be. As it reaches its teens, it starts to develop character, but remains fiery. By the time it is 21 years old, it is fully mature, but without the character further age will bring. By the time it is 40 years old, it has mellowed from a hot plum-like flavor, to a soft nutty taste, full of complexity. As the port continues to age, it starts to lose some of its strength and intensity, but gains complexity and character. 60 to 80 years is often the upper limit of a Vintage Port, and few have the opportunity to taste them this mature, but few forget the experience. Only the greatest Port Vintages make it to the 100 year mark, while lesser years have faded long before this. While I eschew anthropomorphism in wine jargon, for Vintage Port it seems appropriate to make this connection to a human life span.

Viognier *(vee-oh-n'yay)* An exceptional white wine grape that is primarily found in the Northern Rhône region of France. The wines of Condrieu are made from Viognier, and the red wines of Côte-Rôtie sometimes use a little of this white grape to improve their aroma. At one time the grape was much more widespread in France, but with the wine laws that were enacted in the early 20th century, the grape was overlooked in most regions. It produces wines that are highly scented with good acidity. This combination makes it ideal for late harvest style wines. Such was the custom in the 19th century, but again the French wine laws overlooked this use and late harvest Viognier became rare. California has recently become a new bastion of Viognier and producers there are even making late harvest wines (I would like to think that the resurgence of late harvest Viognier was due in part to my campaigning efforts).

Viticulteur *(vee-tee-cul-tuhr)* The French term for a vineyard manager or owner. The person that is in charge of the vines. Sometimes also used for the wine maker. See also Vigneron.

Viticulture The science of grape growing. See also Viniculture.

Vitis That genus of plants to which all grapes belong.

Volnay *(vol-nay)* A wine producing village in the Burgundy region of France. Situated in the southern portion of the Côte d'Or, known as the Côte de Beaune. Most of its neighbors produce white wine, while Volnay is justifiably famous for its red wines made from Pinot Noir.

Vosne-Romanée *(vone-roh-mah-nay)* One of the finest wine producing villages in the northern Côte d'Or region of Burgundy, France. This village, situated in the southern end of the Côte de Nuits is home to five of the most famous Grand Cru vineyards: Romanée-Conti, La Tâche, Richebourg, La Romanée, and Romanée-Saint-Vivant.

Vougeot *(voo-joh)* A primarily red wine town in the Côte de Nuits region of Burgundy, France. It has one large Grand Cru vineyard, Clos de Vougeot, which is notable as an example of how confusing Burgundy can be for the consumer. There may be as many as 60 different producers of Clos de Vougeot alone. A small quantity of white wine is also produced in the village.

Vouvray *(voo-vray)* The region and wine from the Loire Valley in France. Planted almost exclusively to Chenin Blanc, these white wines can range from crisp and dry to luscious and sweet. Sparkling wine from the region has increased in production and popularity of late.

VQPRD Literally: Vins de Qualite Produits des Regions Determinees, it is a European Common Market designation for quality wines produced in specific regions. In theory almost any quality wine from Europe can use this designation, but in practice they use their local terms instead.

W

Waikato A wine region in New Zealand's northern island.

Walla Walla Walla Walla, Washington. The name rolls off the tongue, and for many it is known only as a near nonsense word used by Bugs Bunny. Some of the State's finest grapes are grown here, or near here (Washington State is not a stickler for precise geographic designations).

Washington Along with Oregon, Washington State is often referred to as the Pacific Northwest. The mild climate, and the relatively low cost of land has drawn an increasing number of wine makers to this state. Most of the grapes are grown in the Columbia River basin, in the southeastern corner of the state. Here, shielded from the ocean by the Cascade mountains, an arid plain has been redefined thanks to irrigation and tenacity. Cabernet Sauvignon and Merlot have done well here, as has Riesling.

Wein *(vine)* The German word for wine.

Weingut *(vine'-goot)* The German term for a vineyard estate. If it appears on a bottle the grapes must come entirely from vineyards the producer owns.

Weinkellerei *(vine-kel'-er-rye)* The German term for a wine cellar. If you see this on the label, it may be an off hand way of telling you that the grapes for this wine do not come from the producers own vineyards.

Weissburgunder *(vice'-boor-gun-der)* The German name for the Pinot Blanc grape.

Welschriesling *(velsh-reece'-ling)* A white wine grape that is not related to, but is trying to capitalize on the name of Riesling. It is planted throughout Europe, especially in and near Austria.

White Zinfandel A rosé (pink) wine made from the red wine grape Zinfandel. It tends to be somewhat sweet and easy to enjoy. This is the wine that snobs love to hate. Do not mistakenly call this pink wine Zinfandel, as the red wine made from Zinfandel is one of California's greatest wines.

Willamette Valley *(will-am'-it)* The main growing region in Oregon, and planted primarily in Pinot Noir. Vintages here can be variable, but when the conditions are right, Pinot Noir thrives, and a growing number of wineries are attempting to make their mark with this difficult grape. Even those with concerns in the Mecca of Pinot Noir, Burgundy, France, have thrown in their lots with those gambling on the suitability of Oregon to produce world class wines. While there have been some disappointments, the general trend is promising, and the wines just keep getting better.

Wine Cooler A mix of wine and fruit juices (or lime flavored soda). The practice of disguising bad wine with sweetened juice is as old as wine itself. The name has developed a negative connotation for many wine lovers, since the prepackaged, sweetened and carbonated version is little more than soda pop with a touch of alcohol.

Woody When a wine has had extensive aging in a barrel, it takes on the barrel taste, hence it is "woody." The taste of wood, usually oak, should not dominate the flavor of the wine. It is there to help the wine age, and will diminish over time. Some winemakers disguise the taste of their wines with wood, especially in regions where the grapes do not ripen completely. In the New World this taste has become synonymous with Chardonnay for many wine lovers, although one may debate that this is not a positive thing.

Württemberg *(vur'-tem-bairg)* A good sized German wine region. It is situated around the well known German city of Stuttgart, home of the German automobile industry. The red wines made in the region are of the greatest interest. Besides the usual red wine grape Spätburgunder (Pinot Noir) here you will also find local varieties such as Trollinger, Lemberger and Schwarzriesling (which is not a black riesling at all, rather it is the Pinot Meunier grape which is also found in the Champagne region of France).

X

Xérès *(sair-ress)* The old name for the town of Jerez de la Frontera in Spain, where Sherry is produced. It was the mispronunciation of this word that led to the name of Sherry.

Y

Yakima Valley This region in Washington State is a tiny subsection of the Columbia River Valley.

Yarra Valley Situated just north of the Australian city of Melbourne, this may be the area's best known wine region. Close enough to the city for a leisurely drive, the Yarra Valley is dotted with picturesque wineries that are well prepared for tours and entertaining.

Yeast The single cell organisms that are responsible for fermentation. This is as true in wine as it is in beer or even bread. In the case of wine, the primary yeast responsible for the first (alcohol) fermentation belong to the class sacharomyces. Not all yeast is good yeast, and some can lead to spoilage. Many types of yeast may be found in and around wineries, and due to the need to control the specific yeast in wine, sterility is extremely important in a winery.

Yeasty A wine taster's term for a wine that has a pronounced flavor or aroma of yeast. Reminiscent of fresh bread, this flavor is common in sparkling wines and wines aged "sur lie." For all other types of wine, this flavor should be considered a fault. It should never be too pronounced, and in sparkling wines, it should be more toasty (like burnt bread) than a freshly baked loaf.

Yield When related to wine this term refers to the amount of fruit any given vine or vineyard produces. As with so many things in wine, this is a balancing act. You want to get enough fruit to remain profitable; however, by reducing the yield you attain more flavorful fruit. In Europe the relative yield of a vineyard or vine is often regulated by law. This ensures quality wines. Modern vineyard techniques have managed to increase yields while still maintaining quality. The laws and the world of wine remain in flux as the perfect balance of the number of vines per area and the yield per vine are sought.

Young A designation for any wine that is not quite ready to drink. In the case of lighter wines, this may be directly on release; but, for Cabernet Sauvignon based wines, and others designed for prolonged aging, the period of youth may last a decade or more.

Yquem / d'Yquem, Château *(ee-kem / dee-kem)* The highest rated wine of the Bordeaux region of France. In a land where long lived red wines are common, Château d'Yquem is an even longer lived sweet white wine. Made from the Sémillon grape with a bit of Sauvignon Blanc, this is a dessert wine like no other. As with other wines from the Sauternes district, the grapes achieve their intense sweetness after being effected by the botrytis mold, which removes the water from the grape. The shriveled remains of these grapes are then picked, at their peak of perfection, a task that often takes several "tries" or trips to the vineyard, over a period of weeks to accomplish. While other Sauternes may be described as sweet apricots and figs, I am fond of saying that d'Yquem is "a cornucopia of fruit, that is ever changing in your mouth." There are other Sauternes, and other dessert wines, but nature and man have teamed up to put Château d'Yquem in a class by itself.

Z

Zinfandel A red wine grape found almost exclusively in California. While its origins are undoubtedly European, the exact location and name of its progenitor is one of wine's great mysteries. The Primativo of Italy is often named as the origin of Zin, but some believe that Primativo came from Zin, and not the other way around. Evidence for this is found in DNA testing. Whatever the origin of Zinfandel, it is one of the most planted fine wine grapes in California. These vines are older than most other vines in the area, and for this reason produce some of the most intense fruit. For the uninitiated, Zinfandel means a pink wine. It is important to remember that pink wine can be made from any red wine grape, and that the true red Zinfandel shares little with its pink counterpart. Known for its wide variety of styles, most Zinfandel is not particularly tannic (and does not age well) while having an abundance of fruit, to the point of being "jammy." While Zinfandel is one of my personal favorites, especially in the moderate price range, some find the forward fruit to be too much of a good thing.

Zymase The enzymes excreted by yeast that actually do the work of fermentation. While this is so technical that most books do not even bother to mention zymase, it has yet another claim to fame. It is the root of the word Zymurgy which ends nearly all English language dictionaries.

Zymurgy *(zi'-mer-gee)* The science and study of fermentation.

Common Wine Abbreviations

1er	Premier (as in Premier Cru)
AVA	American Viticultural Area
AOC	Appellation d'Origine Contrôlée
BA	Beeranauslese
CdP	Châteauneuf-du-Pape
Ch.	Château
cl	Centiliter **
DO	Denominación de Origen
DOC	Denominazione do Origine Controllata
DOCG	Denominazione do Origine Controllata e Garantita
IGT	Indicazione Geographica Tipica
LBV	Late Bottled Vintage Port
ML	Malolactic Fermentation
ml	Milliter **
pH	A symbol that describes the alkalinity or acidity of a solution
QbA	Qualitätswein bestimmter Anbaugebiete *
QmP	Qualitätswein mit Prädikat *
SB	Sauvignon Blanc
TA	Total (or titratable) Acidity **
TBA	Trokenbeeranauslese
VDN	Vin Doux Naturel
VDQS	Vins Délimités de Qualité Supérieure *
VQPRD	Vins de Qualite Produits des Regions Determinees *

* *Listed by the initials*
** *Not listed*